THE ALMOST TRUE STORY
OF RYAN FISHER

THE ALMOST TRUE STORY
OF RYAN FISHER

Rob Stennett

ZONDERVAN.com/
AUTHOR**TRACKER**
follow your favorite authors

The Almost True Story of Ryan Fisher
Copyright © 2008 by Rob Stennett

Requests for information should be addressed to:
Zondervan, *Grand Rapids, Michigan 49530*

Library of Congress Cataloging-in-Publication Data

Stennett, Rob.
    The almost true story of Ryan Fisher / Rob Stennett.
    p. cm.
    ISBN 978-0-310-27706-4 (softcover)
    1. Real estate agents — Fiction. 2. United States — Religious life and customs —
Fiction. 3. Satire. I. Title.
    PS3619.T476477A79   2008
    813'.6 — dc22
                                     2008001588

All Scripture quotations are taken from the *Holy Bible, Today's New International Version*™. TNIV®. Copyright © 2001, 2005 by International Bible Society. Used by permission of Zondervan. All rights reserved.

The Twenty-third Psalm is taken from the *King James Version* of the Bible.

Internet addresses (websites, blogs, etc.) and telephone numbers printed in this book are offered as a resource to you. These are not intended in any way to be or imply an endorsement on the part of Zondervan, nor do we vouch for the content of these sites and numbers for the life of this book.

This book is a work of fiction. Actual persons are fictionalized for the use of this story and details are not to be construed as fact.

Interior design by Beth Shagene
Illustrations by Jesse Hamm

Printed in the United States of America

08 09 10 11 12 13 • 23 22 21 20 19 18 17 16 15 14 13 12 11 10 9 8 7 6 5 4 3 2 1

For Dad and Jim Marsh
(and the month we spent eating frozen pizzas)

You are who you pretend to be.
So be careful who you pretend to be.
KURT VONNEGUT JR.

Christian Business

THE AD
WITH THE JESUS FISH

Even though Ryan Fisher didn't believe in God, he placed an ad in the Christian Business Directory. There were a number of reasons Ryan decided to market himself as a realtor to Christians, but the main reason was his desire to become the most successful real estate agent in Denver. Ryan was one of the best natural salesmen to ever work for Phillips and Sons Realty. He could sell ice to an Eskimo, not because he tricked the Eskimo into thinking he needed more ice—the Eskimo was smarter than that. The Eskimo could look around and see there was plenty of ice to build igloos with and to keep sodas cold. But he would buy ice from Ryan because Ryan was so likeable. The Eskimo would find every excuse to run out of ice just so Ryan would come by and they could talk football and joke around. The Eskimo would even catch himself thinking that he and Ryan could build a lasting friendship—the type where they'd have each other's families over for barbecues, and they would watch the kids play croquet in the backyard as the sun set.

Unfortunately, there are very few Eskimos in Denver.

Which was really too bad, because Ryan Fisher was in a slump. His charm and personality didn't seem to be enough anymore. He hadn't closed on a house in a month. Despite his past successes, he was beginning to feel like a complete failure—as if he were a surgeon who'd lost ten straight appendicitis patients, or a guy who'd asked every girl in high school to the prom only to be rejected by them all, or New Coke.

This story begins after another day where promising real estate leads crumbled into disappointing failures for Ryan Fisher. It was his twenty-eighth birthday, but he didn't want to celebrate. He wanted to crawl into bed and disappear. He wouldn't get the chance.

"Surprise!"

Ryan walked through his front door and saw balloons, streamers, friends in pointy hats, cake, and roll-out paper whistles. It was time to party. He should have felt touched that his wife Katherine went to all this trouble. She'd probably spent weeks organizing this get-together. He needed to act grateful. He needed to push the bad day out of his mind so he could mingle with his friends.

His successful friends.

With their exciting careers and great stories.

He was turning twenty-eight, he'd been at the real estate game for five years, and he was average. He'd worked hard and was a great salesman, but things were about as good as they were going to get for Ryan. He never got the lucky break, the right connections; and now his life was destined to spiral into mediocrity. There'd be nothing but work and two weeks of vacation a year (and even then there wouldn't be money for Greek Isle cruises or a Bahamas beach house; he'd have to settle for road trips to Iowa and last-minute discount fares to Delaware). Then, in the end, there'd be nothing to look forward to except retirement and death.

After the party he tried to fall asleep next to his wife, but when he closed his eyes he kept seeing a picture of his friends cruising around on a yacht, sipping fruity drinks with umbrellas, while he and Katherine were in a tugboat. All of Ryan's friends were wearing white pants and laughing at Ryan. Then, thankfully, the yacht cruised out of sight leaving Ryan and Katherine to drift and stare at each other.

Ryan got out of bed, walked downstairs, flopped on the couch, limply aimed the remote at the cable box, and flipped through all late-night television had to offer.

There wasn't much. One channel had cooking gadgets. The next had Chuck Norris pitching exercise equipment. Ryan decided that most people wanted two things late at night: to get fat or skinny.

He finally settled on a rerun of *Dateline* chronicling the journey of a megachurch in Nashville. As Ryan watched he couldn't help but notice that all of the Christians seemed so happy. They laughed at the pastor's jokes as if he were Jeff Foxworthy. They sang songs and smiled and thrust their hands high in the air. It was like they were begging for affordable but classy starter homes.

The segment closed with these magic words, "There are 80 million people in America who call themselves evangelical Christians."

Eighty million people, and every one of them needs a house.

This was it. This was the answer—Christians. These people wouldn't flake out, wouldn't walk out of a deal at the closing table; they would be kind and honest and naïve; they would be extremely easy to sell small, big, and medium-sized houses to. He would be Ryan Fisher, realtor to Christians, and he would be rich and successful. Christians were everywhere and they were going to put him back on the real estate map.

The next morning he was a new man. His coffee tasted richer, the sun looked brighter, his shower made him feel cleaner, and even the traffic jam seemed pleasant, as if it were a big party and all the other motorists were his close Christian friends.

But then Ryan realized he had no idea how to sell to Christians. So when he got to the office, he cracked open the phone book, flipped through the Yellow Pages, and learned how complicated Christianity is. He discovered that all of the churches had names that sounded spiritual, but Ryan had no clue what they meant. There were lists of churches that gathered in different parts of town with similar labels: Assembly of God, Baptist, Calvary Chapel, Episcopal, Evangelical Free, Foursquare Gospel, Lutheran, Open Bible, Our Lady of Guadalupe, Pentecostal Holiness, Seventh Day Adventist, and United Methodist. Then, there were churches that had "church" (or some allusion to church and God) in the title but did not seem to belong to any specific group: Abundant Life Center, Fellowship Christian Church, Fruitful Believers Church, Mosaic, and the Pointing People to Jesus Place. When people converted, Ryan wondered how they decided what brand of Christianity they would join.

It seemed to Ryan that it would take a lifetime to understand all of these versions of Christianity. But he didn't have a lifetime, so he started calling churches. Most of them didn't understand exactly what Ryan was asking. Every conversation went something like this:

"I have an offer for Christians."

"An offer?"

"Something to sell."

"Like—"

"Real estate."

"You want to sell real estate—"

"To Christians."

Click.

But Ryan was persistent, and he wouldn't give up easily. He had already spent twenty minutes calling churches. He could go for another five. His determination paid off when he got on the phone with the receptionist for Fellowship Christian Church.

"I want to sell real estate to Christians." Ryan's spiel had become considerably shorter.

"Oh, you're calling about the Christian Business Directory," the receptionist said.

Ryan could hear the angels singing. "Yes, the Christian Business Directory. That's exactly what I'm looking for."

"What sort of business are you in?"

"Real estate."

"Would you like to place an ad?"

"I would love to."

"What would you like in it?"

"What normally goes in a Christian ad?"

"Well a lot of people put the Icthus on their ad."

"Icthus?"

"It's the fish that symbolizes Christians. You've probably seen it on the back of cars."

"The Jesus fish!"

"Yes, sir. The Jesus fish."

"Yeah, I'll take one ad with my face and the Jesus fish next to it."

The ad worked like hotcakes. His voice mail was flooded with Christians looking to buy and sell real estate.

Ryan quickly learned a couple of things: He learned Christians want to live in neighborhoods with other Christians. They want to move into homes where Christians have lived before so they can be assured their new home doesn't have a history of residents who struggled with "worldly" things like pornography and alcohol and crack.

He learned Christians are thrilled to do business with someone who has the same values as they do. So, being in the Christian Business Directory meant Ryan had to pretend to be a Christian and agree (or at least act as if he agreed) with Christian ideals and values.

Ryan knew he didn't really believe in a higher power, and a client would occasionally make frightening political statements, but those were small things.

What's important is I'm putting good people into good homes, he told himself.

And it was fun being a Christian—it was like being part of a club. It wasn't an exclusive club like a country club or the Mickey Mouse Club; Christianity was a club that was always excited to find new members. When clients asked Ryan how long he'd been a Christian, he was as honest as he could be when he said he'd just recently become one. Ryan was scared they might lash out at him, tie him up to a post, and scream, "How dare you take out an ad with a Jesus fish when you've just recently become a Christian?"

But the opposite was true.

The newer the Christian he was, the better. When he told one client that he'd become a Christian in the last month, she broke into tears and gave him a hug on the spot. Ryan felt so warm inside, he thought his heart was smiling.

All it took was one ad with a Jesus fish and Ryan drummed up more business than he'd ever thought possible.

Just a few weeks ago, finding clients was a great mystery for Ryan. He knew people were buying and selling homes, he just didn't know how they found each other. Ryan loitered around Starbucks and playgrounds and put his name on the sides of benches and bus stops. Then he invested in a billboard; it seemed oddly powerful to have his face hovering over the freeway, smiling at people as they drove to work. But the ads hadn't worked and Ryan could no longer afford to pay for his freeway advertising lifestyle. Soon an ad for Coors covered his face. Other people might have been happy to see his billboard go, but every time Ryan passed those blonde girls in bikinis playing tackle football in the snow, he couldn't help but feel depressed.

But none of that mattered anymore. He was a Christian now. A Christian realtor.

Still, things weren't perfect. Ryan was scared someone would ask him something every Christian should know, and when he didn't know, they would call him a pagan, rip his name out of the Christian Business Directory, put feet on his Jesus fish, and he would have to sell to people who believed in Darwinism. But there was something else, something deeper that bothered him about selling affordably priced real estate to Christians. When he did business with them, it was as if they *expected* something. Christians expected the cheaper deal, they expected not to have to pay as high a realtor fee, they expected to know when the best house was on the market, and they expected Ryan to hook them up. Ryan wanted to confess that he was in this solely for business reasons, but he could never say something like that. If he did, people would know for sure that he wasn't a Christian.

The first question that threw Ryan off came from Stan, a Baptist. Ryan had no idea what it meant to be a Baptist, but he thought the Sanders' house would be perfect for Stan and his family. The outside of the house was painted burgundy with beige trim and had a pond in the backyard where Stan's kids could breed giant goldfish. Inside there were shiny hardwood floors, three-and-a-half bathrooms, and two fireplaces.

Ryan was ready to answer any question about the Sanders' home when Stan asked, "Where do you go to church?"

"Fellowship Christian Church," Ryan blurted.

It was the first name that came to him. He remembered the ad in the phone book had a blue sky, clouds, and a picture of a dove holding an olive branch flying through a window. It was very serene.

"Who's the pastor there?"

"I forget his name."

"Forget?"

"We've just started going."

"Where'd you go before?"

What are you, some sort of interrogator for the Taliban? Isn't where I go or don't go to church between God and me? This is what Ryan wanted to say. But he was learning being a Christian meant never saying what you really thought out loud. So instead he said, "I just became a Christian."

Stan wasn't impressed by Ryan's recent conversion. He simply asked, "How'd you get saved?"

Ryan wanted to think of a clever lie, but he couldn't because he had no idea what Stan was asking.

Ryan didn't know you had to get saved somewhere. He'd decided to become a Christian the way some people become Red Sox fans. He jumped on the bandwagon. He liked the people, the culture, and he wanted to be part of all the fun. He wanted to hang out with and sell real estate to all of the smiling, laughing people he saw on TV.

So Ryan was honest. "I don't know."

"Honey, I think it's great we're going to church. I'm just a little surprised. Now, zip me up," Katherine said.

Ryan zipped up the back of Katherine's brown autumn dress. She looked gorgeous this morning, and the dress made her strawberry-blonde hair, her soft pale skin, and her green eyes stand out. He understood her surprise about church—he didn't want to tell her the reason they were going to church was professional. So one morning at breakfast, he just casually suggested it. And her eyes lit up. It was almost as if she had been waiting for him to ask her to church.

"Okay, which earrings do you like—the emerald or the sapphire?" Ryan hated pop quizzes like this. They weren't quizzes of opinion. There was a right answer. Katherine already knew which earrings she liked and she just needed Ryan to confirm her thoughts.

"I like the emerald."

"Yeah, me too."

Lucky guess.

As he watched his wife put on the emerald earrings, he felt a twinge of guilt. He hadn't told her about the ad in the Christian Business Directory. He didn't say anything at first because he was sure she would shoot down the idea. Since then, there was never really a good time. He told her everything else. He told her how he was the top salesman, how it was a record-breaking month, how he got a special parking place and his picture on the whiteboard at the office.

But still, he felt guilty because before they got married Ryan told Katherine everything. He told her his biggest fears were roller coasters and dying in a car wreck. He told her his favorite movies were all science fiction sequels like *Aliens*, *The Empire Strikes Back*, *The Wrath of Kahn*, and *Terminator 2*. He told her his dream job was to be a sports-radio talk-show host. He'd argue Yanks and Sox, hold debates about the greatest quarterback of all time, and prove once and for all that the Lakers dominate the Celtics. If callers disagreed with him, he'd go Jim Rome on them.

Katherine smiled and laughed at everything he said. She'd

listen and lean closer, she would drink up his stories. He was a puzzle that she couldn't wait to piece together.

And he might not have told her any of that if he had been able to return his library books on time. But he hadn't. Still, he hated paying late fees, so he had approached the student librarian, a girl named Kate, who was wearing black wire-framed glasses and a white wool sweater. She had a ponytail and the cutest smile he'd ever seen. He begged her for an exception.

"I didn't know it was already due. I was so slammed with my paper that I forgot to return it." Ryan was lying to her. The first thing that he ever told his future bride was fiction, but not in the good Jane Austen way.

"You should have renewed the book," Katherine said.

"Yeah, well, I'm just saying, do they have to give us such a short amount of time to read a book?"

"You've had this checked out for three months."

"I'm sorry. You're right. I'm a bad library guy. Let me make it up to you by taking you to coffee sometime," Ryan said.

"I don't like coffee."

Actually Katherine loved coffee. She'd drink it by the gallon if someone sold it that way. The thing Katherine didn't like was Ryan. She knew his type. She knew Ryan was a giant scoop of vanilla ice cream. He was cute and nice and a really sweet guy with serviceable plans for his life.

But who wanted serviceable when there was a guy out there like Coen Jackson? Coen kept just enough facial scruff so it was sexy, he read Milton, and he played guitar at the Coffee Pot's open-mic night. Katherine would go to the Coffee Pot every night of her freshman year and drink caramel lattes while Coen played guitar and sang with his gravelly voice.

During open-mic night Coen sang mostly acoustic covers of Toad the Wet Sprocket and Matchbox 20, but every now and then

18

he'd play a song he'd written. Katherine couldn't tell exactly what his songs were about, but she thought they might be about something he'd lost. Maybe it was something important and meaningful like a parent or a girlfriend, or maybe he had just lost his direction in his life and wouldn't find love until he was with someone who understood him.

Even after all these years, Katherine finds herself thinking about Coen.

She can picture the coffee shop, his curly brown hair, and his green corduroy blazer. She can taste the warmth of her caramel latte and hear his songs buzzing around her. Then she remembers everything that happened next: how she lost her virginity and six months later he was writing songs for Sarah Michaels because she *really* understood him.

Katherine hates when she thinks of Ryan as a rebound, but at the time he was. He was comfort food. He dropped by the library every day and brought her Junior Mints and a sunflower. And every day he asked her the same question, "What are you doing tonight, Kate?"

"I'm busy."

"Okay, see you tomorrow."

And then, finally, one day when he asked, "What are you doing tonight, Kate?" she said, "Something with you."

She was a little nervous when he wouldn't tell her where they were going. Katherine worried that Ryan might take her to a candlelit French dinner, or worse, maybe he'd take her to a picnic in the mountains and see where things went from there.

But Ryan had a first date that was guaranteed money in the bank — Putt-n-Play. They would ride go-carts, play minigolf, share cheese pizza, and he would win enough tickets playing skeeball so he could buy her a plastic promise ring. Ryan stole the idea for this date from the "Karate Kid" himself, Daniel LaRusso, who took Ali on the exact same outing.* And like Ali, Katherine found herself enjoying her date with Ryan against her better judgment. She laughed when Ryan won her a plastic promise ring, and she felt as warm as nacho cheese when she and Ryan strolled around the minigolf course eating a soft pretzel.

Katherine wasn't sure if Ryan was the one. But when she voiced her insecurities to her friends, they couldn't understand how she wasn't madly in love with Ryan. If she would come to them with concerns, they would respond with clichés: He's a dream come true. He's a keeper. Don't let that one slip away. If only there were more guys like him. He's Mr. Right. Mr. Perfect. Mr. Wonderful. He's marriage material.

Katherine did adore how stable and sweet Ryan was. He wouldn't start writing songs for another girl the second he got bored — he would provide for her, he would be a good husband and father. She would never have to worry where Ryan was if he came home late.

Still, for the first few months Katherine was dating Ryan, she thought about what went wrong with Coen. She replayed their entire six months together. Should she have been more adventurous? Was she too prudish? Did she not let him know how much his music inspired her — how it seeped into her soul? She told herself that it was none of these things. Instead, what she loved about Coen made him reject her — he was a free spirit. He couldn't be with one girl, otherwise he'd just be a guy with a girlfriend who went on dates to Pottery Barn to plan what sort of drapes they would hang in their first house. Guys like that aren't scruffy artists who create soul-searching music; guys like that are more like Ryan — handsome, kind, and, well, serviceable.

---

* Ryan knew that if this date could work for Daniel — a poor boy from Jersey who got his butt kicked on the beach the first day of school, and even got beat up on Halloween, the day most bullies took off to smash pumpkins and steal candy from the neighborhood children — it could work for him.

Katherine was about to graduate, and she knew she didn't need a souped-up '67 Mustang like Coen. She needed a Toyota Camry like Ryan. And Katherine felt guilty every time Coen crossed her thoughts, because she knew that with Coen, she felt passion.

With Ryan, she felt safe.

And Katherine's suspicions were right—her life with Ryan was stable. He was a good provider but not very organized, so Katherine paid the bills, checked the mail, and got the oil changed every three thousand miles.

Life was harmonious monotony.

This morning was different. They were up so early they could see the sunrise—well, maybe not the sunrise. It was ten a.m. before they were dressed and in their Jetta ready for church—but it was a lot earlier than they had ever been out on a Sunday morning for as long as Katherine could remember. And as they sat in their car, they felt clean. This Sunday wasn't weighted with the duty of unfinished chores or the gloom of Monday morning around the corner. This Sunday they were going to church. They were dressed up, and they had a purpose.

It wasn't necessarily church that excited Katherine—it was change. Katherine thought about the friends she could make. Church seemed like the place where sophisticated people were, a place where she could meet women who'd drink wine and discuss great works of literature.

Ryan eased the Jetta out of the driveway. He drove his wife through the streets of suburbia, past the lawns littered with crisp orange and yellow leaves, and toward Fellowship Christian Church, where their stable existence would be forever altered—because by Sunday afternoon they would be Christians.

2

THE CHRISTIAN BOX

The first time Ryan identified himself as a Christian was on his college application. They had a completely optional section of the application where the applicant could unveil personal traits — gender, ethnicity, family's income, religion, and so on. As Ryan checked the box labeled Caucasian, he wondered two things.

The first: What is a Caucasian? Initially he thought there had been a mistake and someone had forgotten to put white or Anglo or European American as an option. When Ryan brought this to his guidance counselor's attention, she laughed and told him just to check the Caucasian box. Ryan wanted to make his ethnicity crystal clear, so he told his counselor, "I'm a European American."

"I know, Ryan. But they don't have a European American box. Just check the Caucasian one."

Ryan obeyed, checked the Caucasian box, and wondered if there were any Caucasian clubs he could join, or if he could somehow be the beneficiary of some United Caucasian College Scholarship Fund. But then he began to worry that he'd be ridiculed as a fraud when he arrived on campus and everyone discovered that he was white and not Caucasian.

The second thing he wondered: Is this section of the application really optional? He could picture an application with a completely ambiguous name like Kris Taylor. The application committee would flip to the optional page of Kris Taylor's application, and they would be horrified to see it blank. How could they decipher Kris's ethnicity, religion, sexual orientation, and socioeconomic status? How could they even know Kris's gender? What if they put him/her into the wrong dorm, and he/she sued the university? "How could you not know I'm a boy/girl?" Kris would scream from atop the university's clock tower. Frustrated and frightened by all of the legal ramifications, the application committee would toss this androgynous atheist's application into the reject pile even though Kris had a 3.76 GPA and scored a 1490 on his/her SAT test.

Ryan learned from the tale of Kris Taylor and meticulously filled out every section of his application.

But he hit a third roadblock when he had to check the religion box, because he didn't have a religion he could proudly claim as his own. He knew he wasn't an atheist; that seemed bitter and cynical. He couldn't check "other" because he knew the application committee would assume he belonged to David Koresh's Branch Davidians or Jim Jones or Heaven's Gate, and that would be worse than leaving the section blank.

Buddhism had always appealed to Ryan; it seemed nice to shave your head, wear an orange robe, and meditate in the mountains. But everything Ryan knew about Buddhism he learned from Smashing Pumpkins songs and watching the trailer for *Seven Years in Tibet*, and that wasn't enough to check the Buddhism box on his college application.

By default, the religion Ryan was most knowledgeable about

was Christianity. His parents had taken him to church for Christmas Eve and Easter services until he was eight years old. At that point they noticed that their son never paid attention and decided it was too much of a hassle to get dressed up, deal with traffic, and sit through one of Reverend Harris's dull sermons when all Ryan did in church was draw pictures of cowgirls and Muppets. Ryan hadn't been to church since then, but there were always people holding signs in the street and preachers on TV to remind him of the basics of Christianity: Jesus, a cross, heaven and hell, and the need for Jesus if you wanted to go to heaven. So he checked that he was a Christian on his application because he figured he could wing it enough to answer questions about Christianity if the situation ever called for it.

Ryan occasionally considered his faith after checking the Christian box. He thought about life and death and about God. He wondered if God existed, and if God did exist, he wondered what kind of person He was. But there were always more pressing things to think about: his marketing project, asking Katherine out, the Alpha Chi's keg party, marrying Katherine, getting his realtor license, hitting his sales quota for the month, his inability to get Katherine pregnant.

Is something wrong? Should I be wearing boxers instead of briefs?

With all of these concerns, there was little room for thinking about faith and his place in the universe—God was more of a lingering problem that had to be dealt with later, like taxes or cleaning the garage.

As he and Katherine walked through Fellowship Christian Church's parking lot, they were a little disappointed. This didn't look like a church. There wasn't a steeple or stained glass windows or marble statues of St. Paul—there wasn't even a bell tower. It was just a brick building with some windows, large maple trees, and a sign out front that read, "Fellowship Christian Church." No one could have deciphered this as a place of God if it didn't say so on the sign, and to Katherine, this seemed a little deceitful.

Are they trying to trick me into thinking this isn't a church, that it's something else, just a building where people gather and read the Bible, or whatever it is that happens in a church? she thought.

But maybe this was how all churches looked now. She didn't pay any attention to churches when she drove around Denver; they were just another building on the side of the road, a place where she didn't have any business.

And as they approached the entrance of the church, they didn't say a thing. Katherine was thinking, What if we made a mistake, what if we'd be happier at home in our normal Sunday ritual? What if we walk in and don't know where to sit or how to act? What if the other Christians see us as pagans?

But Ryan wasn't picking up on Katherine's discomfort. He felt great. And if he was feeling uneasy about anything, walking through the front doors of Fellowship Christian Church obliterated any discomfort. How could you feel uncomfortable in a lobby where the walls were painted in pastel blues with canary yellow trim?

Ryan thought, It must be nice to go to church here, it would be like having Easter every Sunday.

Katherine noticed a corkboard overloaded with pictures from a Labor Day picnic. In one corner was a table with teenagers selling freshly baked goods. Church members were smiling and paying large sums of money for blueberry muffins and snickerdoodle cookies — they were doing so because the teenagers were raising money for a fall break mission trip to Mexico.

As the Fishers walked toward the sanctuary, friendly men and women in maroon blazers with carnations on their lapels handed them church bulletins. Ryan hadn't felt this good visiting a new place since the Wal-Mart on Seventh Street opened and their greeter was a happy old man singing show tunes. Sometimes Ryan would make a trip to buy extra fabric softener just so he could hear the old man singing "Phantom of the Opera" as he passed through the swooshing doors.

"Good morning, brother," a smiling usher with a mustache said as he greeted Ryan and Katherine. Ryan wasn't exactly sure why Christians called each other *brother* and *sister*, but he was pretty sure it had something to do with Adam and Eve.

"How long have you been coming to Fellowship?" the usher asked.

"We've never been here," Ryan admitted.

"Welcome. Do you have any kids?'

"Are we supposed to have kids?" Katherine wondered aloud.

"No, no." The usher smiled. "I just asked because we have God's Country upstairs where families can drop off the little ones."

"No little ones here. Yet. We've been trying, but we haven't had any luck. Truthfully, we haven't had any time for sex — "

"Honey," Ryan said.

Katherine blushed, and all three of them stood for a moment in the awkward silence. Ryan never understood why when Katherine tried to ingratiate herself to someone new she would blurt unholy amounts of irrelevant information.

"Well, keep trying," the usher said before he scooted away to pass out more bulletins.

"Good morning, everybody," the pastor said from inside the auditorium. The service was starting. It took Ryan and Katherine awhile to understand the way Fellowship Christian Church's services worked. They didn't know when to sit and when to stand. The only other time Katherine had attended church, there were hymns and an organ player, so she was surprised to see a clean-cut man who looked like Alec Baldwin lead what she later learned was called "praise and worship"—"praise" being the fast songs, and "worship" being the slow songs.

Ryan was engrossed in the service. The people were smiling and singing just like they did on TV, and he knew that he would be Denver's number one realtor in no time. He had finally found the perfect place to meet Christians: church. As soon as the service ended, he would meet Christian bankers, lawyers, stockbrokers, and plastic surgeons. Sooner or later—sooner if Ryan had anything to say about it—they would need to buy and sell expensive homes. Ryan was so busy thinking about all the money he would make from Christians that he forgot to sit down when praise and worship was over. As he glanced around the sanctuary, he saw a few of his current clients: the Speilmens (ready to close on a three-bedroom, two-and-a-half-bath on Maple Street), the Kennedys (moving into their new home with a hot tub in the backyard on Thursday), and the Browns (just put their tan house with burgundy trim on the market).

Ryan's clients watched him continue to stand as everyone else found their seats. The clients were happy to see him at Fellowship Christian Church, and they were impressed that he was so lost in worship that it took him a moment to realize the music had stopped and it was time to sit. This is the kind of man I want selling my home, Dan Speilmen thought.

When Pastor Clark stood behind the pulpit to address the congregation, he began his sermon by talking about the universe: "Light travels at 186,000 miles per second. That's the fastest anything in the universe can travel, unless someone discovers warp speed like they have on *Star Trek*."

The audience chuckled softly. He's no Chris Rock, but not bad, Ryan thought.

"The Andromeda Galaxy, the closest to the Milky Way, is 10 to 12 billion light years from here. The farthest scientists have seen out into the universe is 28 billion light years away, but they assume that if we had a telescope powerful enough, we could see infinitely beyond that. In all of space we continue to discover countless planets and solar systems. And I want you to know something, church—he created all of it."

Pastor Clark went on to say that Jesus Christ, the person who created all of the constellations, solar systems, galaxies, and planets, is the same person who put himself on the cross so we could be forgiven of our sins. Pastor Clark explained that sins "can be as complicated as murder or adultery, or as simple as telling a white lie or lashing out at a loved one. But we have all committed them. Romans 8 explains that every person who has ever set foot on this earth has sinned and that includes every person in this room listening to me right now."

Ryan felt glad to be in a room with other Christian sinners, but he also found that Pastor Clark's sermon made him squirm. It forced him to consider the mistakes he had made: he occasionally fought with Katherine, he had thought about cheating on her—twice he had kissed a coworker at the office Saint Patrick's Day Party. That wasn't really cheating, Ryan thought, but now he wasn't so sure. He'd lied over and over, he ate junk food much too late at night, he claimed tax exemptions when shouldn't have, he'd had crushes on Gwyneth Paltrow, Jennifer Aniston, Angelina Jolie, and whoever else Brad Pitt was dating, he sped through construction zones, he played solitaire during office hours, and once he ran over a chipmunk on the way home. He hadn't even slowed down for little Alvin, and this morning he was sure all of those things were sins.

Ryan couldn't explain the theology behind what Pastor Clark was saying. All he knew was it *felt* true. He was a sinner. He had made the creator of the universe angry, and he knew that God—or all of the gods, Buddha, Mohammed, Zeus, and Jesus—would team up on him and make him pay. Ryan felt very small, powerless, and frightened.

Katherine wasn't thinking any of these things. She was just staring at the Alec Baldwin–looking man sitting in the front row, wondering if he was mistaken for the actor when he was younger. If he was, why was his wife so unfortunate looking? What Kmart did she get that dress from, and why does her hair look like it just jumped out of a time-machine circa 1991? Katherine wasn't trying to be irreverent; she was sure what the minister was talking about was of the utmost importance, but it all seemed too much—these songs, these people, sins, and the creation of the universe. The worst thing was Ryan was so comfortable and loving every second of it. She felt like he belonged here. Had he been sneaking out and going to church every Sunday morning? Katherine's train of thought was interrupted as she watched Alec Baldwin move to the back of the stage behind Pastor Clark and play the electronic keyboard.

"Here's the good news, church," Pastor Clark said. "This God who created heaven and earth, who gave his son to die for you, he wants to forgive you of your sins. All you have to do is ask for his forgiveness, and your sins will be removed as far as the east is from the west." Ryan was impressed by how deep Pastor Clark was. How far *is* the east from the west? he wondered. Did Pastor Clark steal that line from a haiku?

"I know what some of you are saying, 'No, Pastor Clark, you don't understand what I've done. My sins are too big for God to forgive me.' And you know what I say to that? How dare you!"

Ryan was squirming again.

"How dare you be so arrogant to think that your sins are so big that Christ's sacrifice won't cover them? Let me tell you something. Christ's blood will cover your sins, every single one of them, but you have to be willing to believe in him. And you have to be ready to repent and ask for his forgiveness."

Ryan was ready. All of his sins were racing through his mind —lust, pride, greed, anger—and the thought of an all-powerful God reaching down to wipe it all away seemed too good to be true. But it is true, Ryan thought. There is a God who created the earth, who was good and kind and powerful enough to forgive sins. Ryan was ready to believe. He could barely wait for what the pastor would say next.

"If you want that forgiveness, if you're ready to accept Jesus, stand up right now and walk up here."

Ryan's legs were jelly, but he was working up the courage to stand. People around him were walking up to the front. They would all be forgiven. He wanted to grab Katherine's hand and take her up with him; he wasn't sure what exactly he was going up for, but the specifics didn't matter. He knew he had sinned more times than he could count, and something had to be done about it.

"There's no catch," Pastor Clark said. "Just come up here and accept God's forgiveness."

And that's when everything stopped.

No catch? What did he mean no catch? There's always a catch.

Ryan knew if he went home right now and opened his spam folder there would be countless emails offering a chance to meet someone great at hookup.com; credit cards with 0 percent APR; free gift certificates to Applebee's, Target, and Bed, Bath and Beyond; offers for free Viagra, laptops, three-day/four-night vacations to Hawaii, the Bahamas, or Disneyland—and behind every one of those emails was a catch.

Ryan thought, I'm in sales; I only tell a client there's no catch if I have something to hide. So, what does going up there really mean? What is Pastor Clark trying to hide?

Ryan's salvation experience suddenly grew murky—he had a sinking fear that being a Christian wasn't as simple as saying a prayer and going on with the rest of his life. Most of the Christians he sold real estate to didn't go to clubs or sleep around; they were happy and called each other "brother" and "sister"; they acted a certain way when they found out that he was a Christian realtor.

Ryan found himself suddenly overwhelmed with questions and thoughts. What is this all about? Is saying this prayer like signing at the bottom line, agreeing to some fine-print Christian code of conduct? Will everything have to change? What is this I'm really agreeing to?

A line of people now faced Pastor Clark at the front of the sanctuary, but he looked to the rest of the church and said, "It's not too late for you. It's not too late to accept God's forgiveness."

A few more people pried themselves out of their pews and walked toward their salvation. Katherine could see Ryan was struggling.

"Do you want to go up there?" she asked.

"No, I just came here for a client. I'm fine."

"Because if you want to—"

"I don't," Ryan answered.

Maybe he could believe in a God who created earth, the galaxies, the stars, the sun, and the moon. And perhaps there was even a loving God who'd sent His son as a sacrifice to cover our sins.

But no catch?

That was too much for Ryan to believe.

3

HUGS AND HANDSHAKES

Katherine scanned the lobby of Fellowship Christian Church wondering what everyone was chatting about. Were the women trading recipes for Rice Krispie treats? Were the men offering each other advice on how to give their sons fly-fishing lessons?

How can Ryan and I ever compete with these people?

Then she saw a perky man in a pinstriped suit give her husband a bear hug.

"Ryan!"

"Chris!"

Ryan hadn't even seen Chris Meeker when he scanned the sanctuary forty-five minutes earlier. He had just met Chris a few days ago when he was showing him homes on Orchard Avenue, Plum Street, and Sidewinder Lane. Chris's wife had grown sick of homeschooling their three kids and wanted to move into a neighborhood with "godly school districts." Ryan heard that Jefferson Elementary, two blocks from Plum Street, had good teachers; the students even studied French every other Friday. Something like that was probably what Mrs. Meeker had in mind when she said "godly."

"Katherine, this is Chris," Ryan said.

"I didn't even know you guys went here. What did you think of service?" Chris asked.

"Wow," Ryan said. "It was ... man, it was ... wow."

"That's exactly how I felt. Seeing all of those people come to Jesus was—"

"Powerful," Ryan said. He knew that for Christians, a person coming to Jesus was the ultimate victory, but in his short time as a Christian realtor, he had never been able to understand why. What was in it for them?

"After Pastor Clark's message I almost went up there myself," Chris said.

"Tell me about it."

Katherine's Sunday morning at Fellowship Christian Church was becoming more unnerving each passing second, so to clarify who Ryan's new best friend was, she asked, "Is Chris the guy who invited—"

"Nope. Just a client," Ryan said.

"I've got to pick up the kids from God's Country, but it was nice meeting you, Katherine, and good to see you, Ryan." Chris gave Ryan another hug and hustled through the mingling Christians toward God's Country.

Ryan and Katherine watched Chris run off, having no idea that God's Country was a place chock-full of puppets who dressed like cowboys and Indians to teach children the truths of Old and New Testament Scripture.

"Do you hug all of your clients?" Katherine asked.

"No, but sometimes I go the extra mile to provide caring service," Ryan said.

"Ryan!"

Ryan spun around to see Dan Speilmen. Before Ryan could answer, Dan had nearly picked Ryan off the ground with a massive bear hug.

"How long have you been coming here?"

"Just recently."

"Something happen at your old church?"

"No, we'd just heard great things about Fellowship Christian," Ryan answered.

"Wasn't Pastor Clark's sermon—"

"Amazing," Ryan filled in the blank again. He was getting good at this.

"And this must be Katherine," Dan said, looking at Ryan's wife. From time to time Ryan would talk to clients about his personal life, and apparently Dan had the memory of an elephant. Katherine wasn't sure what this large man was doing as he sauntered over to give her a hug, but she could smell Dan's Old Spice as they embraced. As Katherine finished her hug with Dan Speilmen she watched another couple approach Ryan and give him more hugs.

"We close this week," Phil Kennedy said to Ryan.

"Exciting, isn't it?" Ryan said.

"We are so blessed to have a real estate agent like you," Jan Kennedy added.

"Well, it is a blessing to serve people as wonderful as you two." The Kennedys giggled. Ryan was so charming. "Just give me a call first thing tomorrow morning, and we'll work out all the details."

Katherine watched her husband mingle with the Kennedys like they had all been going to Fellowship Christian Church for years, and she was frightened of him.

Frightened in a Hannibal Lecter sort of way.

"Why are so many of your clients Christians?" Katherine asked.

"Probably because his name is in the Christian Business Directory," Dan Spielmen said as if it were obvious.

"The directory is just a place where people advertise to do business with other Christians," Ryan said. They were back in their Jetta driving home.

"But you're not a Christian."

"I know, and I've been thinking about that. I think we should become Christians."

"You don't even believe in Jesus," Katherine said.

"You don't have to believe in Jesus to be a Christian."

"Yes, you do. That's exactly what you have to do to become a Christian."

"Katherine, why do you have to be so closed-minded? Why can't you picture a brave new kind of Christianity? The kind where you're a Christian who doesn't believe in Jesus."

Katherine would not dignify this with a response. She was furious at Ryan. Or at least she wanted to be. But she couldn't help finding his obsession with Christianity attractive. All he ever talked about were interest rates and closing costs and realtor fees; now he was passionate about something bizarre that she didn't understand, but it was exciting.

In the church lobby this morning he wasn't some bland real estate agent; he was more like Donald Trump. He shook hands and gave hugs with the charm of Bill Clinton. People lit up when he walked by; they clung to every word he spoke. Watching Ryan made Katherine want to grab her husband's arm to show that this charming man—this Mr. Wonderful, Mr. Right, Mr. Perfect that all the girls in her dorm had fallen in love with so many years ago—was hers.

"I really liked it there this morning."

"So did I," Katherine said, surprising herself.

Ryan and Katherine went to church for the next month and it was more of the same. Ryan seemed to know everyone while Katherine didn't know a soul. And if someone did know her, they wouldn't address her as Katherine; instead they usually just said, "Oh-you're-Ryan-Fisher's-wife." And they said it just like that, all in one word, as if it were her name. She told Ryan that she wouldn't go again unless they started to make their own friends—people who knew *both* of them. So, Katherine invited Kevin and Jennifer Anderson over for dinner.

The Andersons were the perfect couple, good looking, but not too good looking, sharply dressed, great teeth, and friendly as Mary Kay sales reps. Ryan was a little uncomfortable to learn that Kevin was the associate pastor at Fellowship Christian Church, but as dinner started he settled in. They all had lots in common. There was lots of laughing. At one point Katherine mentioned how she didn't know a lot of people at church.

"Well, you should come to our Bible study," Jennifer said.

"I don't know," Katherine said moving her pasta from one side of the plate to the other.

"Oh, come on, check it out. You'd fit in right in," Jennifer said. Katherine smiled and agreed to come. Maybe she would fit right in.

Overall, the evening went smoothly until Kevin said, "Now I know a lot of people think Fellowship isn't perfect."

"Well, sure, nothing's perfect," Katherine said. But she would have said anything to Kevin and Jennifer. They were so charming and great, she didn't want to say a thing that could jeopardize their budding friendship.

Ryan, however, sat up and was really interested for the first time all evening. "So what exactly do other people think isn't perfect?" Ryan asked.

"Ryan!" Katherine said.

"What? I'm curious." And he was. There were things that annoyed Ryan about church. On Sunday mornings, traffic in and out was unbearable, and there were only four hundred parking spaces for the church's 750 members. The services went too long. The good seats were all taken up unless they got there twenty minutes early. And when Katherine and Ryan first came to the church, the ushers fawned all over them like preteen girls at a boy band concert, but now that they had been faithfully attending for five weeks the ushers only gave them a polite "good morning" and continued to sniff around for first-time visitors.

Ryan knew the church had its flaws. But what surprised him was that *other Christians* thought church wasn't perfect. He sort of just assumed they would smile and love whatever was thrown their way. He didn't understand that it was an age-old tradition to nitpick at how loud the music is, gripe about how the coffee in the lobby tastes, and bicker until the bitter end about who gets to run the committee for the women's tea and tiny muffin brunch. He had no way to know that this view on church was more addicting than nicotine and potato chips.

"Honestly, it could be anything," Kevin said. "Some people think the service is too long. Others think it's too short. People have strong opinions about the music: It's too fast or slow or loud or quiet. People have thoughts about Sunday school or service times. It differs from person to person."

"So, how do you deal with all of those complaints?" Ryan asked.

"Well, that's why I bring this up. We don't look at them like complaints; as a staff we look at it as feedback."

"Feedback?"

"Yeah, room for improvement. Ways we can do church better."

"That makes complete sense," Ryan said.

Kevin went on, "You see, we find — "

But Ryan's thoughts drifted. It never occurred to him that running a church was like running a business. The church had to retain members like customers, the church had to have a business plan, a budget, and so on. Ryan started to think about the things he would do differently if he had a church of his own. The way he would run a church business. He wondered if he could create a church, what would it look like?

But there was no point in thinking about it, it would never happen.

" — and that's the key to maintaining a healthy church."

"No, I totally agree," Ryan said. He had no idea what Kevin actually said, but Ryan was pretty sure it was nice and agreeable. Everything Kevin said was that way.

"Great," Katherine said. "Who's ready for strawberry shortcake?"

— 4 —

EMERGENCY
PREGNANCY TEST

Rain pelted Ryan's Jetta as he sat at a stoplight. He watched children in yellow slickers and red galoshes race newspaper boats down the streams that had gathered in the gutters. They were cute and innocent—for them all that mattered was the pride of knowing that their father had coated the boats with the perfect amount of wax. Ryan wanted to be the dad who would play in the rain and make paper boats, the dad who'd buy Chuck E. Cheese pizza and tokens for the entire Little League team after their victory.

As Ryan listened to the thunder and the rain on the hood of his car and waited for the blurry red light to turn to a blurry green, he couldn't help but face the possibility that he might never get the chance to be any kind of father. Katherine would turn thirty soon, and he wasn't getting any younger. She'd gone off birth control six months ago, and at first he was nervous she would get pregnant right away. He thought of all the annoying things that he would have to do to prepare for a baby: paint the spare bedroom a powder blue or a pink Pepto-Bismol color, make 7-Eleven runs at three in the morning to satisfy Katherine's Rocky Road and pickle craving, and he'd have to deal with morning sickness.

Despite his best efforts, Ryan couldn't stay nervous. His mind would stray toward all of the reasons he was excited about becoming a father. He'd dream about Little League games and Christmas pageants, playing with Barbies or G.I. Joes. Most of all, he thought about how their baby would be this perfect angelic mixture of him and his wife.

Lately, Ryan tried not to think about a baby. He was too worried about why Katherine hadn't become pregnant. He was sure it was his fault. He'd never taken care of his body like he should have, and he'd watched a *20/20* special on impotence that confirmed all of his worst fears. Barbara Walters warned about some of the causes of impotence.*

There was so much to worry about with creating a baby — so much stress, so much that could go wrong. And Ryan and Katherine's inability to conceive started the argument that sent Ryan storming out of the house, into the rain, and driving down the sopping-wet streets without any clue where he was going.

The argument started a half hour ago after Katherine finished taking another pregnancy test. She stared at it as Ryan paced back and forth waiting for the result. Katherine didn't like the packaging of the test she had taken last month, so she bought a new test with better packaging on sale for fifty-eight cents cheaper. Katherine was sure that this new test would change their luck. Her eyes widened as something appeared in the tiny window.

"It's a dash!" Katherine said.

---

*The causes for impotence included wearing briefs instead of boxers (Ryan had loved briefs ever since he received his first pair of He-Man underoos when he was six), consuming yellow dye number five (a prominent ingredient in Twinkies and Mountain Dew; both were fixtures in Ryan's diet from his freshman year in high school to his freshman year of college), stress (Ryan's life had been injected with lots of stress in his attempt to climb the real estate ladder), and steroids (Ryan was a twiggy 164 pounds, but he still thought three out of four was pretty bad).

"It's a dash?" Ryan said. Then, "What does a dash mean?"

"How am I supposed to know?"

"Get the box," Ryan shouted.

"I threw it away." Katherine stated.

"You threw it away? Why did you throw it away?"

"I'm sorry. I didn't know you were collecting pregnancy test boxes!"

Ryan ran into the bathroom and dug the box out of the trash. He flipped it over. He scanned through warnings and disclaimers, over directions on how to take the test (*step 1: Urinate on the stick*; there was no *step 2*) and finally discovered what the dash meant.

"What does it mean?" Katherine asked.

"It's just one dash?"

"Yes."

"One dash means not pregnant." Ryan said.

Ryan stood in silence and watched as mascara dripped down Katherine's face. He hated seeing his wife cry, and he couldn't help but wonder why women always put extra eye makeup on before something really sad happens, like a breakup or watching a movie about a husband who loses his wife to cancer. Ryan decided to say something comforting.

"Maybe the test's wrong."

"The test isn't wrong. They're like 97 percent accurate," Katherine sobbed, not understanding that Ryan was just fishing for something comforting to say.

And Ryan, not understanding that Katherine needed to be held instead of reasoned with, replied, "Maybe we're that 3 percent."

"Are you saying that this is my fault?"

"I'm not saying—"

"I wanted to try a new test."

"It's a generic test."

"It was on sale."

"Because they're desperate to get rid of all the cheap tests that are wrong most of the time. Tests don't go bad like bread and milk, so there must be some reason they put the emergency pregnancy test on sale."

"*Error proof* test," Katherine corrected.

"What?"

"EPT stands for error proof test."

"Well, aren't you so smart? They should put you on *Jeopardy* because you are so freaking brilliant," Ryan shouted.

Katherine and Ryan's argument blossomed into something to marvel at. They started out by arguing about the pregnancy test, then debated the reasons they couldn't get pregnant, and before long, in-laws and sins from the past were peppered throughout their attacks.

The end result left Ryan at this stoplight, unable to think straight because hobbit-sized raindrops were pounding the hood of his car. It was at times like this that Ryan wished Jesus were real — then he could pray for God to make Katherine pregnant like He did for women in the Bible. He nearly rolled the dice and prayed to believe in Jesus at that moment, but he knew if Jesus was out there, Ryan would just be believing in Him in hopes that God could help his wife get pregnant. Jesus was smart enough to see through that. And to punish Ryan, Jesus would make Katherine have a baby with no arms or a bat child like those tabloids always talk about. Still, Ryan felt he needed help. They'd tried everything and it wasn't working. So, he decided to head toward Fellowship Christian Church to ask Pastor Clark to barter with God on his behalf.

"What's God's policy on getting women pregnant?" Ryan asked Pastor Clark.

Pastor Clark had just put his jacket on and was ready to make his way home through the rain when Ryan barged into the office. An undue amount of phone calls and emails had already kept him at the office well past six, and he knew his wife would be upset if he didn't make it home in time for applesauce and pork chop night.

Nonetheless, Pastor Clark was glad to see Ryan. Helping people in times of crisis was one of his favorite things about being a pastor, and he'd wanted to help Ryan ever since they'd met on a Sunday morning a few weeks ago. After the service, Pastor Clark noticed that even though he'd never before seen Ryan at Fellowship Christian Church, Ryan seemed to know everyone. And when Pastor Clark introduced himself to Ryan, he found Ryan clever, funny, fearless, and surprisingly elusive about his history as a Christian. Now Pastor Clark had a chance to understand this charming stranger who'd been frequenting his church. So Pastor Clark took a deep breath and asked, "Did you get another woman pregnant?"

"No!" Ryan said.

"Okay. Good."

"I need God to get my wife pregnant."

"God doesn't really get our wives pregnant," Pastor Clark explained.

"He got women in the Bible pregnant. I've read up on it. "

"He didn't exactly—"

"Like Mary, and Abraham's wife, and Jezebel—"

"He didn't get Jezebel pregnant."

"But he got the other women pregnant."

"Sort of. He helped them."

"Right. So what do I need to do for God to *help* my wife get pregnant? Do I need to give a certain amount to the church or feed the poor or buy Girl Scout cookies?"

"It's not that simple."

"Why not?"

"How long have you been a Christian?" Pastor Clark asked.

Ryan was getting really sick of this question. "Do I have to be a Christian a certain amount of time for God to get my wife pregnant?"

"God doesn't work like that."

"Well, how does God work?" Ryan asked.

Pastor Clark smiled because everyone asks this sort of question in times of crisis. A hurting person will ask some form of the question: Why won't God fix things? Why won't God give me the money for my mortgage payment? Why won't he make my husband love me? Why won't he allow my wife to get pregnant? With one wave of the magic wand, a sprinkle of pixie dust, an abracadabra, or whatever else God does, he could make everything in life better, so why doesn't he?

Pastor Clark didn't understand why this was such an issue for everyone. There was no reason that God should act like our fairy godmother, and Pastor Clark certainly didn't base his allegiance to God on what God would *do* for him. That would be like saying, "God, if you really loved me, you would buy me a new car. God, if you really cared, then you would make this guy or this girl love me. If you wanted the best for me, you'd give me a promotion at work."

This line of thinking made Pastor Clark queasy — we don't base our love for other people on what they can do for us, so why would we hold God to this standard? When Pastor Clark was fresh out of seminary he'd get furious when asked these questions in a counseling session, and he'd examine the theology behind the sovereignty of God. He'd tell, and sometimes read aloud, the stories of Job (God let Satan kill Job's kids, destroy his possessions, and give him boils), Lot (God destroyed Lot's hometown of Sodom and turned his wife into a pillar of salt just for looking back to see the destruction), and Balaam (a minor prophet whose donkey saw an angel and refused to move. Balaam whipped the donkey, and then the donkey *talked back* asking Balaam not to hit him. Balaam's donkey may have been the first-ever member of PETA).

Pastor Clark's message was simple, "God is sovereign and you are not." Pastor Clark had been saying this in counseling sessions for so long that he'd forgotten he originally got the line from a bestselling gospel/rap/heavy metal/country-western/folk/adult-contemporary singer named Carman.

Pastor Clark assumed Carman's point was that sometimes God lets good things happen, sometimes he allows tragedy, and we can never understand his infinite wisdom.

Pastor Clark's intensity usually didn't quell his church members' fears, and as he had grown as a pastor he'd become more empathetic in counseling sessions. But at the moment Pastor Clark didn't feel like sugarcoating. When he stared at Ryan, fire and brimstone churned in his stomach. There was something special about Ryan, but to unearth it he needed a shove in the right direction.

"Ryan, what is your life really about?"

"What am I supposed to say? God?"

"Say what you think. When you get up in the morning, what gives you the strength to get dressed, sit in traffic, deal with people's nonsense, drive home in even worse traffic, only to have to do it all over again tomorrow?"

"Pastor Clark, I came here to feel better."

"You came to the wrong place."

"Apparently."

"If you want to feel better, there are bartenders all over the city that will serve up quick remedies for your problems. If that's what you want, please get out of my office because you're wasting my time and my pork chops are getting cold. If you want to treat your problems and save your marriage, then answer the question: What drives you?"

"Same thing that drives every other American—a paycheck. I want security for my family. I want to have enough money so I can retire, own a big fat yacht, and eat jumbo shrimp all day long."

"Then your problem isn't that your wife can't get pregnant."

"No, I'm pretty sure that's exactly my problem."

"Your problem is that you have nothing outside of yourself. I've heard all about you. You've been fishing for clients from the moment you walked through these doors. As I understand, you've done pretty well for yourself. Congratulations. You're going to get that yacht, and you're going to sail around the seven seas alone because you never took the time to invest in anyone else. We're called to something more—something greater."

"You're the pastor. You're called to something greater."

"Wrong. We're all called to act like pastors. There's a hurting world out there that needs Jesus. Listen, Ryan, I wish I could give you a spoonful of pixie dust that would help you and your wife. But I'm fresh out. So all I can tell you is that I've discovered when we take the focus off ourselves and help those around us, everything else seems to take care of itself."

5

THE NASTY WEBSITES

Ryan could hear the bell jingling from inside Kmart.

Don't look him in the eye, Ryan thought as he burst out of the store.

"Would you care to make a donation to the Salvation Army?"

"No money," Ryan said, not even glancing toward the man in the Santa suit.

"Any little bit will help," the man said, calling Ryan's bluff.

Ryan put his bags in the car, baffled that it was October 17 and a man in a Santa suit was already petitioning for money or change or American Express checks or whatever else he could get his jolly little hands on. For the next two months a simple trip to Kmart for thumbtacks would start and end with having to look at Santa in his whiskey-stained suit. The man would smile at him with rosy red cheeks, not because he was jolly but probably because he had frostbite. And every time Ryan told Santa no, Santa seemed to take it so personally, as if Santa had asked Ryan out and Ryan had told him that he had to wash his hair.

But the worst part about the whole experience was that Santa wouldn't just ask him for money as he entered the Kmart. Santa was too vindictive for that. As Ryan left, Santa asked for money *again*, and Ryan wasn't sure if Santa had forgotten that he'd already asked for money, or if he was just hoping Ryan had grabbed a couple of twenties out of the ATM to drop into the rusty red bucket.

Ryan drove his Jetta a couple of blocks away from Kmart, but when he pulled up to a stoplight he thought, What's wrong with me? I'm furious at a man who dresses like Santa to feed the homeless. Pastor Clark's right—I'm going to hell.*

When the light turned green, Ryan whipped the car around and headed back to Kmart.

"I'm a liar. I told you I had no money. I have lots of it. Here." Ryan opened his wallet to make a generous donation to the Salvation Army, but then he remembered his wallet was empty. It was always empty. Ryan had lots of money in his bank account, but he never carried cash because he hated change.

Change makes everything dirty.

It gets in between couch cushions and car seats, rattles in jeans pockets, clutters countertops, and creates a need for special change holders like glass jars and porcelain pigs. However, as much as Ryan hated having change, he had always loved paying with *exact* change.

He loved paying in exact change so much, that when Ryan was fourteen, he wore a change belt everywhere he went. He would pay exact change for Twinkies, baseball cards, and *Star Trek* paperback novels (he specifically liked the novels that focused on the adventures of Chekov, whom Ryan had always considered to be the most underappreciated character in the *Star Trek* canon).

Still everyone made fun of Ryan's change belt. But it wasn't

---

* Pastor Clark had never told Ryan he was going to hell, but Ryan was pretty sure that's what he had been hinting at with his big "Who are you living for?" speech.

just the change belt—they made fun of everything about Ryan: the *Star Trek* books, the way his hair was parted straight down the middle, his thick glasses, his awkward clothes. They all added up to Ryan having to sit at lunch alone, having go "stag" to every dance, and being tripped as he walked down the hall.

Freshman year was a nightmare.

That summer, Ryan realized things had to change: Contacts instead of glasses, messy hair instead of straight, violent movies instead of space movies, and actual music instead of Weird Al's parodies of it. He needed to be somebody the other kids would like—he needed to be anybody other than himself.

And that meant more than just getting rid of old stuff—it meant he had to become someone new and likeable and charming. He was always funny with just a few friends, but he learned to tell jokes at parties. He was always smart, but he became quick on his feet; he was kind but learned flattery would get him everywhere; and he was shy but he began to understand that if he could act confident enough, even when he didn't feel confident, he could get away with anything. It was a process, and it didn't always go smoothly, but freshman to sophomore year Ryan turned from a caterpillar to a charming salesman of a butterfly. It was then that he learned to do whatever it took to get ahead so he would never have to sit alone at lunch again.

Ryan's paid for everything with a credit card, ever since he was old enough to get one.

He never carried cash, and even though today he could just go inside and get money to give to the Salvation Army, that seemed too easy. Ryan felt he needed to pay some sort of penance for his years of lying to Santa—maybe Jesus would be upset if he just dropped money into the bucket and left. But he'd also heard conflicting reports concerning Jesus' feelings about Santa; some said Jesus was upset that Santa had been trying to upstage him during Christmas, so maybe Ryan was doing the Christian thing by lying to Santa.

Nevertheless, Ryan decided to help Santa and the Salvation Army.

He went inside and bought two giant Christmas bells. When he came back out, he stood next to Santa and rang his handbells with the fury of a hunchback. Ryan wanted people to hear the cry of the bells through their entire shopping experience; he wanted patrons to feel guilty about not contributing to the Salvation Army while they enjoyed blue-light specials.

And it worked. People couldn't help but contribute wads of cash to Santa and the screaming man in a business suit. It was the most entreating thing they had ever seen. After fifteen minutes, a man with a mullet and a mustache asked if he could join in the fun. Ryan welcomed him to the posse, the man took one of Ryan's hand bells and rang it proudly while he smoked a half pack of Marlboro Lights.

The group created a system of what to yell as patrons entered and exited the Kmart. Santa would chuckle, "Ho, ho, ho!" Ryan would shout, "Would you like to make a donation?" and the man with the mullet would bark, "Feliz Navidad!" in an attempt to be multicultural. Ryan had to leave after an hour; lunch was over and he had real estate business to attend to. Santa expressed how grateful he was and told Ryan he was pretty sure that they had broken an all-time record for hourly donations. Santa also said, "No one's ever helped me like this. What made you want to help me?"

Ryan gave an odd answer: "I help people because I'm a pastor."

Katherine accepted Jennifer's invitation and started attending Bible study. She went faithfully every Thursday night for a month straight. She loved it. But on her first Thursday she was anxious about the whole thing. She'd never been to a Bible study before, but she had been part of several book clubs. She missed her book club that met at Mrs. King's house. She missed sipping shiraz and debating the themes in *Sense and Sensibility*. Two years ago, when Mrs. King's book club disbanded, Katherine felt a loss. She feared that she would never again find a group as good as Mrs. King's.

She was wrong. Thursday night Bible study was even better. She'd meet with a group of women, they'd knock back a couple of mugs of instant international coffee, and the discussion would begin. They wouldn't debate—they would glean insights from Romans, Esther, Second Corinthians, and Deuteronomy. These insights would give them practical tools to improve their marriages, their parenting skills, their finances, and their walks with Christ.*

Sometimes the discussions would go off course. At Mrs. King's group when the discussion went down a rabbit trail, they would debate politics and occasionally get as personal as gossiping about their sex lives. But at Bible study, when the discussion would go off course, they would delve into deep and personal matters. They would share their hopes and dreams, fears and insecurities, highs and lows. They would laugh, cry on each other's shoulders, and lean on each other for prayer and support. Katherine didn't think she would enjoy spending her Thursday nights with a group of women who adored Dr. Phil, but she felt so at home.

For Katherine, Bible study became a sanctuary where she could be open and vulnerable. Thursday nights were her reason for living. She wondered if she had been wrong about Dr. Phil.

Maybe she had even been wrong about Jesus.

---

*Katherine never quite understood what "walking with Christ" meant. But there were lots of things like "washed in the blood" and "fishers of men" that Katherine didn't understand. Whenever someone would mention something like that, she would just smile and nod like she was following right along even though she was usually a little scared.

And for the first month, every Thursday went along great — they were perfect evenings filled with laughter, hugs, and growing friendships. But the fifth time Katherine went to Bible study, things started out differently. Marcy Wilkommen was in tears within the first few minutes. "*Sports Illustrated Swimsuit*, Sears, Victoria's Secret … he went to all of the nasty websites," Marcy said through heavy sobs. Katherine offered her the box of Kleenex. All the women of the Bible study leaned forward, waiting for what she would say next. Marcy could only sob.

"Have some tea," Jennifer Anderson said compassionately. She had a way of seeming in control of every situation.

"Did he go to any of the hardcore sites?" Christy asked.

"Christy," Jennifer scolded.

"What? I'm trying to be supportive," Christy said.

"How did you find out?" Jennifer asked.

"He told me," Marcy said.

"That pig," Christy said.

"No, that's good. It means he feels convicted," Jennifer said. "He wants to work this out."

"He does?"

"Sure he does. Wait here, Marcy."

Jennifer walked out of the room with perfect posture and a sense of purpose. The other women leaned in to counsel Marcy, but Katherine wondered where Jennifer had gone. After a few minutes she appeared with Kevin. Kevin crouched next to Marcy, grabbed her hand, and gave it a pastoral squeeze.

"Let's give Dale a call," Kevin said.

"I don't know," Marcy said.

"I know you and your husband love each other. You've just hit a little speed bump. Let's give him a call. I'll put on a pot of coffee, and we'll work through the night until we get this figured out."

"Okay." Marcy dried another tear.

Katherine had to feel her jaw to make sure it hadn't dropped. They're going to just give him a call? They'll work through the night to figure this out? The entire situation was so romantic. Dale and Marcy are going through marital turbulence, while Kevin and Jennifer, supercouple, work through the night to right the marriage that has gone astray. And they would fix the marriage. There is nothing they can't do.

"We're going to have to cut group short tonight," Jennifer said.

Katherine was the last to leave. She sat in her car across the street hidden by the shade of an elm tree. She watched the Andersons' house as the front door opened. She watched Dale's silhouette slightly heave up and down as Marcy stepped out. He seemed sorry and embarrassed he'd ever even heard the words *Victoria's Secret*. Then Dale embraced Marcy. Kevin put a pastorly arm around the couple and guided them inside. When the door shut, Katherine stared through the darkness.

Would anyone ever trust Ryan and me like that? Could we be a supercouple?

Katherine imagined herself as the friend that you would call when everything went wrong. The friend who could say the right things and make the right calls so everything would be okay. She would dress with something from her stylish yet commanding wardrobe. Her house would be perfectly decorated, warm, sophisticated. She would have a cupboard full of twelve different kinds of exotic teas, and she would always pick the perfect one to comfort her ailing friend. When her friend would tell Katherine her problem, she would listen but not enable. If the friend started to wallow in her misery, Katherine would say something like, "You got yourself into this mess, and you're the only person who can pull yourself out. I can help you, but you've got to want it." When her friend nodded okay, Katherine would help create a course of action.

(What is the matter with you? You're fantasizing about doling out advice straight from Dr. Phil!)

Katherine let out a deep breath. She fished her car keys out of her purse and put them in the ignition. She tried not to feel frightened by the person she was becoming. It was true: Jennifer and Marcy were the type of people that she would have made fun of before she and Ryan started attending Fellowship Christian Church. But now the women in her Bible study were her close friends. She wanted to be one of them, but she knew she wasn't. So why had she fallen in love with this group of women? Was it just because she had spent countless hours with them crying about how she and Ryan couldn't get pregnant? They were nice to her, they were kind and thoughtful, but they were so cheesy about it. Every week at Bible study played out as if it were on the Hallmark channel.

(Helping your friends is cheesy?)

Katherine let out another breath. She felt as if an angel was on one shoulder and the devil on the other.

Still, she knew what the real problem was. Her life had no significance. Having a baby gave life meaning. Listening to Coen Jackson's music at the Coffee Pot gave life meaning. What Jennifer and Kevin were doing across the street for Dale and Marcy gave life meaning. But being a loan officer, coming home, ordering out for dinner, and falling asleep while watching TiVoed episodes of *CSI* with Ryan made life seem meaningless. She needed something more. But all her husband was concerned with was growing his real estate empire. He was using these kind, caring people for his financial gain. Ryan would never spend his time doing something kind for someone else.

Before Katherine drove off, she glanced inside the Andersons' house, and she could see the two couples talking — there was even a pot of coffee like Kevin had promised.

She drove down the dark street, unsure of where to go next. But she had already decided she wouldn't come home until two hours later, when Bible study usually ended.

After helping Santa and the Salvation Army, Ryan wondered why he'd never done anything like that before. It was like nothing he'd ever felt. Maybe it was similar to the way someone felt after skydiving for the first time or the way hippies felt rolling in the mud listening to Jimi Hendrix at Woodstock.

Whatever this feeling was, Ryan grew crack-cocaine addicted to it. There was something intoxicating about random acts of kindness. So, he committed one every Monday through Friday on his lunch hour. The part he loved most was watching people's reactions. It was like they had been reverse Punk'd.

One Thursday he got a few rolls of quarters from the bank, walked around downtown, and paid up on every parking meter that had twenty minutes or less in it. When Sandy (a middle-aged woman who'd been embarrassingly lonely since her divorce five years ago) saw Ryan drop the quarter into the meter, she nearly cried on the spot.

"Thank you. Wow. You're just dropping quarters into people's meters?" Sandy asked.

"Only during lunch hour."

"Well, thanks," Sandy said, still a little awestruck.

"Don't mention it. It's the least a pastor could do."

On Mondays Ryan approached the cashier at McDonald's and told him, "Here's my card. I'll pay for the next six people in line." Ryan stood back and watched one customer after the next stand in shock as the cashier heroically announced that their Filet-O-Fish value meal had already been paid for.

Some customers would ask, "Who paid for this?" and the cashier would point to the corner and say, "Pastor Ryan did."

On Tuesdays Ryan stopped on the side of the road to help stranded victims with broken-down cars. On Wednesdays Ryan read stories to elementary-school children.

Ryan loved performing acts of kindness, and he was starting to feel oddly comfortable with telling people he was a pastor. Initially he had good reasons. After all, hadn't Pastor Clark suggested that everyone is called to act like a pastor? And since Ryan was acting like a pastor, why couldn't he just tell people he *was* one? He supposed he could tell people he was a Christian, but he never accepted Christ, so that would be as big of a lie as telling them he was a pastor.

And there is also a stigma attached to telling people you're a Christian. He had tried it once after he had spent his lunch hour dishing out mashed potatoes at a homeless shelter. The coordinator running the shelter told Ryan, "Thanks for all your help." Ryan responded, "I was just trying to be a good Christian." The coordinator jumped a little, as if Ryan had admitted that he was really a vampire and he was volunteering in the kitchen so he could suck the homeless people's blood after the day was over. Ryan thought he could say nothing after an act of kindness, but the few times he'd tried it, it seemed even more devious—his acts of kindness were not met with gratitude and smiles, but suspicion, as if there were some sort of creepy reason he was acting so nice. Maybe he had put razor blades in the cheeseburgers, or maybe he had put change in women's car meters so he could pick them up. So, he resolved that telling people he was a pastor was the only way to feel good about committing acts of kindness.

But there was a bigger problem. When Ryan told people he was a pastor, they would often say things like: "Where's your church?" "I would love to come hear you speak on a Sunday morning." "You're the coolest pastor I've ever met."

All of this made Ryan think he could be a pastor. He could picture a large sanctuary with brightly colored stained-glass windows, a huge wooden pulpit, an organ that would play thick heavenly pipe music, and he could see himself standing there in a silky white robe with a blue sash, addressing the masses. He would tell jokes and read the Bible, and they would be moved. But Ryan knew that no church was just going to make him a pastor. The only way to become one would be to start a church of his own. But that would be crazy.

Crazy like a fox.

Ryan had always wanted to go into real estate for himself. He had been reading for years about how to start a small business. He knew the importance of strong goals, a mission statement, a financial plan, a killer website, creating a brand, and finding the perfect location. In his real estate dealings he had seen a lot of advertisements for other churches—many of them looked like they were designed by the same agency that did the print work for *Miami Vice*. The websites weren't much better; some of them would play synthesized versions of "Amazing Grace" that sounded more like Super Mario Brothers.

But, if there was a church with a sharp professional website, a prime location, a clean memorable brand, and a focused mission statement, it could compete, couldn't it?

No, it wouldn't just compete—it would explode.

People would flock to it every Sunday as if Bono himself were preaching the sermon. And it would give Ryan the chance to devote more time to acts of kindness. It was simple: He would tell jokes and warm anecdotes on Sunday mornings, he would make sure his ushers took the time to make everyone feel welcome on their second and third Sundays (not just their first), and he would be kind during the week. His life would be perfect. At parties Ryan would seem significant. When some self-important lawyer would say, "It took six months, but I saved someone from going to jail," Ryan would just sip his martini and then reply, "It took me one hour on Sunday, and I saved fifty souls." Everyone would walk away from the trite lawyer and huddle around Ryan, clearly the most interesting person at the party.

Ryan tried to stop himself. He didn't really want to become a pastor. He didn't want to plant a church. He didn't want to become a community hero. A legend in the church world. To be adored by women and children. A savior to everyone who crossed his path.

He didn't want any of that.

6

THE PROPOSAL

The summer after second grade, Ryan had a clear plan of what he was going to do with his life. He was going to dig to China. Ryan asked his father, "Has anyone ever dug to China?" "Don't think so," Mr. Fisher replied without looking up from the newspaper.

That's all young Ryan needed to hear. He began drawing maps, gathering tools, rallying the neighbor kids and telling them how they were going to do the impossible. They were going to dig to China. News coverage would soon follow, and they would be heroes and legends like Christopher Columbus or Magellan.

When all of the neighborhood kids gathered around the sandbox, Ryan told them how, when the project was complete, they could jump into the hole and go to China every single day. They could walk upside down, enjoy buffets filled with fresh Mongolian beef and piping hot won ton soup, and they would end every day watching those parades where fifteen people are all dressed up like one giant dragon. Every kid in the neighborhood bought into the plan. And for three straight days Ryan was General Patton commanding his troops, overcoming problems, and refreshing his friends with ice cold red Kool-Aid when the heat got unbearable.

At the end of the third day of digging, Ryan's father came out to see the giant hole Ryan created in the sandbox.

"What is this?" Mr. Fisher asked.

Everyone gathered around the hole next to Ryan, proud to show Mr. Fisher their progress.

Ryan announced, "We're digging to China. We're going to be the first kids to dig there."

"Grownups haven't even dug to China."

"That's because they haven't tried," Ryan said.

"No, it's because it's impossible. The middle of the earth is solid rock, and if you somehow get through that, the earth's core will melt you and your friends. And even then you would only be halfway to China."

"Oh," Ryan said as the wind was kicked out of him.

The next day, less than half of the neighborhood kids showed up for the dig. By the week's end everyone had grown disinterested and found Nintendo or Little League Baseball to fill up their summer days.

Ryan was left to dig alone.

He spent another two weeks trying to prove his father wrong. But eventually he grew too tired and embarrassed to keep digging.

And now, over twenty years later, Ryan didn't tell anyone he was seriously considering planting a church. It'd be like telling them he was digging to China. He knew he couldn't utter his plan out loud. Even Katherine

(especially Katherine)

would shoot the plan to pieces. She would say the obvious: He was too young, inexperienced, immature, unprepared; he had the wrong motivation, knew nothing about God, didn't believe in Jesus, and so on.

There were a million reasons it wouldn't work. So, before Ryan would let his plan see the light of day he wanted to make sure it was bulletproof.

First it had to have a solid foundation. Ryan felt he couldn't plant the church in Denver; there were too many Christians who saw him as just a real estate agent. They'd have a difficult time believing that he was a pastor. Worse, Pastor Clark and Fellowship Christian Church would probably frown on the idea and tell all of the Christians to stay away.

That's why Ryan decided they would have to move. But where? Another big city? Chicago, Houston, Atlanta? They all had big successful churches that could smoke Ryan's little operation.

As a matter of fact, nearly every major market in the United States now has a big powerful Christian church. They are as much a part of the landscape as the local Major League ball club.

Therefore, the only thing left was a small town. They were littered all over the western plains of the United States. And very few of them had a church that could compete with Ryan. They wouldn't be nearly as slick and polished as the church Ryan was planning, and he could go into a small town and wow the locals with his charm and business savvy.

Still, the question was where? Should he tack up a map and throw a dart and see where it lands? No, the thing that made the most sense was to go to a state with the most Christians. And when Ryan did a little research, he stumbled onto a few surveys and census results that pointed to a clear-cut favorite: Oklahoma.

The state was crawling with Christians. Seemed like as good a place as any. Oklahoma, the state rich with history, the place where all of the Native American tribes were once moved to because the white man wanted the rest of America to himself. "We want Kansas, Nebraska, and New Mexico!" the white man shouted. "But you can have Oklahoma." Then, later, the white man decided he wanted Oklahoma as well. So there was a race and all one had to do to gain a chunk of the state was to be the first to run up to it and plant a flag there. One man placed a flag down and shouted, "I shall call this Tulsa!" And then a far less creative man planted a flag and shouted, "I shall call this Oklahoma City." Oklahoma was kind of like America's version of Australia.

Ryan had only been there once to visit a cousin named Jeff who lived in a small town. But that's all he could remember. He called his mom to see if she could help him remember any more details.

"Mom."

"Hi honey. How come you never call your mother anymore?"

"Sorry, I've been busy. But I have a quick question: Remember that cousin who lived in Oklahoma?"

"Yes, Bridgett's kid. Jeff."

"Yeah, Jeff."

"How big was the town he lived in?"

"You know, it was medium-sized to small."

"Mom, I have no idea what that means."

"It's smaller than Denver."

"But it's smaller than most of the big cities in Oklahoma, isn't it?"

"Yeah, I think so."

"But is it big enough to have a successful business?"

"I think they have a Wal-Mart," Mrs. Fisher said.

"And what was the name of that town? Browingland? Bakerton?"

"Bartlesville."

"Yes, Bartlesville. Thanks Mom."

"You're welcome. Now, how's Katherine? Are you two doing okay? I mean are you *really* doing okay?" Mrs. Fisher asked.

This was the price for calling his mother. Calling her about anything always led to a conversation about how he was *really* doing. "How is your marriage ... *really?* How is your job ... *really?*" she would ask. Ryan hated this question because it implied that what he'd told her was a lie, or at least he was masking his true feelings about life. And even though this usually was the case (He wasn't going to tell his mother everything; who tells their mother everything?), it was still irritating.

So Ryan updated his mother on his life, editing out the juicy details. But for the remainder of the conversation, the predominate thought echoing around in the back of his mind was — Bartlesville. It had a nice friendly ring to it. It sounded like the perfect place to plant a church.

Katherine had been worried about her marriage ever since last Thursday when Marcy's husband's Internet scandal brought Bible study to an abrupt end. As she drove around the city she realized something was wrong, and she immediately figured out what it was: Ryan was having an affair. It was probably with Natasha, that perky new blonde realtor. She had the million-dollar smile, the perfect body, the adorable giggle, and she was fun to be around. The thing that irritated Katherine the most was that she hadn't seen it earlier. How had she not realized that Ryan was just as absent from this marriage as she was? She wasn't the only one disinterested in every conversation. And she obviously wasn't the only one who had noticed their sex life had turned into a science experiment, with thermometers, calendars, textbooks, ovulation sticks, and pregnancy tests.

The only question was how long had the affairs been going on? Weeks? Months? Years? Earlier, she had been fantasizing that she and Ryan could be a super-couple — she could picture them having late-night life-altering conversations with couples on the brink of divorce. Now, they'd need Kevin, Jennifer, and a pot of coffee just to save their own marriage.

And Katherine didn't think anything could be worse than infidelity until she discovered Ryan's Church Plant Proposal. She discovered it completely by accident. She may have never learned of the plan, and Ryan probably would have never gone through with it, if it wasn't for her copper earrings. But she needed those earrings. They were the only things that went with her bronze belt and her bronze purse, and she wanted her outfit to really stand out at church (Katherine had actually become a little obsessive over her Sunday morning attire).

She'd scoured the jewelry on her dresser with no success, and her last resort was the office, a room she almost never entered, to look through an old jewelry box in the closet. But when she entered she found something that made her forget all about her earrings—a packet of paper on the desk in the office. She probably wouldn't have noticed it, but the packet's title was hard to ignore: "The People's Church. A Church Plant Proposal." She picked the packet up, and in complete shock, read the following:

THE PEOPLE'S CHURCH
A Church Plant Proposal

Written by Pastor Ryan Fisher

Mission Statement
The People's Church is a cutting edge revolutionary church where all are invited to enjoy everything that's great about being a Christian.

Location
Bartlesville, Oklahoma.

Advertising
The two most important parts of a business are advertising and

location. Once I find a prime location for the church, we'll need a website with a captivating design that's easy to navigate. The church will also need a gripping corporate logo, and perhaps even a catchy jingle that can be played during radio ads. Maybe eventually the church could afford celebrity endorsements, perhaps not A-list endorsements, but we could probably afford *Full House's* Dave Coulier or Steve Urkel himself, Jaleel White.

Katherine then flipped the page to read what seemed to be a questionnaire* for someone thinking of planting a church:

Hello, future Senior Pastor. The following questionnaire will help you determine if you're absolutely ready to plant a church. Please be as honest as possible in answering the following questions:

1.) *Is my principal motivation for considering church planting something other than dissatisfaction with my present situation?*
I like to think of myself as an optimist. My life probably isn't perfect, but I try not to dwell on that and instead think of how satisfying it will be once I have a successful church of my own.

2.) *Have I had enough exposure to church planting situations to know what the life of a church planter is like?*
No, but there's a first time for everything.

3.) *Do I know what my personal long-term goals are?*
A. Become a rich, successful, heroic pastor.
B. Learn how to play the banjo.

4.) *Do I have all the training I need in order to do church planting effectively?*
The Purpose-Driven Life (bought but as yet unread)
Your Best Life Now (going to get to this one any day now)

---

* © Copyright 2000, J. Allen Thompson, International Church Planting Center. Used by permission. Adapted from original, *Is City Church Planting for Me?*

Rich Dad, Poor Dad (I've read it three times)

Who Moved My Cheese? (lost count of how many times I've read this one)

5.) *Do I have plenty of energy for my work and little trouble with personal discipline in the use of time?*
Nothing a little Starbucks can't fix.

6.) *Is my spouse willing, even enthusiastic, about our planting a church?*
Haven't talked to her yet, but I'm sure she'll love the idea.

7.) *Am I a people person?*
Who isn't a people person?

8.) *Does God use me to lead people to Christ on a consistent basis?*
If that's the same as changing people's days with inspiring acts of kindness, then that's a big yes, God uses me to do that.

9.) *Do people follow me as their leader?*
I haven't had a lot of opportunities, although I was elected Student Body Vice President junior year, and I think people would have followed me as the leader if the Student Body President had been assassinated.

10.) *Am I comfortable with people of various church backgrounds and able to accept them joyfully into membership, being patient when they are slow to grow spiritually and doctrinally?*
I don't really understand this question.

11.) *Can I describe in some detail the church I'd like to plant?*
Yes. The People's Church—

"Did you find your earrings, baby?" Ryan shouted from the hallway. "We've got to go. It's time for church."

"Yeah, okay," Katherine managed to say as she put the proposal back on Ryan's desk exactly as she had found it.

Pastor Clark was teaching on Galatians. "Brothers, if someone is caught in a sin, you who are spiritual should restore him gently. But watch yourself, or you also may be tempted."

Katherine tried to listen to Pastor Clark, but all she could think about was Ryan's proposal. She wanted to bring it up on the ride to church; she wanted to ask Ryan what he possibly could have been thinking by writing a proposal for a church plant. Where does an idea like that even come from?

She wanted to ask, but she was scared of the answer—frightened he might say something that would jeopardize their marriage. After all, affairs are normal. There are support groups, books, and counselors that walk couples through infidelity. But what sort of advice would Dr. Phil have for a wife who discovered her husband was planning on planting a church behind her back? She thought that if she called Dr. Phil, he would probably book her for tomorrow's show. Pastor Clark continued to preach, and Katherine shifted in her seat, uncomfortable in her own skin, and next to a husband she no longer trusted.

Ryan didn't notice though—he was too busy watching Pastor Clark and imagining himself up there and what it would be like if this was his church, if all of these people came to hear him speak. And for the first time, the thought of pastoring his own church made lukewarm beads of sweat crawl down his face.

I would be lost, Ryan realized.

This snapped him back to attention and made him study Pastor Clark's every move from the pulpit. Ryan noticed Pastor Clark would stroll from one side of the stage to the other, hands in his pockets, stopping occasionally to gaze into the soul of someone in attendance as if he were talking directly to them. His vocal inflection would bounce up and down—at times he would rapid fire his sermon like an AK-47, but when he really wanted to hit a point home, he would stop, lean in, and whisper it. Every now and again he would flail his hands around, and when the audience belly laughed after a good joke, he would take a slow drink of water, letting everyone bask in the glow of his delightful anecdote. Suddenly it was clear to Ryan—preaching is about *how* something is said as much as it is about *what* is said. A sermon is 70 percent style and 30 percent substance.

Pastor Clark was teaching that a good way to keep sin out of your life is to have someone trusted, like a teacher, small group leader, or a pastor to confess your sins to. He warned that this person should not have the same struggles as you; otherwise you may end up trapped in the sludge of sin, embarrassed and with no escape. But what was amazing was how he said it—the look in his eyes, his posture, and the tone of his voice—it made you *believe* that what he was saying was true.

After every F.C.C. service was over, a long line of groupies waited to speak to Pastor Clark. Ryan waited with the others, and when it was his turn, Pastor Clark smiled and gave him a big hug.

"Your sermon delivery this morning was right on. You brought your A-game today," Ryan said.

"Um, thanks. So, how are you? You and your wife okay?"

"Oh yeah, right. My wife. Stuff's great. We're great," Ryan said, annoyed that Pastor Clark was bringing up something they had talked about on a rainy night nearly three weeks ago. Ryan was a different person then, an immature Christian—those were the days before he had discovered random acts of kindness, before he'd had the ingenious idea of planting his own church. "Tell me, how do you do it?"

"How do I do what?"

"Preach like that. You had them, Pastor Clark. They were like gummy bears in your hand. It was brilliant. It was magic."

"I don't really know what to say," Pastor Clark answered. "I just pray, study the Word, and the rest just kind of happens."

Later Ryan sat on the couch watching the Broncos play the Chiefs, and stewed over Pastor Clark's reluctance to tell him how to preach a great sermon. But he couldn't stay angry for long — the more he thought about it the more it made sense. Jerry Seinfeld never shared the secrets to his stand-up routine, Mick Jagger never showed up-and-coming rock stars how to mimic his dance moves, and Larry Bird wouldn't teach his opponents how to shoot his patented can't-miss fade-away. Ryan realized how naive it was to ask Pastor Clark how he preached with such style and technique. He was flattered that Pastor Clark wouldn't tell him.

He sees me as competition, Ryan realized.

And that's when the TV shut off.

"We need to talk," Katherine said.

In the five years that they'd been together, Katherine had only twice shut off the TV to initiate a fight. Ryan didn't know what the problem was, but he was already annoyed that he would have to spend the next few nights on the couch, or in a motel room if things really spun out of control. Ryan stood from the couch and saw Katherine clutching the business proposal for the People's Church.

"I've been meaning to tell you about that," Ryan said. He really had been, but he knew how unbelievable it sounded. *You want to do what?* she would say. She would shoot down his idea; she would be his father destroying the dig to China, and that's when the dream would die. That's when his fantasy would shrivel in the light of the truth — successful real estate agents don't just quit their jobs to start churches. He had chosen his career path. He had checked the box marked real estate agent, and he would do that for the next fifty years until he was too senile to do anything else. The church proposal was at best escapism, at worst a delusion of grandeur, but either way it was fantasy. He knew it, and it was time to admit it.

"Okay, this whole idea, planting a church, it's crazy," Ryan said.

But not being able to completely back down he added, "But just for the record, I would make a great pastor."

"You don't know anything about being a pastor."

"Actually, I do."

"How?"

"There's a lot you don't know about me Katherine."

"Apparently."

"During my lunch hour I've been doing acts of kindness. Random ones. I'm amazing at it, and people love me."

"Okay—"

"Half the time people assume I'm a pastor." Ryan forgot to disclose that people thought he was a pastor because that's what he told them he was. He worried it might weaken his argument.

"You can't fake being a pastor."

"Then what if I actually became one?"

"And you can't just become a pastor. There's a lot of training required."

"There are other ways to get ordained. I've looked into it. And I'll learn what I need to on the job." Ryan was surprised to hear himself defend his position so vehemently. He had meant to say that this was all just a mistake. That he'd been going through his first midlife crisis. But there was no backing down now.

"Pretending you're a pastor is like pretending you're a doctor or a lawyer," Katherine said.

"It's nothing like that. If you don't know what you're doing as a lawyer, people go to jail. If you're an incompetent doctor, people die. But if you happen to mess things up as a pastor—"

"People go to hell," Katherine said.

Checkmate.

Ryan looked at his wife, this woman whom he loved more than anything on the planet, whom he honored and respected, whose father he promised that he would protect her from anything and everything. She stood in the doorway, quivering, with tears rolling down her cheeks.

"You're right," Ryan said.

"Ryan, what's wrong with you? You're scaring me."

"I know, I'm sorry. I'm just a little unhappy right now, baby. I can't get you pregnant, I hate my job, and you seem distant. I guess I've just been looking for something to give our life purpose."

Ryan took the church plant proposal from her. "This isn't real. I typed it up one day when I was bored. Have I been thinking about it? Yeah, I have. It seemed like an adventure. You and I could go somewhere new, start this life together, and we could be anything we wanted. We wouldn't just have boring jobs crunching numbers and doing business, we could do something profound and important. Something eternal. I should have told you about it — I didn't because it's insane. I mean, why would I actually be thinking of planting a church? I wanted to tell you, I was just scared you wouldn't understand."

Katherine walked over to her husband, put her face on his shoulder, and began to sob. Ryan put his arms around her and they stood in silence, both feeling guilty that they weren't able to express themselves earlier, feeling guilty that they had let everything build up so much.

Twenty minutes later, when Katherine finally brought herself to talk, she looked at her husband and told him something completely unexpected — she told him he was right; they should start a church.

CHURCH PLANT

7

BARTLESVILLE

It was breakfast, and on the edge of Bartlesville,* Oklahoma, pop. 23,000,† the Greasy Spork was buzzing with commerce.

Not a single citizen has ever had anything disparaging to say about the Greasy Spork. Its parking lot is never empty and the sign above the joint always has something inspirational to say, like, "We become what we give ourselves the power to be." The outside of the restaurant is constructed from dark weathered wood with a forest green trim. It looks like a combination of a log cabin and a Denny's. For the town of Bartlesville, the Greasy Spork is more than just a place where patrons can dine on chili Frito salads and mushroom onion burgers. It's a social hub where one can

---

*Bartlesville, Oklahoma is an actual place with real people, businesses, and landmarks. The author of this novel has only visited once, and he barely remembers anything about the place—but the name. It's the best named town in the United States of America. Therefore it is the name of the town in this book. However, outside of the name, most other things about this town are completely fabricated for the purposes of this story. If anything, this town is much closer in resemblance to Pampa, Texas. But clearly Pampa is not as good a name as Bartlesville.

† For instance, this is not the actual population of Bartlesville.

catch up on the daily events in the lives of friends and neighbors, where the women can play canasta and exchange juicy gossip, and on every third week of the month, the Greasy Spork also has "Romance Saturdays" where couples can enjoy a candlelit dinner and listen to the music of the local mariachi band.

On the morning that would change Bartlesville forever, Sheriff Somersby sat in his usual corner booth and scanned the dining room of the Greasy Spork while Cammy Miller refilled his mug with tar-black coffee. Cammy, the restaurant's head waitress, had worked there for fourteen years and knew every regular by name. She never had any lofty career goals—all she really wanted was a big family for whom she could cook waffles, bacon, eggs, and sausages on Sunday mornings before church. Such a family would take the perfect father, the type of person who could be a loving family man, yet someone with career goals who could provide for her and the kids. In Cammy's youth she wasn't gorgeous, but she was cute; she looked a bit like the high school version of D. J. Tanner from *Full House*. Cammy went on quite a few first dates, but she was unbearably picky about potential suitors. At some point during the date, Cammy almost inevitably had a conversation like this:

"What I really want is a large family."

"How large?" the young man would ask with his voice quivering.

"Nothing outrageous. Just like eight or ten kids."

"Anything else?"

"I'd also like a little barn out back where I can churn butter and pickle jelly," she would reply.

Cammy had never been on a second date.

She started waiting tables at the Greasy Spork the summer before her senior year, and she thought she'd earn a little extra money and pass the time before she was whisked away by her cowboy in shining armor. Now, fourteen years later, Cammy lived for her job—her maternal instincts fulfilled through delivering patty melts and cups of coffee with a smile. She loved and cared for every one of her regulars, but none more than Sheriff Somersby. There was something irresistible about him. She loved his light brown mustache, his stern protective eyes, his sense of justice, and how adorable he looked in his uniform.

He's perfect, Cammy thought. God had his own sense of timing, and maybe God allowed her to be so unreceptive to men in the past because he had someone better for her. Someone like Sheriff Somersby.

Cammy and Sheriff Somersby had been on a date a little over a month ago. Cammy invited him to a "Romance Saturday," and they dined on a fajita platter for two, drank margaritas, and had the most enchanting conversation. During the date, Sheriff Somersby (Cammy tried to call him Roger, but the Sheriff let her know, "I prefer Sheriff Somersby, if that's okay with you") told Cammy all about his job as the town authority. He talked about the raging battle of crime versus law and order that he was in the middle of every day. Cammy wanted to reach over the table, grab Sheriff Somersby, and give him a passionate French kiss. Maybe she would have if it wasn't for his walkie-talkie, or C.B., or whatever it's called.

"Sheriff Somersby," the walkie-talkie said.

"Yeah, Kirk." Cammy could see the look that was creeping onto the Sheriff's face. He was no longer her adorable date, he was turning into the Sheriff, distributor of justice and protector to the town of Bartlesville. Cammy felt as if her heart was dropping like an elevator in a high-rise because she knew her date was about to be called away for business.

"We've got a code teal," Kirk said. Sheriff Somersby invented his own color code shorthand for different types of law enforcement situations. No way the criminal element can crack our code, he would often tell his staff.

"I'm on my way," the Sheriff said. As he got up and put on his jacket, he told Cammy, "Sorry, duty calls."

"Do you have to go?" Cammy asked.

"Normally I wouldn't, but this is a code teal," the Sheriff said. As it turned out, it wasn't a code teal, there was just a group of high school boys shooting BB guns at Billy Finn's cattle. "Thanks for the lovely evening," Sheriff Somersby told Cammy, threw fifty bucks on the table, turned, and left the Greasy Spork.

Cammy was disheartened, but she knew there was magic between them. He'll make it up to me, she assured herself. But Cammy had spent the last month greeting the Sheriff with a smile and always keeping his coffee mug piping hot. He always politely thanked her, left an 18 percent tip, and every day Cammy hoped the Sheriff would ask her for a second date. But before he could get around to it, the walkie-talkie would call out a code beige, teal, maroon, or turquoise, and the Sheriff would throw money on the table and rush out of the Greasy Spork without even telling Cammy good-bye.

"What's a brother got to do to get a patty melt around here?" Jimmy Buckley asked.

"Hold your horses," Cammy told Jimmy like a teacher instructing a kindergartener.

Jimmy sat in the booth across from the Sheriff, alone. Two weeks ago Jimmy would have been eating breakfast with his wife Megan and his daughters Stacy-Ann and Lisa.

But that was before Jimmy discovered pokerpros.com.

His life changed and his marriage began to crumble at two a.m. one morning when he was playing Texas hold 'em in an online poker room. Jimmy had wanted to play professional poker ever since he started watching the World Series of Poker on ESPN. Jimmy would sit on the couch and watch hand after hand, noting the critical mistakes the players made. He fantasized about how he would act if he were there, how he would bluff, go all in, win millions of dollars and become a celebrity. But then, as if reading his thoughts, a commercial appeared on the television that said, "Think you could hang with the poker pros? Try your luck at pokerpros.com."

At first, Jimmy just played for fun. He was amazing. In his first six hours in the poker room, he had gone from 1,000 chips to 14,354 chips. Jimmy wasn't sure, but he thought it could be some kind of record.

If only I was playing for real money, Jimmy thought. Maybe this is what I'm supposed to be — a poker pro.

When he started playing for real money, he was just as good. He started in the low stakes rooms and went from $20 to $120 in the course of an hour. He wanted to play with the big boys in the high stakes online room. Just for a hand. Just to see what would happen.

And that was the hand where, by the end of the turn, flop, and river, there were four diamonds on the table, and Jimmy happened to have the king of diamonds in his hand. There was only one card that could beat him, the ace of diamonds, but Jimmy thought that Randolf815 probably had the 10, jack, or the queen of diamonds when he laid down a bet of 375 dollars.

No way he had the Ace. What are the odds? Jimmy thought as he clicked a button sending 375 dollars of his hard-earned money onto the Internet poker table.

And as this story is bound to end, Randolf815 did have the Ace of diamonds causing Jimmy to lose a grand total of $581 in a single hand of poker. Jimmy could have been discouraged by the loss, but he crawled into bed at 2:13 a.m. with a proud grin on his face.

You had balls of steel. Nine times out of ten, the King of diamonds wins that hand, and you had the guts to make the call. It was the call a real poker player would have made.

In his hours on the couch watching the World Series of Poker, Jimmy had watched poker greats like Howard Lederer and Chris "Jesus" Ferguson lose tough hands even though they always made the right calls. That's what being a poker pro was all about. Still, Jimmy knew Megan would kill him when she saw that their account was a couple of hundred dollars light.

And the next day when Jimmy told Megan, "Pumpkin pie, I got the flu or something, I need to stay home today," he had the best of intentions. He was going to skip work and win the money back. Break even, that was the goal. He had poker ability and he knew if he used it, he could win all of his money back, maybe even a little more, and Megan would never have to know what happened.

That evening Megan was at the grocery store with a shopping cart full of food for the week. Lisa (five years old) was crying because Megan told her she couldn't have a Kit Kat, and Stacy-Ann (three years old) was throwing food out of the cart. Megan had to manage her daughters in line behind six other carts full of groceries because it was a little after five, which was rush hour at Safeway. When the grocery clerk rang up all of Megan's groceries, Megan ran her debit card through the machine only to have the clerk say, "Your card's been denied."

"That's impossible."

"Do you have another card?"

"No my husband and I cut up all of our other credit cards."

"Do you have any cash?"

"No, but we have over three thousand dollars in our account.

Try it again." Megan handed the clerk the card and he carefully swiped it through the card reader.

"Sorry. It's declining it again."

Megan stood for a second, unsure of what to do next. The line behind had grown to eight shopping carts long, Lisa wasn't really crying anymore—she was now screaming between breaths, and everyone in the store stared at Megan with puppy dog eyes. Megan could feel everyone's looks, she could feel that they were sorry for this mother who had grabbed one more box of Pop-Tarts than her debit card could handle, and she felt dirty, ashamed, pathetic.

The manager walked over and told Megan, "We are sorry about this mistake. Listen, we'll put all of your groceries in the cart while you call your bank to clear this up."

"We have three thousand dollars," Megan said realizing that her daughters were now not the only ones crying.

When Megan got home grocery-less, she saw her husband in the office, in his boxers and a dingy white tank top with bloodshot eyes. The room was pitch black except for the soft blue glow from the computer monitor, which gave Jimmy's face a pale, ghostly look.

"How are you feeling?" Megan asked. Her voice was so cold Jimmy thought he could see her breath.

Jimmy confessed everything to his wife. He told her about pokerpros.com, he explained how he was so great at first until he lost the 581 dollars. He said that his goal today was to win the money back, but to win that kind of money back he had to play in the high stakes rooms, and after a few bad hands, it was easy to find yourself down a couple of thousand dollars. "But I'm going to get it all back, baby. You have to trust me," Jimmy said.

Megan didn't say anything. She just nodded and gently closed the office door. She packed a few things and took her daughters over to her mother's house. And for the next two weeks, every time Jimmy called Megan, Megan forced her mother to lie and tell Jimmy, "Sorry. Megan and the girls aren't here right now."

Cammy placed the patty melt on the table. It was made just like Jimmy always ordered it: onions, cheddar cheese, special sauce, and a sausage patty snuggled between two pieces of Texas Toast. "Thanks Cammy," Jimmy said as he stared at his breakfast. The patty melt was all he had left to look forward to.

But that wasn't anything special. Most in the Greasy Spork didn't have much to look forward to. This was a diner full of people that needed God.

Everyone had a story. Bob Woods ate French toast with strawberry syrup as he scoured the help wanted section and worried about how he was going to pay this month's rent or even pay for his breakfast. Tiffany Blake, the other waitress on duty, took an order for hotcakes and grits while she debated how long she should wait until she told her parents that she was pregnant. Leonard Wilson was depressed because he had to take his wife to a hospital in Tulsa for more chemo this afternoon and he didn't know how much more she could take.

Luckily, hope was on the way.

When Ryan and Katherine pulled into town they were hungry and thought the Greasy Spork would be a quaint place for breakfast.

It took them half an hour to park the moving truck (Ryan insisted they could park in front of the dumpster, Katherine refused because it was illegal, and they finally found a place three blocks away and walked to the Greasy Spork). After they were seated, Ryan acted like he was glancing at the menu, but he was really surveying the restaurant.

These are the people who are going to be coming to my church. This is my flock.

Ryan had been reading up a lot on being a pastor, and for some reason he found a lot of shepherding terms for the relationship between a minister and his church. He was the shepherd and they were the flock. He wished there were more manly terms that described the relationship between a pastor and his congregation—maybe something like he was their gladiator and they were his Roman citizens, or he was their Captain Kirk and they were his crew on the *Enterprise*. But Ryan had yet to find any analogies like that.

"Welcome to the Greasy Spork. Could I interest you in some heavenly hash browns?" Cammy asked. Heavenly hash browns were the Greasy Spork's most ordered breakfast item. They consisted of three melted slices of Kraft cheese, chili, ranch, sautéed onions, mushrooms, and a dollop of guacamole, served with a side of bacon.

"I'd just like to start with a cup of coffee." Katherine said.

"I'll have heavenly hash browns with a side of flapjacks. And I'd also like to pay for everyone's check," Ryan added.

"You want to what?" Cammy said.

Ryan handed Cammy his MasterCard. "Breakfast is on me for everyone in the restaurant. If they ask who paid for it, just say it's on Pastor Ryan."

"Okay." She walked away, staring at the MasterCard.

"Ryan!"

"Yeah, babe?"

"We've been in town for ten minutes and you're buying people's breakfast."

"Kind of a rush, isn't it?"

"You can't just pay for everyone all the time. We don't even have jobs anymore."

"Honey, I have the best job on earth. I'm a pastor."

"Without a church."

"Exactly, which is why I'm paying for everyone's meals. To let them know there's a new pastor in town."

Katherine continued to argue about how you can't buy people's allegiance. That's not how a real pastor would act. Ryan wasn't really listening, but he still nodded in agreement, like a man whose wife asks him to take out the trash during the fourth quarter of the Rose Bowl.

Ryan smiled in anticipation. Cammy was approaching the tables to inform the customers that their breakfast had been paid for. As she spread the news, they all stared at Ryan in disbelief, but not with the grateful smiles he had encountered when he did this at Starbucks and McDonald's. If Ryan didn't know better, he'd think they were scowling at him. Even some innocent-looking boys in coonskin caps seemed to have furrowed brows; their father, a beefy man in a John Deere trucker hat, locked eyes with Ryan, stood, and stomped over to Ryan's table.

"What is this?" the man asked.

"An act of kindness," Ryan answered.

"You think I would take my family here if I couldn't afford it?" He clutched the crumpled receipt in his hand.

"I was just trying to do something nice."

"I pay for our breakfast."

"It wasn't anything personal. I bought breakfast for everyone."

"Why? Because we're all poor?"

"Because I'm a pastor," Ryan said, standing from the table and realizing that this man was six inches taller and fifty pounds heavier than he was. But he didn't care. He had spent his hard-earned money to show a little kindness and this was the thanks he got? Ryan would take this joker on in a cage match if given the chance.

Every patron in the Greasy Spork now stared at Ryan. Katherine didn't know what everyone else was thinking, but for the first time she was a little frightened. Yes, she liked that Ryan was being impulsive like Coen Jackson, but now he wasn't stable. Maybe a person can't be reliable *and* adventurous. She wanted Ryan to be just a *little* more exciting, but buying everyone breakfast and making

(you can't have your cake and eat it too; you have to decide: do you want him exciting or bland?)

a big scene, that was a little much.

The man in the trucker hat asked Ryan, "So what, you're paying for breakfast so I will accept Jesus?"

"I don't care if you accept Jesus," he said honestly. "I just want you to come to my church. Services start in two weeks," Ryan announced to everyone in the restaurant. But everyone just stared at their food as if they hadn't heard Ryan.

The Sheriff had watched this go on long enough and didn't want to see the situation escalate. He drank the rest of his coffee as if it were a shot of whisky, stepped between the arguing customers, and said, "Carl, go finish breakfast with your family."

"Sheriff, I wasn't trying to ..."

"Carl, don't make me call in a code aquamarine on you," the Sheriff said with fire in his eyes.

Before Carl went back to his booth, he told Ryan, "Don't let me catch you buying breakfast for my family again." But Ryan just smiled back at Carl, thinking how foolish he would feel once the People's Church had blossomed and Ryan had become the most adored man in the county.

Ryan turned to the Sheriff and said, "Thank you. I'm glad you can accept an act of kindness."

"I'm not letting you pay for my breakfast either. Pastor, you watch yourself. This is not a town that's likely to accept candy from strangers." The Sheriff then paid for his breakfast, left Cammy a tip, and sauntered out of the Greasy Spork.

Ryan went back to his table and picked at his heavenly hash browns and bacon. Paying for breakfast had not gone as well as he thought it would, and for the first time Ryan started to worry. What if starting a church was something God took seriously? Ryan had been going around telling people he was a pastor, which was essentially like telling everyone that he was one of God's agents, and now maybe God was about to punish him. During his time at Fellowship Christian Church, Ryan heard Pastor Clark read stories from the Old Testament, and Ryan knew that God had flooded the earth, used fire and brimstone to destroy cities, and God had even swallowed all of Pharaoh's army with the Red Sea. What if God decided to destroy Ryan with a semi-truck, or a flood, or a bolt of lighting, or by dropping a piano on him from heaven? Perhaps everything that happened this morning was a warning, and if Ryan kept walking this path, God would destroy everything around him.

Ryan ate a forkful of flapjacks and laughed at himself. He realized that if God was real, he had to take care of galaxies and wars and global warming and everything else that was going on around the world. There is no way that God would care what an ex – real estate agent was doing in the middle of Oklahoma.

God had bigger fish to fry.

Ryan stopped thinking about God and began thinking about his flapjacks. The butter had melted into the maple syrup and Ryan didn't know if he'd ever tasted a better pancake. With each bite of his breakfast Ryan started feeling better about the way the morning had gone. Sure things hadn't gone exactly as he planned, but he figured he had created a buzz and soon everyone would know there was a new church in town.

And Ryan was right. By that afternoon most of the citizens of Bartlesville would hear the gossip about the new pastor, and about his confrontation with Carl and Sheriff Somersby.

Ryan went to pay for breakfast and discovered that no one had decided to take him up on his generous offer except for Jimmy Buckley. And Jimmy took Ryan up on the offer only because he had no money — his only choices were to accept a free meal or spend the rest of the morning washing dishes. Jimmy wasn't about to wash dishes. So he took the meal, and to repay Pastor Ryan, Jimmy decided that he would check out this new church.

When Jimmy told Ryan that he wanted to come to his church, Ryan smiled back at Jimmy proudly, like a business owner who'd just earned his first dollar bill.

8

WHERE A KID
CAN BE A KID

There is no map for planting a church. But there are a lot of theories.

Most church planting experts agree that the key to a successful plant is to have a leadership team executing administrative and interpersonal tasks with the efficiency of a NASCAR pit crew. The ideal church plant team would consist of a senior pastor (well versed in theology and proficient with Scripture), an accountant/administrator, a worship leader/music director, a children's pastor, and a team of intercessors (people who pray fervently for the church's success). The church planters should also have a stable "mother church" that backs the team financially and spiritually. Finally, the church planting team should scout the location of the church plant for at least six months, getting to know the landscape, the people in the area, and potential areas where the church can hold services.

Ryan had not read any of these theories. Had the authors of these theories watched the way Ryan was going about planting his church, they probably would have told him that his church was failing before it started. The People's Church had nowhere to conduct services. His team consisted of himself, his wife, and an unemployed man named Bob who followed them around for lack of anything better to do. These authors probably would advise Ryan to pack it up, count his losses, and go back to real estate.

But Ryan would be too busy to listen to them. There were too many other things to worry about.

At the moment, priority number one for Ryan was to secure a place for the People's Church to meet on Sunday mornings. Ryan knew it would be about six months before he could afford to build a church of his own, so he drove his U-Haul around Bartlesville looking for a place to conduct services. The first place he met with was the beautiful Hotel Earl, a three-and-a-half-star resort off Highway 134. It was the type of place with thick cotton bathrobes in every room. The Hotel Earl prided itself on being the nicest re-sort for seventy-five miles in either direction of Highway 134—a haven for travelers who wanted more luxurious accommodations than a Super 8 or a Motel 6 could offer. Ryan imagined his church holding services on the veranda while ushers offered new mem-bers freshly squeezed orange juice and cheese Danishes. But that dream died a quick painful death when the concierge informed Ryan how much the Hotel Earl would charge the People's Church to hold services there every Sunday.

So, Ryan continued his search. For three days he met with schools, the Veteran's Hall, restaurants, churches, hotels, and motels. But there were always reasons it wouldn't work. Other obligations, too high an asking price, or the business proprietors were just uncomfortable with the idea of a church meeting at their establishment. Ryan was right. By that afternoon most of the citi-zens of Bartlesville had heard the gossip about the new pastor, and about his confrontation with Carl and Sheriff Somersby.

At the end of the third day, Ryan found himself in the lobby of Chuck E. Cheese's around midnight, talking to a twenty-two-year-old named Nancy who was wearing a golden nametag.

"I don't think you really want your church to meet here," Nancy said.

"Of course I don't want to meet here, Nancy." Ryan explained.

"You don't?"

"No. But we have to meet here."

"Why?"

"Because everyone else has turned me down. I'm going to have to preach on a stage with a six-foot robotic mouse behind me. This is not exactly my first choice."

"We can close the curtains," Nancy said.

"Thank you."

"But I don't think I can let your church meet here before I talk to the general manager."

"No one's ever going to have to know. Just open the doors Sunday morning at eight and we'll be out of here by eleven," Ryan said.

"Ten."

"Ten?"

"We have to prep the dining hall before the customers start getting here at eleven," Nancy said.

"Ten would be fine."

"Listen, I really want to help but—"

"Nancy," Ryan said, "I sold my house, my car, and moved with my wife out here to chase a dream ... a dream that's going to die without your help. This is your chance to help someone out—your chance to be the manager, make a call, and help a dream blossom into reality. This is your chance to be a hero."

"Like Wonder Woman?"

"Exactly like Wonder Woman."

Speeches like this were Ryan's gift. Everyone who does something great has some ability—some superpower—that propels him to greatness. Superman leaps tall buildings, Spider Man flings webs, Batman knows the perfect bat gadget for every situation, and Ryan had the ability to become irresistibly suave and convincing to the person sitting across from him. Ryan would have to rely heavily on this ability, this ice-to-an-Eskimo charm, if his church plant was going to survive.

Nancy blushed, took a deep breath, and asked Ryan, "When do you want to start meeting here?"

Katherine was in charge of finding the music director for the People's Church.

She was excited about her task because she could be the Paula Abdul for some local musician and help him blossom into a star. Still, when she was feeling honest, the thought of picking a worship leader for the church intimidated her. During services at Fellowship Christian Church the musical portion was the time that confused her the most. Watching the worship band perform at the church reminded her of a rock concert. There were a lot of similarities: the audience loved some songs, and just sat through others waiting for the hits. Some audience members watched quietly with their hands in their pockets, others would sway back and forth and passionately sing with the band. There were highs and lows in music, and a good worship band, like a good rock band, knew exactly where they were taking the audience.

And that's where the similarities stopped.

The best rock concert Katherine ever attended was during her junior year in high school when she saw Guns N' Roses. They were in their prime. Their set consisted of "Paradise City," "Welcome to the Jungle," "Knockin' on Heaven's Door," and "Sweet

Child o' Mine." There was one legendary song after another. The arena was packed with fans and everyone was there to see the band. Katherine loved watching Axl Rose dance across the stage, marveled at the way Slash slid his fingers across the electric guitar strings, and screamed until she was hoarse during Steven Adler's drum solo. Katherine had been to a number of rock shows since, and even though none were as good as the first time she saw Guns N' Roses, everyone was still always—*always*—there for the same reason: to see the band.

It wasn't the same during the music at Fellowship Christian Church. The audience appreciated the band, but they didn't focus on them; when the lead guitarist played an impressive chord progression, no one would even blink. The focus was on something else—as if God were

(in the room? looking down from heaven?)

at the center of everyone's thoughts. During certain musical numbers it felt as if everyone in the room was pondering God—attempting to fathom how he worked, how loving he was, and what he thought of their sinful lives—just like Katherine was during her first Sunday at church. Worship was much more pensive and boring than a rock concert, but moments of worship were powerful. Almost as powerful as a Guns N' Roses concert, Katherine thought when she was feeling honest.

Katherine entered the Greasy Spork. It was Thursday, the Spork's karaoke night, and Katherine hoped maybe she could find a worship leader here. As she entered she saw a woman named Sandy belt out the chorus to Bonnie Tyler's "Total Eclipse of the Heart":

"And I need you more tonight. And I need you more than ever."

Sandy was not an amazing vocalist; she actually botched a few notes badly, but tears rolled down her cheeks while she sang the song as if the lyrics were her own, pouring out from her soul. If Katherine had still lived in Denver she would have walked over, given Sandy a hug, and invited her to Bible study. Katherine knew that if Sandy went to Bible study she could drink hot tea, while the collective wisdom of the women in the group would solve any problem she had.

But Katherine wasn't in Denver. She didn't have a group to invite Sandy to anymore. Loneliness started to put its claws on Katherine as she faced reality—she didn't have a friend in this town. Her friends were far away and moving on with their lives. Bible study was going on at this moment, and someone else was sitting in her chair, drinking tea out of her favorite mug, the one with kittens playing in sunflowers on it. The women of Bible study might not even be missing Katherine—truthfully they'd probably forgotten all about her.

And Ryan, the only other person she had, was too consumed with his own church planting vision to care.

"Thank you, Sandy. That was moving," Andy, the young man with the microphone, said. He couldn't have been much older than twenty. He was pimply and stick-figure thin, but Katherine noticed how confidently he stood on the stage. This was his show and he was proud of it. He would tell jokes, anecdotes, and would give last night's top ten lists between the acts. He knew that the customers were there to see the performers. They loved to watch their friends sing covers of Bon Jovi and Tina Turner songs.

But they've also come to see me, he would think. He was the glue between the acts, and his entertaining segues did move the night along seamlessly. Occasionally, he would entertain thoughts that he could be the next Dick Clark or Ryan Seacrest—that he was meant for stardom. He thought his quick wit and impeccable comic timing could earn him millions of adoring fans and dump trucks full of money. But he knew he'd probably spend most of his life in this town working as a beat writer for the *Bartlesville Post*. He only wished he had something interesting or different or exciting to write about. The most exciting thing that ever happened to him was when during the week while working on a story, someone would occasionally stop him and say, "Aren't you the guy from the Greasy Spork?" And he would answer, "Yes, I am," because he knew exactly what they were talking about.

"Our final performer of the night is one of my favorites. He's a karaoke Thursday regular. And if you've ever heard him sing, you're probably as big of a fan of him as I am. So, can we please give a big Greasy Spork welcome to Cowboy Jack!" Andy shouted.

The diner burst into applause as Cowboy Jack sauntered onto the stage. Katherine could already tell he wasn't the worship leader she was looking for.

He walks like he's God's gift to women. How can someone possibly be that arrogant? Who does he think he is? He's probably just going up there to get a good look at every woman here so he can decide who to take home.

Other women might have been attracted to his skintight Wranglers, denim shirt, and white snakeskin hat, but his cocky swagger turned Katherine off. At least she thought it was a cocky swagger until he looked up. Then she saw something so attractive in his crystal blue eyes that she couldn't help but like him.

He was afraid.

Katherine noticed Jack's hand shake, just a bit, as he grabbed the mic from its stand. He was more than afraid. His eyes were glued to the monitor waiting for the karaoke lyrics to appear. Butterflies began to dance in the pit of her stomach. It seemed like all was lost.

Then Cowboy Jack changed. He ripped his eyes from the monitor and began to sing a Toby Keith number. It was heavenly—his voice was a little bit country, a little bit rock and roll—half Garth

Brooks, half Dave Growell. He hit every note with a precision that would have made Simon Cowell smile. Cowboy Jack commanded the attention of everyone in the diner. Conversations went pin-drop silent. Waitresses froze. Cooks and dishwashers crept out of the kitchen like zombies to brains. When the song ended, the room was in a paralyzed silence. No one could even clap. Cowboy Jack had done more than put on a great performance—he'd turned the Toby Keith song into something profound and moving and beautiful—and they'd all been lucky enough to witness it.

"Thank you," Cowboy Jack said as he awkwardly put the mic back into its stand.

Later, Cowboy Jack sat across the booth from Katherine.

"Tell me a little about yourself," Katherine said, a bit more adoringly than she had intended to.

"Not much to tell really," Cowboy Jack said. "I take care of the cattle on Dan Henderson's farm during the week, and during the weekends I like to go to the movies."

"What kinds of movies?"

"Um, I like the scary ones. Dracula, Freddy, and the one about the little blond kids with glowing red eyes. I also like romantic comedies."

"Have you ever thought about singing professionally?"

"From time to time."

"And?"

"And it never gets past the thinking phase. What am I supposed to do, move out to Nashville? I'm a dime a dozen out there. There's more cowboys that can sing than prairie dogs on a quail hunt."

"Not ones that can sing like you," Katherine said.

"Appreciate that."

"I mean it."

"Well, thanks. But for now, I guess I'm happy here. Gus gives me a free beer every time I sing, it's fun, and there's no real pressure."

"Have you ever thought of singing somewhere else?"

"Like—"

"Church."

"Not my thing. I'm not a religious man."

"That's what's great about this church. It isn't religious," Katherine said hoping Cowboy Jack wouldn't ask for further clarification, because she couldn't give it. She knew that the People's Church wasn't religious, but if he asked her what it was, she would sit there dumbfounded. They didn't know what they wanted to do as much as they knew what they didn't want to do in their new church. They knew they didn't want to treat people as numbers, or to have church services that were boring and stiff. She assumed they wanted their services to be exciting, and she knew they didn't want to put lots of pressure on people to accept God.

God is more of an idea, Ryan told Katherine recently. His new theology (theology is being used here in the loosest sense of the word) was that most people accepted God because he helped make sense of things that they couldn't explain. People didn't necessarily believe that there was an actual man with a long white beard holding lightning bolts and sitting on a cloud, but they did believe that things happened for a reason. They did believe that when someone was taken from this life too early, it wasn't simply the end. That there was something more, some greater purpose they didn't understand. And that makes sense, Ryan said. But Katherine was frightened that he was figuring all of this out on the fly. He was going to give his first sermon in a week, and he could easily offend everyone in the room. They could call him a heretic. After all, wild theories about God and the nature of the universe are not things that most Christians take lightly.

"—entail?" Cowboy Jack asked.

"Excuse me?" Katherine said, a little embarrassed she hadn't heard his question.

"This church gig, what would it entail?"

"You know, just lead the church songs for us every week."

"Like what?"

"How should I know?"

"Because you're the one asking me to sing in a church. So, I'd think you'd know what songs you want me to sing."

"You know, churchy songs. Songs about Jesus."

"Who are you anyway? Is this your church?"

"Sort of, it's my—" Katherine couldn't bring herself to say *it's my husband's church*, because she wanted Cowboy Jack to still think she was single, even if he would only think so for a little while longer. So she corrected herself by saying, "I'm the pastor's assistant. My name's Katherine."

"Cowboy Jack."

Katherine smiled as he said this. She liked the way he said his name. "Look, I'm just going to be honest. I like the way you sing. You would be the perfect worship leader for our church. I think you'd make the church grow right away, and I don't really care what you sing. You could sing Beatles songs all morning long, and I wouldn't care. I just think you'd be great to have around."

Cowboy Jack drank the rest of his beer, flashed a confident smile, and said, "All right then Kate—you've got yourself a worship leader."

9

Sunday
Bloody Sunday

Chuck E. Cheese looks especially frightening at 6:13 in the morning.

But there he was, a robotic six-foot rat with his creepy all-knowing grin, watching Ryan set up chairs in the sanctuary of the People's Church. Ryan thought about how Chuck E. sings those same five songs, in a loop, over and over, to children's birthday parties and Boy Scout troops. And during every song, Chuck E. would have that grin, that scary looking grin that coolly said, "I see you."

Today was the first Sunday of the People's Church, and Ryan's first Sunday as a pastor. He was ready, ready for his coming-out party, ready to prove to Katherine, Pastor Clark, and the town of Bartlesville that he wasn't going to be a good pastor, he was going to be a great one. A legend.

This would not be a Sunday to forget.

Ryan had done nothing but work on creating buzz for the People's Church since arriving in Bartlesville. He created a flier with people from every ethnic group on the cover, all wearing the traditional garb of their ethnicities: Nigerians in ornate robes, Asians in decorative smocks, and Australians dressed like the crocodile hunter. The only text on the flier read:

The People's Church
Everyone's Welcome

And there was a map to Chuck E. Cheese's on the back. Ryan stapled these fliers to telephone poles, pinned them up on corkboards in coffee shops, and placed one on the community board of the Bartlesville library. After Katherine recruited Cowboy Jack, he wrote a jingle that played on all three radio stations in town during Bartlesville's morning rush hour. It was to the tune of "I Love Rock and Roll" and went like this:

Here comes the People's Church
It's comin' at ya' this coming Sunday
Here comes the People Church
So, bring your whole family and come to church with me.

Ryan assumed his advertising blitz would go over great in a small town like Bartlesville. After all, nothing ever happened there. The town would come to check out his church because that's what people in small towns do. It happens in every movie: There's a mysterious stranger in town, everyone gossips, and eventually they embrace him and make him one of their own. Ryan had always assumed this was the script. This was how things would turn out. At least a hundred people would come to his first service, he'd be a hit, and things would just grow from there.

"Boss?" Cowboy Jack had just begun setting up the sound system.

"Yeah, Jack?" Ryan said.

"It's Cowboy Jack."

"Sorry, um, yeah, Cowboy Jack?" Ryan said.

Ryan wasn't sure about the worship leader that Katherine had picked out. He'd never heard him sing, and he looked nothing like the worship leader at Fellowship Christian Church. Ryan wasn't sure if all worship leaders were supposed to look the same, but Ryan knew that all the worship leaders he'd ever seen had worn suits on Sunday while Cowboy Jack looked the same as he always did: boots, faded denim shirt, snakeskin hat.

"What songs do you want me to sing this morning?"

"I don't know. That's your job. You're the worship leader."

"I've never led worship before."

"Neither have I. Why don't you sing 'Amazing Grace'?"

"Okay, I think I can remember a lot of the words to that," Cowboy Jack said.

"Great."

"What else?" Cowboy Jack asked.

Ryan took a slow drink of his orange juice, stared at Cowboy Jack, and finally asked, "What other songs do you know?"

"I know 'Mr. Jones' by the Counting Crows."

"That's a Christian song?"

"I think it's sort of about Jesus."

"Mr. Jones is Jesus?" Ryan asked.

"Yeah, maybe so. I'm not sure. I never really think about what songs are about. I just like the way they sound."

"Okay, great. 'Mr. Jones' and 'Amazing Grace.' A little bit of an old song, and then something new and hip. That's perfect," Ryan said.

Cowboy Jack started unpacking sound equipment until Ryan asked, "Where's your guitar?"

"I don't play the guitar."

"You don't. What do you play, the piano?"

"The harmonica."

"That's all worship is going to consist of? You singing and the harmonica?"

"That's what it seems like, chief."

"No, cool, I like that; it's organic," Ryan said.

Cowboy Jack went back to setting up the sound, and Ryan forgot about him. He didn't matter. Jack was the warm-up band. Ryan was the main event. This Sunday morning would rise and fall on how well his sermon went. He could feel it was going to be a home run, out of the park. The People's Church would laugh, cry, be moved, and soon, after the service was over, the entire county would know about this new preacher and his influential church.

Katherine walked in and began placing bagels on the back table, arranging the bagels from saltiest to sweetest. She was humming and looked smoking hot in her new sea-green dress with a slit cut a little higher than should be allowed for a pastor's wife. Ryan stared at her, smiled, and thought how lucky he was to be married to her. She had been more supportive and caring about the church plant than he could have ever asked, and this Sunday morning would have never happened without her. He was going to walk over, kiss her, and tell her that — when Nancy the manager came up and said, "Curtains won't close."

"What do you mean, the curtains won't close?" Ryan asked.

"Some sort of malfunction with the wiring."

"I have to preach with Chuck E. behind me?"

"Won't be that bad."

This is not the image I want everyone to have of The People's Church, Ryan thought as he stared at the all-rodent band consisting of Chuck E. on guitar, a possum on the drums, and a crazy-eyed squirrel on the tambourine.

If visitors to The People's Church didn't have to walk through the lobby, past the skeeball machines, racecar games, and ticket counters cluttered with stuffed animals, they might have thought they were in an actual church. The dining room had been completely transformed into a sanctuary. Nancy had clipped black sheets in front of the rodent band; Cowboy Jack had organized the sound equipment around the pulpit; Ryan had hung a banner that read, "The People's Church," and Katherine had created a reception table with orange juice, coffee, bagels, Apple Jacks, and milk.

When Jimmy Buckley walked in, he didn't bat an eye. It was as if he assumed that all churches meet in children's restaurants and he was just wondering when the music and Bible teaching would begin.

Jimmy was not dressed in his Sunday best, partially because he didn't really own any clothes with dressy things on them like buttons and collars, and partially because he had been sleeping at the Rugged Creek Motel for the last week and half. Megan still hadn't forgiven him for gambling away all of their money, and when she moved home with her daughters, she told him he needed to find somewhere else to live for the rest of his life.

Ryan noticed Jimmy wasn't dressed nicely, but he remembered that part of The People's Church's mission statement was to always make people feel welcome. So he smiled and told Jimmy, "Good morning!"

"Guess so," Jimmy grunted.

"Would you like some orange juice?" Katherine asked.

"Does it have pulp in it? I don't like pulp. It tastes unnatural."

"Sure. I think we have some without pulp," Katherine said.

As Katherine took Jimmy to the reception table, other visitors entered the sanctuary. They included Clive and Wilma Wilson and Cammy Miller. By 8:09, nine minutes after the service was supposed to have started, there was a grand total of seventeen people in the room. Ryan didn't want to start the service yet because he was sure more people were coming. They must have been held up by the weather.

Problem was, while everyone was waiting for the service to start, the room felt like a junior high dance. People were milling around the snack table and staring at their shoes. Ryan didn't understand why people weren't friendlier. This was church and church people live for small talk. At Fellowship Christian Church there was a small talk epidemic. Everyone slapped each other on the back, hugged, smiled and laughed, and talked about how great it was to be a Christian. And Pastor Clark never went out to make sure the conversations were going okay. They just happened. So he wondered, what is it that makes people feel comfortable at church? Why is it so awkward here?

At twelve minutes past the hour, Cowboy Jack started out the service by saying, "Thanks for coming out tonight." This was how Cowboy Jack always greeted the audience at karaoke night, and he was too nervous this morning to vary from his routine. He then blew an E-minor into the harmonica and began to sing "Amazing Grace." Everyone in the room sang the words along with Cowboy Jack, but limply, as if they didn't believe them, as if the grace wasn't that amazing and the sound wasn't very sweet.

Then Cowboy Jack ended the song by belting out the final words with a force that would have made Clay Aiken proud. Jack sung, "Was blind, but now I see-ee-ee." He sung the last *e* in *see* for nearly thirty seconds, bouncing his voice up and down, snapping the congregation awake. Almost involuntarily, every person in the church smiled. No one was smiling wider than Katherine.

When Cowboy Jack finished the song, there was a reverent hush in the room. It felt almost like God had stopped whatever he was doing to peek down on these people singing inside a Chuck E. Cheese's in the middle of Oklahoma.

This feeling was obliterated when Cowboy Jack piped the

opening note to "Mr. Jones" into the harmonica. Cowboy Jack's performance wasn't bad, but the staunchly religious folks in the room could not believe that a pagan song was being performed in church. They had no idea how singing

Mr. Jones strikes up a conversation
With a black-haired flamenco dancer

brought them any closer to God. Cowboy Jack's performance was impressive. There was no denying his vocal talent and his ability to swivel his hips like John Travolta, but no one really knew how to respond to the song. The room was again silent, but not in the awed silence of five minutes before. It was more the contemplative, how-do-I-sneak-out-of-this-room-without-being-noticed sort of silence. After Cowboy Jack finished the number, Ryan walked in front of the crowd, closed his eyes, and began to pray.

"Heavenly Father, we come to you today ..." Ryan said. And then there was a pause. Ryan's thoughts were as blank as a freshly erased chalkboard.

Why do we come to you today? Is there a right thing to pray here? *If I pray the wrong thing will they all know that I've never done this before?* Ryan had seen Pastor Clark and the preachers on TV pray dozens of times and it always just came to them. Ryan didn't think that they were reading off note cards or that they had something scripted, because Pastor Clark had always said that prayer came from the heart. Ryan was horrified to discover that when he opened up his heart there was nothing inside. Ryan tried to stutter on. He thought, these people believe that God created everything, so maybe I should just thank God for all of his creations.

He prayed, "Thank you for the mountains and the stars and for food and drink. Jesus, thank you for Tang, which is just like orange juice but better ..." Ryan felt naked. He was supposed to be blowing everyone away with his pastoral charm. And he was tanking. He had his eyes clinched tight as a fist, because he was scared to open them, scared to face this group of people that he conned into coming here this Sunday morning. So he just kept praying, "We thank you for the electoral college, for all of Elvis's music in the pre-Vegas years; we thank you for long walks on the beach, and puppy dogs, and Rocky Road ice cream." When Ryan realized that his prayer had turned into an Internet dating ad, he decided to utter the word "Amen."

The congregation of seventeen people (if seventeen people can be called a congregation) opened their eyes, squinting, as if sunlight had flooded into a pitch-black room. Most in the room looked befuddled—everyone else looked horrified or on the brink of laughter.

Ryan scanned the congregation of The People's Church for the first time. It looked depressing. No one was dressed up, and everyone seemed pale and hopeless. These were not the types of people that could be the building blocks of a successful church plant, Ryan thought. These were not the types of people that Jesus would have preached to. Ryan wasn't sure, but if Jesus were alive today, his church would have been packed to the brim with attractive, successful people. Jesus would have preached his sermons to millionaires and rock stars and NBA players.

Ryan began to read from Matthew 7, "Do not judge, or you too will be judged. For in the same way you judge others, you will be judged, and with the measure you use, it will be measured to you." When he finished he looked up and said, "Jesus was a wise man. And you know who else was wise: Batman. So, for those of you taking notes, my sermon is titled, 'Why Jesus Is Just Like Batman.'" Ryan then launched into a twelve-minute discussion on the similarities between the Son of God and the Caped Crusader. The connections were weak at best as Ryan tried to compare the bat belt to the Holy Spirit. Ryan had always liked sermons that used pop culture to explain greater spiritual truths. He thought that he could do the same.

He was wrong.

After twelve minutes (Ryan didn't have a watch and thought that he had been preaching for about forty-five minutes) Ryan looked at Cowboy Jack and said, "Why don't you lead us in a closing number?"

Cowboy Jack looked startled — he was glancing around the room to make sure that Ryan was talking to him. Then he said, "I don't have a closing number."

"You're the worship leader. You're supposed to have a closing number."

"I have to do opening *and* closing numbers?"

"Yes. That's your job. Haven't you ever been to church?"

"No, I haven't." Cowboy Jack said as if he were getting ready for a bar fight. "I could sing 'Mr. Jones' again."

"You know what — it's getting late," Ryan said. He didn't realize that the service had only been going for twenty-seven minutes. "Thank you all for coming. Enjoy bagels and Apple Jacks at the welcome booth. See you next week." Ryan strutted off stage and behind the curtains. He stood there in the dark with Chuck E. and his robotic band. He didn't want anyone to see him right after service. He wanted to seem like a mysterious celebrity; after all, rock stars and great comedians don't mingle with the crowd after they perform. But for a while it seemed as if nobody moved. Everyone was just waiting to see what would happen next.

In the end there were two types of people who left The People's Church on that Sunday morning. Half of the people that attended the first Sunday felt that every moment of the service was like fingernails slowly screeching down a chalkboard. These people were offended and outraged. They wanted to run Ryan out of town. They wished that they could find a memory-erasing device, like in all the sci-fi movies, that could wipe their minds clean of what they had witnessed. They would tell everyone in town to avoid this church at all costs.

The other half thought The People's Church was the most entertaining thing they had ever seen. And they knew they could never miss a Sunday again.

GOD'S MOUTHPIECE

Katherine assumed things had to get better. Every service couldn't be as disastrous as the first week. Ryan was making mistakes because he was new at this. But after four straight Sundays, services and her life in Bartlesville were getting worse not better. Sunday mornings were all over the place, the attendance was sparse, and the offering nonexistent. And she couldn't really do anything to help. Ryan was doing everything on his own. With each passing week she felt more and more trapped, as if she were a child who initially wanted to go on a roller coaster, but now that she was strapped in and the coaster was climbing up the tracks, there was nothing more that she wanted than to get off before the whole thing went plummeting down.

"Honey, I'm off to work," Katherine said as she kissed Ryan on the cheek and walked out of the apartment.

Katherine had gotten a job as a clerk at the First Bank of Bartlesville because she knew they were going to need to make more than the $35.86 that The People's Church's average offering had produced. In Denver, she was a loan officer at First Bank and she'd had a cubicle where she could display pictures of herself and Ryan on the beach in Hawaii, and she had Strawberry Shortcake paraphernalia placed in key locations across her desk.

There was no cubicle now.

There was just a window that she had to stand in front of from nine to five where she would receive deposits and dish out withdrawals. That's all she did, over and over, and sometimes, if she were really lucky, she would accept a withdrawal *and* dish out a deposit all in the same transaction. She graduated cum laude with a BA in economics from the University of Colorado and now all her skills and talents were wasted every time she smiled and asked, "Do you want to make that deposit into checking or savings?"

When Katherine arrived at the First Bank of Bartlesville, she put her sack lunch—consisting of a tuna fish sandwich, Yoplait yogurt, and skim milk—into the fridge in the break room. Then the bank's manager checked her in and she spent the first part of the morning assisting mostly the town's merchants as they did all the necessary transactions to get ready for the day's business. Katherine got through the morning rush and checked the clock. It was 10:43. The day was crawling by. She didn't know if she could make it to the end.

But it all changed when Cowboy Jack strutted into the bank. He let someone pass him in line, waiting until Katherine's window was open so he could do his banking with her.

"Morning, sunshine," Cowboy Jack said.

"Hi," Katherine smiled.

"I like that blazer," Cowboy Jack said referring to the stiff navy blue blazer Katherine was wearing. All of the bank employees had to wear it, but the blazer's bulky shoulder pads and cheap stitching made Katherine feel plain and awkward.

"They make us wear these."

"Well, you wear it better than anyone else."

Katherine blushed. "So, um, how can I help you today?"

"I need to make a deposit."

"Will that be into checking or savings?"

"Would you like to have lunch with me? Oh, and checking."

"What?"

"I'd like to make the deposit into my checking account."

"I know, but lunch?"

"Yeah, would you like to have lunch? We could talk about church music or something."

"Yeah, sure," Katherine said.

Ryan left for work shortly after Katherine. And as he left he looked at the meager apartment that they now called home. In Denver they'd had a three-bedroom, two-bathroom mansion compared to this current shack with its one bedroom, stand-up shower, and a kitchen so small that the open silverware drawer easily stretched from one side of the room to the other.

He'd mortgaged everything to plant his church: his money, his security, and his career.

And he couldn't have been more excited about it. This is what great men do, he thought. They start computer empires by tinkering around with machines in their garage; they leave their high paying jobs to open their dream business; they quit the rat race and carve out their own destiny.

Still, most new businesses and business owners fail within the first year. But the great ones—the ones who succeed and become the innovators of how life is lived in America—don't quit and they never give up. Ryan Fisher wanted to become that type of businessman/pastor. Once he had a goal he would not be stopped, he would overcome any obstacle, leap any hurdle, and face any challenge until his task was accomplished. He would be much like the Terminator in that respect, except unlike the Terminator, if Ryan were shot he would have to be taken to the hospital, and if Ryan were shot too many times, he would die.

But this isn't that type of story. Very few people, if any, will be shot.

Ryan started his car and headed off to work, and since he didn't have an actual office he'd made The Greasy Spork the place where he crafted sermons and conducted the other business of The People's Church.

He was a little disappointed every time he walked in because no one seemed to recognize him. When he'd planned on moving to Bartlesville he'd done so because he was going to be a big fish in a small pond. It never even occurred to him that he would be a small fish in a small pond. How embarrassing was that? If he couldn't feel significant in a small town, where could he feel significant?

Ryan clutched his cup of coffee and sipped it while he looked around the diner. He knew he should be doing something to make his church successful, but what was there left to do? He'd spread the word, created radio ads, fliers, and a website. He'd personally invited every soul he'd run into over the last couple of weeks, and all he could muster up was around twenty people a week for services.

He'd tried to make a splash and failed.

Ryan figured there must have been other successful church plants in the past. But how did they happen? What makes a person choose a church? Obviously different churches focus on different leaders: some follow Buddha, Mohammed, Jesus, Joseph Smith and/or Brigham Young. But after that it's just flipping through the phone book. There are different dominations, but for the most part, Ryan assumed all Christian churches offer the same thing—sermons and songs about Jesus. He assumed that the only real difference, the thing that separated a huge church from a tiny one, was the advertising. And that was Ryan's sweet spot. Remember the ad with the Jesus fish? Ryan had checked every advertisement and website for all the other churches in town, and his branding and marketing blew everyone else's away. It wasn't even close.

Maybe these things just take time.

"Pastor Ryan?" Cammy said. She poured Ryan a cup of coffee and he looked at her a little uneasily, still not used to being called Pastor Ryan without an act of kindness involved. "Can I talk to you?" Cammy asked.

"About?"

"Love."

"That's not my specialty."

"But you know what God says about love," Cammy insisted.

"I suppose that's true," Ryan said, growing more uncomfortable with this conversation by the second. "What do you want to know?"

"Does God want me to get married? Or did I do something to make God mad so that men won't love me?"

Ryan didn't even know where to begin; the next thing Ryan would say wouldn't be his advice—he was about to be the mouth-piece for God. At least, to Cammy Miller he would be. And he didn't know what sort of dating advice God would give Cammy. Actually, how was any pastor supposed to decide what God would say? Perhaps the Bible gave sound dating advice, but Ryan wouldn't know. He didn't read the Bible much, and the couple of times he tried, he found it boring and confusing.

So what do I say to this waitress who is pouring her heart out?

Ryan remembered a time when he asked Pastor Clark a question in a similar vein, and Pastor Clark told him a Bible story. Ryan thought maybe he should do the same.

"You know, the Virgin Mary thought that nobody loved her when she was pregnant with baby Jesus," Ryan said. Off the top of his head he only knew three Bible stories: the story of the Virgin Mary, Noah's ark, and Jonah and the whale. None of those stories were about love. Mary's was the closest. "But it turns out someone did love Mary. Joseph did."

"That's true."

"Who do you love?" Ryan said, feeling the need to get away from the Bible story.

"I can't tell you that."

"Then I can't help you."

"Okay, fine." Cammy gave a mischievous look around the restaurant. Then she smiled. Her eyes lit up as she leaned in and whispered, "I'm in love with Sheriff Somersby."

"The cop with the mustache?"

"Yeah," Cammy said. "I think it's sexy."

Katherine decided she had no reason to feel guilty about going to lunch with Cowboy Jack. Why should she? Cowboy Jack asked her and she said yes. It was innocent. She was a grown woman—she was simply going to dine with another adult whose company she enjoyed. She shouldn't have to ask Ryan's permission to go to lunch with someone else.

(So why didn't you tell him about your lunch date with Jack? And why didn't you tell Ryan your favorite part of Sunday was Jack's worship?)

The angel on her shoulder asked. She wouldn't even dignify the angel with a response. She didn't need to. This wasn't a date, and it wouldn't do any good to tell Ryan that she thought Cowboy Jack was a lot better at singing than Ryan was at preaching.

This wasn't a competition. Ryan would get better, and in the meantime

(*you'll spend every moment with Jack and not tell your husband about it*)

she would support Ryan any way she could.

"We're going to lunch, that's all. I would never do anything else with him," Katherine said aloud in the empty car.

Inside The Cactus Rose, the local Tex-Mex cantina, Katherine saw Cowboy Jack in the booth looking at the menu. He had three days worth of facial scruff (for some reason his scruff looked rugged and manly, while Ryan's looked like the beard Teen Wolf would have grown if he'd lost his razor) and when he looked up his crystal blue eyes pierced through her. She was worried she might melt on her way to the table.

"Afternoon, Kate," Cowboy Jack said.

"Good afternoon," Katherine said, taking a seat across from Cowboy Jack. She flipped through the menu and then asked, "Is there anything on special?" She was embarrassed by her pedestrian question. She wanted to say something much more interesting and charming, but what do interesting and charming people say on first dates?

Not that this was a first date.

"How hungry are you?" Cowboy Jack asked.

"Hungry, but not super hungry," Katherine said wanting to give an answer that made her seem neither obese nor anorexic.

"What do you say we grab a bite real quick and spend our lunch hour doing something else?"

"Um, yeah, okay," Katherine said. She was visibly sweating for the first time in recent memory.

"You have to tell him how you truly feel," Ryan told Cammy.

"I can't."

"God doesn't like people who say can't."

"What if Sheriff Somersby doesn't like me?"

"Then he doesn't like you. Cammy, there are more cops with mustaches in the sea. If he doesn't like you, then you can stop wasting your time on him and find someone who sees you the same way God sees you: like a beautiful flower on a spring morning."

"That's how God sees me?"

"Every single day."

"Wow, you're a wise man. How long have you been a pastor?" Cammy bubbled with admiration.

"Nine years," Ryan blurted. It just kind of came out.

He knew that people would ask him about his past, and he'd been meaning to create some sort of backstory. But the key question always revolved around how long he'd been a pastor. He knew that Christians were really happy when he told them that he'd just become a believer, but he had a sneaking suspicion that it wouldn't be the same about a pastor. Maybe if he'd had eighty people on Sundays instead of eighteen he would have been more confident. But The People's Church was small—fragile as an egg—and it needed a leader with experience and confidence, not some fresh idealistic guy who didn't know what he was doing.

"Well, we're blessed to have you," Cammy said.

"Thank you," Ryan said, and meant it.

"So, how should I talk to him? Should I be forceful? Tell him everything I think?"

"You like this guy, right?"

"Yes, Pastor," Cammy giggled.

"Don't do any of that. Be forceful with a customer who doesn't tip. Speak your mind to the drive-thru guy who gives you small fries even though you ordered them extra large. But if you want the Sheriff to like you, be enthralled with his stories, be honest

115

and warm about how you're feeling, flirt with him a little, and laugh at all his jokes," Ryan said.

"Is that what the Bible says to do?"

"Probably," Ryan answered.

Cowboy Jack wouldn't tell Katherine where he was taking her. He wanted it to be a surprise. About a half mile ago he jumped out of his rusty Ford pickup and opened a weathered white fence in front of what looked to Katherine to be more of a hiking trail than a paved road. Cowboy Jack didn't seem to care. He hit the gas and the truck flew down the road, popping off the ground like an overweight man in a high jump contest whenever it hit a really bad pothole. Cowboy Jack punched his tape deck and Johnny Cash sang "Jackson"

(*Jack has voice just like Coen's doesn't he? Maybe even better.*)

and Cowboy Jack sang right along, crooning just as handsomely as Mr. Cash. When it came to the part of the song that June Carter sang, Katherine jumped in and sang with the passion and energy Whitney Houston had in her pre–Bobby Brown days. In the final chorus Cowboy Jack and Katherine sang together, playing the parts of Johnny and June perfectly. When the song came to an end, the tape deck on Cowboy Jack's truck clicked to a stop.*

"Didn't know you could sing like that," Cowboy Jack said.

"I don't sing much."

"Why's that?"

"When does a regular person sing outside of the shower or their car?"

---

*Cowboy Jack still had a tape player because he hated CDs. It was too easy to skip through an album. With a tape he had to listen to an album from front to back, "the way it was meant to be listened to."

"You're saying I'm not a regular person?"

"No, you're not a regular person. Regular people's voices belong inside showers and cars. Yours belongs out in the open for everyone to enjoy." There was silence until Katherine added, "Are we almost there?"

"Yeah. We're real close."

She regretted her question right away. But she couldn't help herself; she was always bad with changes in plans. Whenever Ryan tried to surprise her, it went wrong. On the morning of her second anniversary, Ryan told Katherine he was taking her out. He wouldn't tell her where. He wanted it to be a surprise. Katherine spent the whole day asking questions: What should I wear? Is it expensive? Can we afford it? Do we have reservations? What time are we going? Should I eat a light lunch so I'll have room for dinner? By three that afternoon Ryan gave in; he told her that he was taking her to a spot in the mountains where they had their third date—the place of their first kiss. Ryan brought some champagne and a picnic up into the mountains, they ate dinner, kissed for a bit, then Katherine got cold so they went back to the car.

She fell asleep on the way home.

But driving down the dirt path, Katherine realized that even though she didn't like surprises, she needed them. That was why she let Ryan uproot their life for a church plant in Oklahoma. Wasn't it? And wasn't that why she now found herself in the middle of something out of a bad romance novel? She was sitting on a seat with a sheepskin cover, in a cowboy's pickup, soaring through the wilderness off to something mysterious. It all made sense—she felt alive when

(just a lunch, nothing else, right, Kate?)

she didn't know what to expect.

The rusty truck came to a stop right outside of a horse stable. Katherine followed Cowboy Jack into the stable and he said, "I

117

want you to meet two of my best friends. This is Saddie and this is Phil."

"These are your horses?"

"Yeah."

"And is this your land?"

"Did you see what kind of pickup I drive? I couldn't afford this. My buddy Jasper owns this land. He just lets me keep the horses here. Technically, they're his. But he never rides them. I take care of 'em, groom 'em, feed 'em, and I can take 'em out anytime. We can go for a ride if you want."

"I'm married," Katherine said. She hadn't heard a word of what Cowboy Jack said. She couldn't let herself drink in the magic of this situation any longer. She wasn't allowed to. This was wrong.

"I know," Cowboy Jack replied.

"I love my husband."

"He seems real nice."

"I'm a pastor's wife. People watch us. I mean, do you know how bad this looks?" Katherine asked.

"I've never been a pastor's wife."

"You're the worship leader and I'm sneaking off with you to a horse stable."

"I didn't know we were sneaking," Jack said.

"Life's different for me now. I can't act like I used to."

"You used to sneak off to horse stables with cowboys?"

"No! I've never done anything like this."

"Right. Neither have I. What are we doing again?"

"It doesn't matter."

"Oh, okay, great. Do you want to feed the horses?"

"All that matters is what it could look like to other people. It could look," she took a deep breath, "it could look bad. Like we're in sin. And it's not the truth at all. I'm married. Happily. If my husband weren't working so hard I would be having lunch with him. But he's a very busy man."

"All right, now I'm going to be honest. I've never liked church. Never seemed like my type of place, because there are all these rules."

"The rules are there to help keep people from sinning."

"Sure. Great. Let me finish. I like your husband. He's a good guy. He talks about Batman and I've never known a preacher who talks about Batman; they mostly just talk about Abraham and Israel and boring stuff like that. But even better, you both trusted me to sing at your new church. No one's trusted me with something like that before. So, I guess I need to say thank you."

"You're welcome."

"The other day you said you were bored and didn't know a lot of people in town. So today I thought I'd take you to lunch. But here's the thing, I hate sitting in a booth and eating lunch. I wanted to go somewhere I was comfortable. I'm comfortable out here with my horses. Now you're telling me that's a sin. Maybe you're right because you know a lot more about God and Jesus than I do, so I'm sorry that I made you sin with me and the horses."

"That's okay, really, this is my—"

"But honestly, I don't care. I don't understand why this is a sin. I just like spending time with you. And if *that's* a sin, well, I guess I'm going to hell."

Katherine found her face inches from Cowboy Jack's. She could smell his Dakar Noir mixed with his sweat; it was intoxicating, as if it were a scent Satan himself had concocted to draw Katherine in. She closed her eyes and waited—knowing he was about to kiss her, knowing it would take God himself stepping down from heaven to stop Cowboy Jack.

But God didn't say a thing.

He just watched it all unfold.

11

MEET THE PEOPLE
OF THE PEOPLE'S CHURCH

Ryan decided that he should stay the course. Keep up the great advertising, the relevant and charming sermons, and the church would grow. He was much like a politician with his philosophy, "If at first you don't succeed, keep trying the exact same thing until it works." For the next six weeks he preached one culturally engaging sermon after another. And they all had catchy titles like: "Punched by an Angel"; "Jesus: The Fifth Beatle"; and "The Holy Spirit: Better than Chocolate."

He wanted these sermons to be controversial yet warm—a challenge, yet a breath of fresh air. He wanted the citizens of Bartlesville to experience church in a new and different way. And for the first two months, between seventeen and twenty-three people showed up for church every week. They all had their reasons for coming.

Some came to watch how Ryan was going to deliver his sermons. His delivery was always evolving; some weeks he would stand on chairs and tables and scream, others he would wear glasses, sit on a stool and read his notes. Some sermons were filled with jokes; others were loaded with inspirational anecdotes. But no matter how he preached, he always seemed to be in a little over his head, like an algebra teacher who doesn't know the answers to the problems without the teacher's edition textbook.

But most people didn't come to The People's Church to watch Ryan's awkward sermon delivery. Most of the members had never regularly attended church. The only reason they came to this church was because they felt welcome. They didn't feel the need to contort their lives and personalities to what the pastor said was acceptable. They could come as they were, (compared to all of the other churches in town, they were the Bad News Bears) and they all found comfort in that. They had a community, a place where they felt accepted and everyone pitched in to make the church work. Different folks would volunteer to help set up and tear down every week, and usually everyone stayed around with their families after the service to eat pizza, play video games, and watch Chuck E. and the band perform.

Ryan smiled and laughed and played right along with everyone. He ditched his rock star persona and decided he should just hang out with the people who came to his church. No one was ever able to tell how he felt every Sunday after church. He did not leave Denver to run this little social club. He thought if he preached the right sermons his church would grow. But no matter how terrific or how awful his sermons were, the church stayed right around twenty members. It wasn't growing. It wasn't even shrinking. It was stable and it was puny.

Ryan didn't know what more he could do. He tried more than just different styles of sermon delivery. He'd tried reordering the events in the service. For instance, one week he started with preaching and ended with worship, while another week he tried what he called a sermon sandwich. This entailed preaching, followed by twenty minutes of Cowboy Jack singing, and then back to more preaching. None of it worked. Ryan decided that there is a tried and true, sacred and holy reason that every church in America starts the service with singing and then follows it with announcements and preaching. Maybe this was how Jesus ran his church services in the Bible. Ryan made a mental note to check into that.

The only experiment Ryan tried that really seemed to work was called "Meet the People of The People's Church." It was actually Katherine's idea. And Ryan didn't have the heart to tell her how lame and clunky the title was. But the idea was fantastic. Simple, but fantastic. It involved Ryan bringing one of the members up and interviewing them, getting to know about their careers, families, hopes, and dreams. The interviews were never that engaging, they were more like small talk that everyone else got to watch. "Meet the People of The People's Church" segments never delved too deep or got too personal, but they made Sunday mornings feel warm, as if everyone was part of a family.

That all changed on the morning of Cammy Miller's interview. The interview started out innocently enough as Ryan said, "Tell us a little about yourself, Cammy."

"Well, I've been working at The Greasy Spork for fourteen years, and I'm, um, single, and I really enjoy jigsaw puzzles."

"Wow, that's great," Ryan said, even though it wasn't that great at all. He hoped he wouldn't fall asleep during the rest of the interview. It went on like this for a few more minutes with Cammy unraveling one trivial piece of information after the next. Finally he asked, "Is there anything you can tell us about yourself that we might not know?"

"Not sure if I really have anything that interesting."

"Come on, there has to be something."

"Well, um, I'm in love with Sheriff Somersby."

"Wow," Ryan said.

And Sheriff Somersby sat up. He was a first-time visitor to the church—Cammy invited him because she was going to be on "Meet the People of The People's Church" this morning. The Sheriff did not expect this.

"How long have you felt like this?" Ryan asked.

"I don't know. I guess ever since I laid my eyes on that big teddy bear of a cop with his cuddly mustache," Cammy blushed.

Sheriff Somersby was sneaking out the back.

"Sheriff, why don't you come on up here?" All twenty-two members of that morning's congregation clapped wildly, egging the Sheriff on. He couldn't leave now—he'd look like a fool. Even worse he'd make Cammy look like a fool.

"Sheriff, I'm sorry to put you on the spot like this," Ryan said.

"Quite all right. I look lawbreakers in the face every day. I can handle this."

"Listen, I just want to set things straight. Cammy is paralyzed by her feelings for you." Cammy gasped a little at this. "I'm sorry, Cammy, but it's true. You can't see another man in the world. Even if there was another great eligible bachelor in town, you wouldn't notice him because of your feelings for the Sheriff. Isn't that the case, Cammy?"

"Yeah, I guess it is."

"Sheriff, I'm going to ask you a question and I need you to be honest. Do you like Cammy?"

"Um, well, it's not that simple—"

"Because if you don't, it's okay. You're not obligated to like her. You have every right not to like her. I'm fine either way. I think we're all fine either way," Ryan said gesturing to the church. "Well, all of us but Cammy. Still, you have to let her know so she can get on with her life."

"It's like I said, it's not that simple. My career is very important to me. And I don't know if I have room for another person in my life. What if I was hurt or killed? What if I'm just too busy to be a good husband?" Cammy turned crimson red when he said "husband." "What if—"

"—being with Cammy brings your life meaning in a way you never thought possible? What if she gives a reason to be excited about coming home? What if a lot of things, Sheriff. Life's a gamble and it's dangerous—you and I know that. Don't tell all of us what you're thinking." Everyone in the church was on the edge of their seat. They wanted to know how the drama was going to play out. "This is between you and Cammy. But you have to tell her what you're feeling one way or the other. If you're the decent man I think you are, you'll let her know," Ryan said.

Cammy and the Sheriff stepped down from the seats and joined the other members of the church. Ryan then looked at his congregation and said, "We have a lot to learn from Cammy. You see, the Bible calls us the bride of Christ. But in this day and age, we often think of marriages as stale and lifeless. So, that's why if the Bible were being written today, it might call us the girlfriend of Christ. Because look at the passion that Cammy has. She's willing to make this big declaration about the Sheriff and she doesn't know how he's going to respond. He could have shot her down in front of all of us. The Sheriff didn't because he's a good guy, but he could have, and that was a risk Cammy was willing to take. You see guys, we've got to take risks like that for Jesus. We've got to shout, 'I love Jesus!' or 'I love The People's Church!' And we can't care what the 'Sheriffs,'"—Ryan made quote marks with his fingers as he said "Sheriffs,"—"of this world will think about us. Are you with me?"

The congregation nodded yes. A few even said, "Amen."

"Okay, now it's time for part two on the series, *Harry Potter, The Ultimate Evangelist*."*

During the first two months of the church, Katherine continued to have lunch with Cowboy Jack, and she had strict rules:

They could only have lunch once per week.

They could only make out during lunch hour and they could never go past second base.

They would always have an agenda for the things that they were supposed to have talked about during lunch. Katherine would brief Cowboy Jack on the agenda items in case Ryan or anyone ever asked what they talked about during lunch. Then they would be ready to give a reasonable and sensible answer.

The structure made the affair a lot more enjoyable for Katherine —it was a game with rules that could not be broken. The rules made it so she wasn't being wild and careless. And if they kept to them they wouldn't get caught being seen or doing something they would regret.

The affair didn't really have anything to do with Ryan. She still loved him very much. It was just escapism. Ryan got to cash in on his midlife crisis ten years early by starting this crazy church in Oklahoma. Shouldn't she get to have a little midlife crisis of her own? Shouldn't she be able to escape to her own fantasy world one hour every week?

(No, you shouldn't. Your husband is trying to make his dream work and this is how you treat him? How can you really think this is okay? Do you even have a soul?)

Katherine decided that she needed an outside opinion. The

---

* Ryan learned to create catchy titles by looking online and discovering that the most successful preachers in the country also had clever sermon titles. So, Ryan would usually think up a catchy title for his sermon and then figure out what the sermon was going to be about.

angel was being opinionated again. So she decided to call Jennifer Anderson, her brave and perfect leader from Fellowship Christian Church in Denver, to get some advice.

"Katherine! Hello. How are things out there in Oklahoma?" Jennifer asked. Katherine didn't like the way Jennifer asked the question. It felt almost like she was asking, "How's Siberia?" or "Have you made any good friends in the penal colony?" Still, Katherine felt warm talking on the phone to her former women's Bible study leader—it made her want to drink exotic tea and tell Jennifer her darkest secrets.

"Things are good," Katherine said. "We're missing Denver, but we're making it."

"How's Ryan's new business going?" Jennifer asked. Ryan decided not to tell anyone exactly why they were leaving Denver. He simply said it was to "start a new business in Oklahoma," and when someone would ask for more details, Ryan would get skittish and change the subject.

"It's slow, but it's tough starting a new business," Katherine said.

"And where in Oklahoma are you?"

"Bartlesville."

"Why Bartlesville?"

Katherine couldn't count the times she'd asked herself the same question. "I couldn't really tell you. Listen, I kind of need some advice."

"Sure, what's going on?"

"There's this new friend that Ryan and I have. He's a real great guy."

"Okay."

"I've been spending some time with him, and he's a great listener—"

"And you have a crush on him," Jennifer said.

"What?" Katherine could feel her hands getting tingly and numb.

"You like him, don't you?" Jennifer asked. Katherine had spent thirty seconds explaining Cowboy Jack to Jennifer and she could already tell exactly

(Ryan's going to figure it out soon too)

what was going on. She had assumed her crush was a little more mysterious, that her feelings for Cowboy Jack were well shrouded, and now she wasn't so sure.

"You can be honest with me," Jennifer said.

"Okay. I um ... you know, I like him."

"It makes sense."

"Really? It does?"

"Sure, you're in a new city, and you don't know a lot of people. It's natural that you would form an attraction elsewhere."

"So, it's okay that I like him?"

"No. It's very *not* okay. I said it's natural." Katherine knew that as a Christian if something feels natural, it's probably wrong.

"Sure, I mean, I don't want to like him."

"Have you done anything with him?"

"No!" Katherine said so passionately that she almost believed herself. "I would never cheat on Ryan."

Talking with Jennifer made a tidal wave of guilt wash over Katherine. Her game, her fantasy world, was collapsing. Katherine was forced to contemplate what she was doing and what would happen if Ryan caught her.

My marriage will never be the same, she thought. He trusts me and when he finds out what I've done, that trust will be gone. He'll wonder what's really going on every time I take a little too long to grab something at the store. He'll wonder if it's all started again. Or what if he won't even forgive me? What if he leaves me, and I have to start over? What if everywhere I go the scarlet letter brightly burns on my forehead because it's so obvious that I'm "that divorced woman who cheated on her husband." No man will ever love me again. I'll spend the rest of my life going on blind dates with truckers named Al. And in between those dates I'll spend my time in a run-down apartment watching *The Price Is Right* and taking care of cats. The cats will be the only things that can bring themselves to love me, and even they will have their doubts.

"I'm glad you've controlled yourself. I'm glad you called me before you did something you would really regret," Jennifer said.

"Yeah, so am I."

Katherine wanted to tell Jennifer the truth. She knew Jennifer wouldn't be furious with her. But their relationship would change. They were supposed to be peers now. Ryan was a pastor just like Kevin was. But Jennifer wouldn't look at Katherine as a peer if she knew the truth—she would look at her more like a therapist looks at their patient: sympathetic, understanding, and distant. Katherine, of course, was forgetting that Jennifer didn't know that Ryan was a pastor like Kevin. She assumed one day Jennifer would know. And then they could all be supercouple friends. And as Katherine thought this she realized another reason, perhaps the real reason, she wanted to move out here in the first place. She wanted to do important life-changing things with Ryan. And she was robbing herself of that chance by messing around with some cowboy. Maybe she could get out. Maybe there was still hope.

"What am I supposed to do?" Katherine asked.

"I know he's been a good friend to you, but you can't spend any more time with him. Try to slowly cut him out of your life, but most importantly make sure you're never alone with him. You don't want to give *the Enemy* any room to operate."

By "the Enemy" Jennifer meant Satan himself. It was a common belief at Fellowship Christian Church that Satan actually interfered with people's lives, luring them into sin and wickedness. Some members even believed that Satan would use his supernatural powers to wreak havoc, as if he were a twister in the plains of Kansas shredding the wooden shacks of their lives to pieces. When Katherine first heard the theology of Satan at Bible study she was terrified. She couldn't believe that there was an actual underworld being with an insatiable hunger to destroy Christians. As she told this to the other girls they just giggled at Katherine's innocence, telling her she had no reason to be afraid. "Jesus is stronger than Satan," they assured her.

But I'm not stronger than Satan, she thought.

"—So can you?" Jennifer asked again.

"Can I—"

"Stay away from this man. This—"

"Jack. Actually his full name is Cowboy Jack."

"That's kind of cute," Jennifer said.

"I know, isn't it?"

"Okay, but you can't call him that anymore," Jennifer said. "As matter of fact, don't call him anything. Stay away. No long talks. No discussions of feelings. That will just lead to ungodliness."

"Sure, okay," Katherine said, knowing that even if she wanted to, she couldn't stay away from the worship leader at her husband's church.

Next Sunday, as the service started, Cowboy Jack blew an E-minor into the harmonica and began to sing Bob Dylan's "Knockin' On Heaven's Door." Or at least that's what it sounded like. But Cowboy Jack had rewritten the verse and it went like this:

Jesus take these sins from me
I don't need them anymore
It's getting dark and I want to see

So I'm knockin' on heaven's door

The chorus went the same as it did in Bob Dylan's version "Knock, knock, knockin' on heaven's door," four times in a row. As always, Jack sang the song beautifully and Clive Wilson was so moved that he thrust his hands in the air with his palms toward heaven as he swayed back and forth. Cowboy Jack didn't know there were *other* Christian songs besides "Amazing Grace" so in the next month he would become the Weird Al of christianizing songs. It's tough to say what's worse: Weird Al distorting classic songs like "American Pie," "Smells Like Teen Spirit," and "Achy Breaky Heart" or Cowboy Jack changing the lyrics of the AC/DC hit to "God Shook Me All Night Long." He would find all of his favorite songs and change the lyrics to something spiritual so he'd have something new to sing every Sunday morning. If anyone else had tried this it would have been a disaster, an embarrassment, but Jack was so genuine about it. He was worshiping God the only way he knew how. He rewrote songs with so much flair and passion that everyone almost forgot "Hit Me Baby One More Time" wasn't always a church song.

When worship was over, Ryan was ready to launch into his sermon. But first he had to do the weekly "Meet the People of The People's Church" segment. And he was a little nervous about this week's. It involved Clive and Wilma Wilson. As Ryan called the Wilsons forward, Clive helped Wilma into her seat. This was the first time Ryan had seen Wilma in public. She was wearing a red bandanna and her skin looked yellow and brittle; the chemo had clearly taken its toll. But when Ryan first looked at Wilma he didn't notice her frail body or her bald head. The only thing he could see was how bright her eyes were, as if there were tiny Care Bears inside them shooting beams of light toward whatever she fixed her gaze on.

Ryan couldn't believe she seemed so happy and unfazed. She

should be bitter. She hadn't done anything to deserve this affliction, but the cancer didn't care. It had latched itself onto her liver, and the rest of her life was going to be dominated by it. Not that she had much longer to worry: the doctors told her she should be around for another six months at most. Ryan knew if this had happened to him, he would throw things and scream. He would drop pianos and titanium safes off large buildings. He would light anything he could find on fire to prove a point: this isn't fair. Wilma didn't seem to care about proving that point. And neither did Clive. They just sat in their chairs and waited for Ryan to ask them questions. It was almost like they were ordinary people.

"Good morning," Ryan said.

"Good morning," the Wilsons responded.

"So tell us a little about yourselves."

"Well, I've been selling car insurance, for golly, I don't know, how long has it been, Mother?"

"Twenty-two years," Wilma said.

"That's right, twenty-two years. And my goal has always been to provide security for all of my clients. And Wilma, she's always been a housewife."

"Homemaker," Wilma said.

"Homemaker, that's right. I always forget what you're supposed to call it," Clive said.

"Well, let me tell you something, Pastor Ryan, it was a full-time job. I had to raise our four beautiful children, three of them boys, and you know what a handful boys are," Wilma said.

"I sure do," Ryan said, pleased that the subject of cancer had not been brought up yet.

"But I wouldn't trade that time for anything in the world. And now our kids are all grown up and in different parts of the country. It happens so fast, doesn't it, Clive?"

"Sure does, honey bee. Sure does."

"Well, great, sound like things are good then?"

"Yeah, for the most

(the elephant is staring everyone in the face. You have to ask her about her cancer. You can't just act like she's not sitting next to you, dying. You'll look completely inhuman. They'll lose all respect for you)

part," Wilma said.

"How are you feeling, Wilma?"

"There are good days and bad days, but God is good," she smiled.

Clive grabbed her hand. His eyes were welling up. "She's been going to chemo, but the cancer won't budge."

"I'm sorry to hear that," Ryan said, right away feeling lame, as if he were saying I'm sorry you got a flat tire, or I'm sorry you couldn't come to the party last night. He felt weak and phony—he felt like he was not a mature pastor who could deal with heavy subjects like cancer.

"What can we do for you?" Ryan said trying to pull the service out of the nosedive it was in.

"Well, we've been looking for someone to pray for her."

"I'd be happy to pray for her," Ryan said.

"We want someone to pray for her healing."

"Oh, right. Well that's okay, I mean, I can pray for her healing too." Ryan didn't quite understand why, but the room was suddenly filled with electricity. Everyone whispered and smiled and looked at Ryan as if he were a prophet.

"Do you really think God will heal me?" Wilma said as a tear rolled down her cheek.

"Yes, I do."

The room was buzzing again.

Wilma and Clive jumped out of their seats and gave Ryan a hug. Ryan was surprised Wilma had the strength to hug him as hard as she did.

"Thank you so much, Pastor Ryan," the Wilsons said.

"You're welcome," Ryan said, pleased with how sunny and warm the service suddenly felt. He opened his Bible and began to shuffle through his notes. He could preach a great sermon when the room felt like this.

"Are you going to pray for her right now?" Clive asked.

"No, I've got to get to my sermon."

"Oh, then when are you going to pray for her?"

"How's Wednesday?"

"Sounds perfect," Wilma said. She hadn't stopped crying.

"Can everyone here come?"

"Sure, I don't see why not. Let's plan on Wednesday at three in the afternoon, everyone."

At that everyone began to cheer.

"We'll meet at the Wilsons' house. I will pray for Wilma Wilson. And she will be healed."

12

MIRACLE MAN

There are still some people in Bartlesville who remember the Miracle Man. They remember how weeks before he would come to lead a revival meeting, there would be white vans that cruised around town announcing, "The Miracle Man is coming!" They remember posters slapped over every inch of town announcing his arrival as if he were a king or a senator or the Beatles. The posters were of a red, white, and blue background and the face of the man himself, Rev. Richard Sizemore. Underneath his face there were bold letters that asked a profound question:

Do You Need a Miracle?

They remember how the Miracle Man would set up his large tent on the outskirts of Bartlesville and how everyone from Taldega, Wasougge, and Blaine counties would come to watch the Miracle Man perform in revival meetings for five nights straight. At the meetings there was music, preaching, and every night ended with breathtaking miracles. The crippled would walk, the blind would see, the deaf would hear, and those afflicted with emphysema would get home and realize they were emphysema free.

Everyone who was around in those days remembers the Miracle Man. And Clive Wilson remembered him as well as anyone. Whenever he looked at the lot that now holds a Costco and a Bed Bath and Beyond, all he had to do was shut his eyes and he could see the large white tent and hear the passionate words of the Miracle Man.

Clive had seen a lot of pastors and been to a lot of churches since those days in the tent. But no one reminded him of the Miracle Man as much as the new pastor in town did. That's why he was confident that Pastor Ryan would be just the man to perform a miracle. Just the man to heal his wife.

When Clive asked Ryan, Ryan agreed so confidently and graciously, it was almost as if he had been waiting for weeks to perform a miracle, and all he needed was for Clive to show a little faith and ask.

And now Pastor Ryan was in Clive's living room standing over Wilma. He was about to pray for the healing power of God to wash over her body. And there was quite the audience to watch the miracle, including the entire People's Church as well as six of Clive's good friends from the insurance office, Clive's brother Lionel, Wilma's entire quilting group, and the Boy Scout troop he was den leader over. Everyone in the room had heard of the Miracle Man, and when Clive started spreading word around town that Pastor Ryan was the second coming of the Miracle Man—that he was going to perform a miracle just like the ones Rev. Sizemore did in the olden days—no one believed Clive, so they had to see it for themselves.

When Ryan arrived, he walked up to Clive Wilson's porch and

saw that there were three times more people in Clive's living room than there ever were at Chuck E. Cheese's on a Sunday morning. Ryan stood on the porch with his Bible in hand and felt the weight of the glares, as if their collective mistrust was seeping through the screen door and strangling him.

Clive opened the door and gave Ryan a hug.

"Hope you don't mind, I invited a few more friends over. You know, 'where two or three are gathered' sort of thing," Clive said.

Ryan nodded politely. He had no idea what Clive was talking about. Ryan didn't know of the passage in Matthew that read, "For where two or three come together in my name, there am I with them." Ryan didn't know that it was a custom in many Christian circles, when asking for something like a miracle, for a group to come together and pray in agreement for the request. Problem was, most people in the room were not there to pray with Ryan in agreement. They were there to watch.

As Ryan stepped into the house, the crowd of onlookers parted like the Red Sea. The room smelled old, like rotting black Jujubes; there were porcelain dolls on shelves all over the room — leprechauns and Precious Moments kids and Eskimos — and they all seemed to be glaring at Ryan too. In the corner there was a TV that looked ten years older than Ryan, and the couch Wilma was laying on was circus peanut orange and bathed in dust.

Every soul in the room leaned forward to watch what the pastor would do. People were putting kids on their shoulders so they could see; it was as if Ryan was Santa Claus at the Bartlesville Christmas parade. Ryan sat on the couch next to Wilma and grabbed her hand. "How are you doing?" Ryan asked.

"I'm getting scared, Pastor Ryan," Wilma said. "I don't feel good at all."

"She's gotten a lot worse since Sunday," Clive said.

"I'm sorry."

"Not your fault."

"I just wish there was something I could do," Ryan said. Everyone in the room gave one another confused glances and whispers.

"Something more than pray, I mean."

"You're going to pray and God's going to heal her. What more is there than that?" Clive said.

"Right," Ryan said.

Silence. Clive and Wilma closed their eyes for the prayer. Ryan just looked around, trying to think of a way he could sneak out.

"Okay, so I'm going to pray now to ask God to heal her," Ryan said in a tone that made it seem like he was asking more than telling.

"It's just like when you talked about faith a few weeks ago," Clive Wilson said.

But Ryan hadn't talked about faith. He talked about *faithfulness*. He was noticing his church actually had thirty or so members but only fifteen would show up at a time. The rest just came and went, skipping Sundays here and there. So Ryan talked about the importance of faithfulness, of never missing a Sunday, and he did his "Meet the People of The People's Church" interview with a loan officer named Sandy who hadn't missed a day of work in over five years. "Think of all the chances to put people into new homes Sandy would have missed," Ryan had said.

It was one of the more lame Sundays at The People's Church.

Ryan understood faithfulness, but faith—especially a faith like Clive had—was foreign to Ryan. Truthfully, Ryan thought putting that much faith in anything was naive. He used to put faith in things: he had faith that the Cubs would win the World Series, that the stock market would make him rich, that a father wouldn't hurt his son—wouldn't leave his family to pursue his own selfish needs. Ryan didn't put faith in much of anything anymore.

"We're right here with you. We're going to agree with every word you pray," Clive said.

Ryan took a deep breath. He couldn't stall any longer. There was nothing else he could do but bow his head, close his eyes, and pray.

To fully understand how Ryan got himself in this predicament it is important to note that last Sunday Ryan had completely misunderstood what Clive was asking.

When he agreed to pray for healing, he did so because he was sure that Clive had meant a spiritual healing. Something like her last rites, or a confession; he wanted her soul to be "healed" before she went to heaven. Ryan wasn't qualified to lead this sort of prayer either, but he could fake it—there had to be some sort of Dummy Book or Idiot Guide on the subject, and after the prayer no one would know if it worked or not. How could they? How could you tell if someone's soul was actually healed?

But Ryan didn't feel like spending all day researching the topic of spiritual healing. He needed the CliffsNotes. He needed to call another pastor. He needed to call Pastor Clark and pick his brain on the subject. Pastor Clark could probably walk Ryan through the steps of spiritual healing, or whatever kind of healing Clive was looking for. The only trick for Ryan would be asking for this advice without letting Pastor Clark know that he now called himself a pastor.

Ryan called Pastor Clark and they spent the first five minutes of the conversation catching up on each other's lives. As the conversation went into a lull, Ryan asked, "Can you answer a hypothetical question for me?"

"I'll do my best."

"Let's say someone has liver cancer. They ask for a prayer for healing. They mean a spiritual healing, right?"

"They could mean that," Pastor Clark said in a tone that implied they don't mean that.

"Okay, I'm sorry, I don't know the exact terminology. I'm a new Christian. If you were going to call it something besides a 'spiritual healing,' what would that be?"

"Actual healing."

"What do you mean, actual healing?"

"I mean, a lot of times people want to actually be healed from their sickness."

"People can actually be healed?"

"That's a debated topic. There's always Lazarus . . ."

Who's Lazarus? Was he in a band? Ryan thought. But he just said, "That's true." Then he added, "But cancer. God can't actually heal people from cancer."

"It's happened before."

Now Ryan was sure Pastor Clark was lying through his perfect teeth. People can't be healed of cancer. It's one of those unbeatable things. Trying to stop cancer is like trying to outspend the Yankees, or going to the farewell tour of Aerosmith, or watching the final James Bond movie. Some things can't be defeated—can't even be slowed down. Cancer is one of those things. And if God *could* heal one person from cancer, why wouldn't he heal everyone from cancer? Why wouldn't he make cancer as obsolete as a VHS tape?

"So, you're saying if someone's asking me to pray for healing from cancer, they mean when the prayer is over the cancer will be gone?" Ryan asked.

"Yeah, something like that," Pastor Clark said.

"I'm sorry, but that doesn't make sense. People don't get healed from cancer. I had no idea what I was agreeing to."

"Who's asking you for that sort of prayer? What are you doing out there, Ryan?"

"It's just a friend, and I'm running a Christian real estate company."

"A Christian real estate company?"

"We sell, uh, Christian houses and uh, we also sell churches."

Ryan didn't like where this conversation was going.

"Listen, Ryan, are you—"

"Hey, I've got to run, Pastor Clark. Nice catching up with you."

Ryan hung up before Pastor Clark could respond.

Ryan had no idea what he was doing amidst all of the people with their heads bowed in prayer. He didn't know how a healing prayer sounded, but he had a hunch everyone else in the room did. Pastor Clark made it sound like healing prayers were commonplace in the church.

So Ryan had to make a decision, to take action, to pray, or to say or do something that would get him out of this situation.

I'm supposed to heal this woman of cancer in the next five minutes? How is that going to happen? Scientists have been looking for a cure for an awfully long time and they haven't had any luck, Ryan thought.

Luckily for Ryan, he'd learned at an early age how to process options in a difficult situation. He learned this by reading Choose Your Own Adventure* stories, and as he read through them he would always go back and reread all the other choices, paying careful attention to the way they all played out. Some choices

---

*Choose Your Own Adventure is a series of children's books written from 1979 to 1998 in a second person point-of-view, with the reader assuming the role of the main character. After an introduction to the story, the reader is given choices of how the story should progress. For instance:

If you decide to start back home, turn to page 4.

If you decide to wait, turn to page 5.

Depending on the reader's choice, the plot would unfold in different ways and eventually lead to many different possible endings (www.wikipedia.org).

would get the character out of a jam while others would be met with disastrous consequences. If Ryan's life at the moment was a Choose Your Own Adventure story, here's how it would look:

If you think Ryan should pretend he knows exactly what he's doing, turn to page 43.

"Father God, we come to you today because ... we need your healing power!" Ryan would exclaim. Then he would continue to lie his way through the prayer, acting as if he knew exactly how it was supposed to go. When the prayer was over, someone would challenge him and say—

"I've never heard a prayer like that."

Ryan would respond, "I've healed sixteen people from cancer and that prayer has worked every single time."

"Sixteen people. Seriously? Wow!"

"Yep, if Wilma doesn't get healed, the problem is with her, not the prayer."

When word got out that Ryan had healed sixteen people from cancer, everyone would come to him for prayer. And he'd continue to lie. He'd say that he could heal people of any and every type of sickness. But it would never happen; people would come to Ryan sick and they'd leave sick *and* disappointed. There would be no healings, and Ryan would continue to insist that the problems were with the people of Bartlesville and not his prayers.

The whole town would grow so angry that they would grab torches and would chase Ryan out of the town and into the nearby forest. Finally, Ryan would be destroyed either by robots or dinosaurs.

If you think Ryan should be honest and tell everyone he does not know what he's doing, turn to page 37.

"What am I doing?" Ryan would say, confusing everyone in the room. Ryan wouldn't know how to be tactfully honest. Once he started being honest he wouldn't know when to stop. "I don't belong here. I've been lying. I'm not a pastor. I should not be praying for your wife's healing. Clive, you're a good man, and she's a good woman, and you shouldn't trust me. I can't heal your wife from cancer because I've never seen it done. I don't even believe it can be done."

Clive would say, "Pastor Ryan, you have the anointing. You are just like the Miracle Man."

And Ryan would say, "No, I'm not. I'm nothing but a fake. I'm a magician with a bag full of lame tricks. And now I'm going to perform a disappearing act."

All would watch in silence as Ryan limped out of the Wilsons' living room like a man condemned.

Next, Ryan would drive straight to the bank where his wife worked and tell her he wanted to go home; it was time to go back to Denver. Katherine would not understand Ryan's dramatic change of heart. She would be so exhausted by her husband's up-and-down behavior that she would decide she had no choice but to leave him. She would hook up with Cowboy Jack and eventually marry him. They would start their own ranch and she would finally get to be mother of three strapping young boys.

And Ryan would live in Denver as an unsuccessful real estate agent. He would never remarry. He would spend every night in his apartment eating Apple Jacks and wondering where exactly his life went so horribly wrong.

If you think Ryan should bluff his way through the prayer, turn to page 34.

"Father God, we come to you today because ... we need you," Ryan would pray.

After considering his options, Ryan knew he had to be honest but not exactly truthful. Faking it would get him out of the moment, but then things would get worse later. And Ryan didn't know how to be honest *and* discreet in this situation. It would be too difficult to admit that he didn't know anything about cancer-healing prayers, but also keep up the front that he was a seasoned minister. He had to bluff, to use everything he knew about prayer and Christianity to make him appear knowledgeable, but not too knowledgeable. After all, Ryan had agreed to pray for Wilma but he'd never claimed that he'd had a lot of experience with such prayers.

He prayed, "We need you to heal Wilma Wilson of cancer. Wilma is your faithful servant, and she is in pain. Science cannot help her, medicine cannot help her, and truthfully God, I can't help her. We need you. We need you to come down from heaven, or however you work, and take this cancer away."

All in the room who could remember the Miracle Man peeked their eyes open and gave each other confused looks. This was not how the Miracle Man prayed for people. The Miracle Man would reach his arm toward heaven and scream, "HEALING! WE PRAY FOR HEALING, FATHER!" and then he'd slap the person on the forehead. The power of God would be so strong that the person would fall on the floor for a long stretch, and when they woke up they were healed.

"God, I don't know what else to do or to say, but please have mercy on us. And have mercy on me. I know that I might not be the perfect person to pray for this woman, but don't take that out on her. Wilma loves you, Clive loves you, and they have followed you their whole lives."

As Ryan was praying he thought he could actually feel the presence of God Himself in the room. He felt as if he were being slowly dipped into a large vat of all-knowing, all-caring, all-powerful love. He'd never felt more confident that God actually existed and that He was going to bail Ryan out of this mess and heal this lovely woman of cancer.

"Thank you God for this healing. We are honored that you would do this. We worship you in your Holy Name, Amen."

"Amen," all the onlookers echoed.

The only sound in the room was the steady ticking of the Wilsons' grandfather clock.

Wilma smiled at Clive; then she locked eyes with Ryan. It's working, this is what a person looks like when they are being healed of cancer, Ryan thought.

Wilma grabbed the back of Ryan's neck. With all her strength she whispered, "Thank you." Her fingers slipped off his neck and fell to her side.

Everyone stood in the silence. The grandfather clock continued to tick and the room began to feel cold, as if the sun was setting and the room was being swallowed by large shadows. Ryan waited for Wilma to wake up, or stir, or move, because God was going to heal her—it was the surest Ryan had been of God's existence and wisdom and power since his first Sunday at Fellowship Christian Church.

Ryan had never watched someone pass away. He'd heard stories of white lights and tunnels, but it didn't seem like there was anything like that here. It didn't feel like someone had just gone to heaven; the room just felt a little more empty and hollow without Wilma's soul in it.

And, like Ryan, for almost all of the fifty-four people in Clive's living room, this was the first time they had seen someone pass away right before their eyes. They had seen it in movies, but people in movies weren't real. Wilma Wilson was real. She was their friend, their neighbor, she had the best Rice Krispie treats every Halloween, she was a staple volunteer in the PTA long after her own kids had graduated, and she had one of those smiles that always made the day go a little better.

She was alive thirty seconds ago. Now she was dead.

Her soul was in God's hands.

BEING OPRAH WINFREY

13

WILMA'S WAKE

The paramedics slammed the doors to the ambulance with finality, shattering any hope that Wilma would spring back to life, any hope that she would give Clive a loving hug as she said, "I'm alive! God wiped the cancer out of my body! Pastor Ryan's prayer healed me!"

Shortly after Wilma died, Cammy Miller had called 911, and soon there were ambulances, firefighters, and police officers swarming around the Wilsons' home. They wanted Ryan to tell every detail of the story exactly as it had happed.

Clive was trying to stay composed as the reality of Wilma's death was sinking its teeth into him. He was now a widower. He would have no one to come home to, no one to watch *Jeopardy* with, and after supper he'd have to take long walks through the neighborhood alone. Clive watched the paramedics slide a thin black sheet over Wilma.

Ryan had put a pastorly arm around Clive and told him it was going to be okay. But when Clive turned and looked at Ryan, Ryan had felt Clive's thoughts interrogating him: Why didn't God heal her? I thought you were the Miracle Man. But you're not, you're a liar. How many more people have you been lying to? What else have you been lying about?

Most of Clive's friends stood in the front yard scattered amidst the pink flamingos and green lawn gnomes as the ambulance pulled away. All watched as the ambulance crawled down the dirt road, and no one spoke until it had completely vanished into the dark.

Then, like a group at the end of a museum tour, the crowd began to ask questions. Everyone had just watched their friend pass away and they had lots of questions for God, but since God wasn't around they would have to ask Ryan. He would have to serve once again as God's mouthpiece. He was the pastor, this was his show, and even though he couldn't heal Wilma of cancer, the crowd thought that surely he knew the right things to say and do in this situation.

He told Wilma's friends and family, "You should go home now; Clive's had a long day—he needs to get some rest."

No one questioned Ryan.

And when there were only a few close family members left at the scene Ryan began to leave. Clive hadn't said a thing to him since Wilma had died, and Ryan wanted Clive to say something. He wanted him to say something like, "I forgive you. You did all you could. Thank you for trying." Ryan gave Clive one more opportunity to be grateful as he shook Clive's hand and told him, "I'm here for anything you need."

But all Clive could do in response was muster up a friendly nod.

When Ryan got home he collapsed on the couch. Katherine had heard about everything and she kissed her husband on the cheek and asked, "Are you okay?"

Ryan stared straight ahead. He told his wife, "I'm the Dr. Kevorkian of prayer."

"You are not."

"God killed her to teach me a lesson."

"What were you really trying to do over there?"

"I was there to heal her."

"You heal people?"

"It's part of what pastors are supposed to do."

"Since when?"

"I don't know, since the Bible days," Ryan said. "Clive asked me to pray. So I prayed. And she was supposed to be healed—"

"Just like that?"

"Yes, just like that."

"You can't just heal someone from cancer."

"That's not what Pastor Clark told me."

"So, what is this going to do to the church?"

"Besides destroy it?" Before Katherine could answer her husband, the phone began to ring. Ryan snatched the phone out of cradle and said, "Yes."

Katherine couldn't imagine who would be calling at a time like this. All she knew was whoever had called was doing all of the talking. The only things Ryan said were, "Really? Sure. I'd be honored to. You too." And then Ryan hung up the phone.

He looked up at Katherine and said, "Clive wants me to do the funeral."

"But you've never done a funeral."

"I'm sure it's like doing a wedding. Only sadder."

Two days later the Lutheran Church on the north side of Bartlesville was a picture of the scene Ryan had hoped to see when he first decided to become a pastor. The pulpit was made out of solid oak and had a commanding presence. Whoever stood behind it would have undeniable authority, much like the person who sat in the captain's chair on the bridge of the *Enterprise*. The pews were packed with hundreds of folks wearing their nicest clothes. The sun was beaming through the stained glass windows making the room feel holy and angelic. Music danced out of the organ pipes while latecomers were squeezing into the final seats at the end of the pews. Best of all, everyone was waiting to hear Ryan speak, to lead, to read the Bible, to recite prayers and give words that could provide comfort and guidance.

Unfortunately, the mahogany funeral casket hovering on the center of the stage made it impossible for Ryan to enjoy the moment. And as he peeked out from the sermon prep room and saw men and women staring at Wilma's casket, he began to feel every symptom of stage fright. Butterflies were dancing in his gut, cold sweat was trickling down his face, and his mind felt cloudy and slow. He'd forget everything that he'd prepared to say. He couldn't even concentrate enough to read his thoughts off of the note cards.

Then Ryan looked at Wilma's casket. All the feelings of guilt he'd wrestled with for the last few days flooded back to him. Ryan had murdered the old woman. Maybe he hadn't actually pulled the trigger, or strangled her, or hit her over the head with a pipe wrench,* but she was still dead. A couple of days ago Wilma had been crying and hugging Ryan while imagining a cancer-free life. One prayer from Ryan and she was dead. Surely this would be the end of his ministry. This would cause even the small contingency

---

*The image of the pipe wrench came to Ryan's mind because of the Milton Bradley game Clue, where characters with colorful last names like Mustard, Scarlet, and White were supposed to have killed an innocent victim with ordinary household items like ropes, wrenches, and thimbles. Or maybe thimbles were from Monopoly. Either way Ryan couldn't believe parents allowed their children to play such a violent game. Children would be much better off drowning in the molasses swamp of Candyland than bludgeoning one another with the pipe wrenches from Clue.

of The People's Church to leave, to swear off God and church forever. Ryan tried not to think of himself, about how this would affect him, because he knew he should be focusing on the task at hand.

The more he thought about Wilma's death the more it seemed to him as if there was no chance her death could have been a coincidence. There was a reason she died at the time she did. Ryan had no idea what the reason was. He hadn't had the luxury of processing her death because for the past two days he'd been busy acting as the strong comforting presence for everyone else. But it was taxing him. Sucking him dry. He was the shoulder to cry on one second, the comforting voice that would explain the bigger picture the next. And the way he explained the bigger picture was by saying, "God had a greater purpose with Wilma's death." Then he braced himself. Waited for the next logical question, "What? What could God's purpose be in killing someone? What could justify that?"

But no one ever asked that.

So Ryan learned there was an easy out. He learned that there was an answer to all difficult questions like, "Why did God allow Wilma to die from cancer?" The answer was, "It's part of His plan." And this answer worked every time. If a church member had the audacity to ask: "Why did God let my cousin die in a car accident? Why did I lose my job? Why are gas prices soaring so unbelievably high?" There was always one simple answer, "I just know God's in control." And who are you to question the almighty God?

That was where the argument ended.

Every time.

"They're ready for you," Reverend Whitlock said.

Ryan followed Reverend Whitlock out onto the stage. Ryan could feel the butterflies dancing violently in his insides as hundreds of eyes focused on him, but the congregation couldn't tell. To them, Ryan was the picture of calm—a man who looked like this was another day in the office. The expression on his face said, I've buried many people before and I'll bury even more in the future.

This was another of Ryan's gifts, of his special X-Men skills. Unlike Jimmy Buckley, Ryan could have made a lot of money on the World Poker Tour because he had the special ability of communicating one thing with his face while something much different was happening in his head and his heart. When he was on the verge of losing the sale of a house that badly needed to come off the market, his face said, I could care less, and thus the buyer thought, If he doesn't care about losing the sale there must be lots of other buyers and this house must be a great deal. Ryan would get the sale. If Katherine was pouring her heart out to Ryan, he had a look that said, You have my complete attention, even though Katherine only sometimes had his attention.

As Ryan stepped behind the large oak pulpit, he could see tears stream down the faces of the congregation. He could hear sobbing in the room and he understood he was the final step, the end of the process. Wilma was already dead, but when he finished the service it would be official. He felt as if he needed to be soothing again.

So he began to say the things a preacher is supposed to say at a time like this. He said, "We come here today to remember the life of Wilma Wilson. But this is not a sad occasion; this is a happy one, because

(how do you know it's a better place?)

Wilma is in a better place."

Ryan couldn't help but notice that the tears began to dry up and the sobs went quiet. He continued, "Please, turn with me to the Twenty-third Psalm. 'The Lord is my shepherd; I shall not want.

(it's not like anyone's ever come back from heaven to affirm it's a better place)

He maketh me to lie down in green pastures: he leadeth me beside the still waters. He restoreth my

(maybe heaven's not as great as we claim it is; maybe the only music there comes from Kenny G. and elevator soundtracks; maybe the only shows on TV are reruns of The Golden Girls *and* 7th Heaven*)*

soul.' "

Ryan flipped the page in his Bible, looked up, and noticed that people's eyes were glazing over. They were supposed to be remembering Wilma, this great woman, and he was offering nothing but clichés and trite spiritual advice. He was trying to tell everyone about heaven

(maybe heaven doesn't exist at all; maybe we die and then there is nothing)

but he didn't know what to say. Not that it mattered. He was realizing something horrible was happening here. He was one of those pastors that he hated, he was saying things that were cold and lifeless, and worst of all, boring. He wasn't letting people grieve; he was just numbing their feelings.

And that's when Ryan felt something unusual: an overwhelming urge to be honest.

He wanted to say what he was really feeling—God had abandoned Wilma; he could have snapped his fingers and let her live, but he sat in heaven with his arms folded and let her die. Ryan knew he should have just continued to say what he was saying, that she was in a better place, that they could rejoice because the cancer was gone and Wilma was now square dancing in heaven with Jesus and the archangels. But as he stood in front of this packed house of mourning souls, Ryan began to wonder if maybe saying the right and proper thing isn't what is supposed to be done. Maybe he should just say everything he really thought to this group of onlookers.

What Ryan didn't know was that he was exactly right. As bizarre as he seemed to the people of Bartlesville by bursting into town and obnoxiously trying to start a church, nearly everyone still liked him. And they liked him because he was so imperfect. He didn't have lots of money and a solid corporate plan; he was starting a church like they would have: He was meeting people, hanging up fliers, and meeting in the only place he could afford. Ryan was like the lovesick teenager who comes to the bedroom window of his dream girl and serenades her by singing a song badly. The teenager can't sing and can't play, but he is willing to make a fool of himself for the girl and that's why she'll fall for him.

Ryan didn't understand that he was growing more and more popular because he was unpolished. He didn't understand that today more than any other day they wanted him to be authentic and real, to act like he was hurt, like he cared about Wilma, like he was one of them.

Ryan was halfway through reading the Twenty-third Psalm when he looked up and said, "You know what, this really sucks."

Silence.

Everyone looked at each other. The glaze over their eyes had washed away — their expressions asked, Did you hear what I just heard? Did he really say that? Ryan was letting the words sink in as he searched his thoughts for the next honest bomb that he would drop in the funeral service.

Then he said, "See, here's what I really think. Wilma should be here today. She might be in a better place, but right now, I don't care. I just wish she were here. I wish she were sitting in that pew right next to Clive smiling at me, and I really wish that God would have healed her like I asked him to, like we *all* asked him to that day at Clive's house. But he didn't. He took her up to heaven with him, and maybe that's because he was really selfish and wanted Wilma all for himself.

"But I want her back. I've never wanted someone to live so bad only to have them taken away from me. I know I'm new here. I know what Wilma meant to all of you, so I'm sorry for your loss. For me, it's tough to know where to go from here."

Everyone was leaning forward in the pew. They were glued to every word Ryan spoke. They had never seen a minister act like this at a funeral, and they loved it. He wasn't talking down to them; he was saying what they all felt. He was confused and vulnerable like they all were, and that took real courage.

"I'm not saying that we should give up on God or Jesus or anything like that," Ryan said. "I'm sure that he's got a plan in all of this. I just don't see how any plan without Wilma Wilson in it could be a good one."

No one moved as Ryan closed his Bible. He had to collect himself before he could step away from the pulpit. In those brief moments Ryan was sure that he had failed, that he had gone too far, that his career was now over, and he'd pounded the final nail in the coffin. But right before Ryan stepped away from the pulpit he heard a single person giving him applause for his speech. He smiled as the one person clapping turned to a few, to half the audience, to everyone. Then he watched as one person after another stood from their pew and passionately clapped, giving him his first ever standing ovation.

14

A THREE-RING
SUNDAY

For a traditional nuclear American family (father, mother, 2.4 kids) getting to church on a Sunday morning is a harrowing ordeal. The whole process starts at the crack of dawn with Mom—she is usually the engine, the driving force to get everyone to church. This is probably because she realizes that church is a place that brings families together by teaching about wholesomeness and good deeds. And because it gives her a chance to dress her children up in dresses, blazers, and slacks, and parade them around. Then she'll meet up with the other mothers and they'll compare and compliment each other on which children have the cutest clothes and most adorable outfits, and they always frown at that one little boy who comes dressed in jeans and a faded Teenage Mutant Ninja Turtles sweatshirt with Cheeto crumbs all over his face. They all whisper, "What type of parents does that boy have?" The mothers usually assume that the little boy with Cheeto crumbs comes from a single-parent home, or maybe his parents deal crack or own a chain of pornography stores.

Church is a place where people get judged. Even children.

Knowing this, the mother will spring to action at the crack of dawn, before the rooster crows. Missing church will mean furrowed brows and whispers from all the other women in her canasta group, and that is not an option. My family will go to church, the mother thinks.

So she starts her day off by brewing a pot of coffee and making a game plan for getting everyone to arrive at God's house on time. She knows that her husband is the hardest sell; he always tells her that getting to church is too stressful: the parking, the people, and those overcrowded pews. Can't we just have church at home? This is the weekend; shouldn't we be relaxing? After she gives her husband *the scowl*, the one that squelches all questions, the one that she has worked on for the last fifteen years of her marriage—he stops fighting and starts to get ready for church. As a small reward for his obedience, the wife tells her husband, "Bacon and eggs are on the table."

Next, the mother goes one room over and is pleased to discover that her daughter is already out of bed. The daughter usually wakes up on time, sometimes even earlier than the mother, but when the mom walks into her teenage daughter's room, she sees a sixteen-year-old still in her pajamas, tossing her clothes from one side of the room to the other.

"It's time to get ready," the mother instructs.

"I've been getting ready," the daughter replies.

"You need to pick out an outfit."

"I hate all my clothes!"

"What about your pink sweater?"

"Oh my God, are you actually serious? That pink sweater is gross. I look like a life-sized bottle of Pepto Bismol."

"Could you wear your tan velvet jacket?"

"There is no way Steven Catrisano is going to notice me in that."

"Okay, well, we need to leave in an hour."

"It is totally humanly impossible for me to do my hair, makeup, and find an outfit in one hour."

"Then you better get started," the mother says, cruel as Scarface, and she closes the door.

Her eight-year-old boy has the least reluctance. When the mother tells him to wake up and get ready, he does so without any protest. Problem is, ten minutes later she finds him in front of the TV snacking on a bowl of Lucky Charms and watching *Transformers*. The mother shuts the TV off, snatches the Lucky Charms away, and yells, "Everybody ready now!"

And somehow, thirty minutes later, the family pulls out of the driveway and heads down the street past all of the similar looking houses to head to church. They don't say a word as they drive, they're too tired and angry from the morning's events to attempt to drum up any small talk.

Ryan remembered how tough it was getting to church with his family. He was amazed anyone ever made it to church.

But this morning, what made him more amazed was that ten minutes before church was supposed to start, the dining hall of the Chuck E. Cheese's was packed. There were twice as many people in the room as the fire codes allowed, and as Ryan peeked out the window into the parking lot he was thrilled to see that cars were lining up and fighting for spots. People were parking in front of fire hydrants and in handicapped spaces because that was all that was left.

Ryan thought this might happen. He'd heard the buzz all week.

He'd performed Wilma's wake on Monday, and by Tuesday he was all the talk in the Greasy Spork. On Wednesday and Thursday, folks were asking each other if they were going to Pastor Ryan's service this weekend. By Friday the question wasn't, are you going, it was simply, how early are you going to get there? And everywhere Ryan went he felt like a rock star. He no longer had to pay for a cup of coffee at the Spork, he got 15 percent off of his oil change at Pete's Automotive, and when he'd walk down the street, strangers would stop him, tear up, and say, "Thank you for your honesty. Wilma's funeral changed my life."

Ryan was startled that his message at Wilma's funeral had that much of an impact.

What he didn't understand was the town of Bartlesville had been looking for a hero for quite awhile. The days of the Miracle Man seemed far behind them, and the town had been searching for something to bond them together, a person and institution with whom they could find their identity. Especially the teenagers and twentysomethings were sick of hearing about the good old days—they wanted their own hero, their own legacy to be excited about. They weren't sure if Ryan was the hero they were looking for, but they were willing to give him a shot.

And Ryan could sense what the town was thinking. They were wondering, is he just going to be a flash in the pan, a person who gets fifteen minutes of fame, or is he the real deal? Is there something to this church?

Ryan was ready to step up. He wouldn't let this deal fall through. That's why when Katherine said, "We have to turn people away," he simply replied, "Not an option."

"We can't fit any more people in here."

"Then we think of somewhere else to meet."

"You can't just move an entire mass of people somewhere. That is not possible."

"We have to think of a plan B."

"Okay. Fine. What is plan B?" Katherine said.

Ryan had no idea. He barely understood what plan A was.

But Ryan had read *Good to Great* and *The Tipping Point*. And he'd learned for a business to succeed there is nothing, absolutely not one thing more important than a customer's first impression. And he had only moments to devise a plan that would leave all of these first-time visitors with a feeling that The People's Church was the place they wanted to spend their Sunday mornings.

He had to act. Now.

"We're going to have the church service in the parking lot."

"What?" Katherine said.

"Tell everyone to grab every chair out of here and take it to the parking lot. Then run up to Wal-Mart and buy every chair that they have: lawn chairs, camping chairs, little kid plastic chairs; if it has four legs, buy it."

"We can't afford all of those chairs."

"Put it on a credit card. It's Wal-Mart. They take anything back. We're not buying them; we're renting them. Except, you know, for free."

Katherine had to bring Cowboy Jack with her to get all of the chairs. He was the only one with a Chevy truck. It was awkward. They hadn't been alone together for weeks. They hadn't talked (or *really* talked as Ryan's mother would say) since Katherine decided she and Cowboy Jack should no longer have lunch together. Katherine broke things off shortly after her conversation with Jennifer Anderson.

"Did I do something wrong?" Cowboy Jack had asked.

"We both did something wrong," Katherine had said.

"I thought you said this was just innocent and fun."

"That's exactly what Satan wants us to think."

"What?"

"I don't really get it either. You'd have to ask Jennifer Anderson."

"Who is —"

"My old Bible study leader."

"And your old Bible study leader told us that Satan wants us to have lunch together?"

"Pretty much."

"Kate, this is really —"

"And she's right Jack. I don't know what I was thinking. I was confused. But this has to stop. We have to act like this never happened. That's what Jesus would want us to do."

And Katherine really did think that's what Jesus would want them to do. She remembered Pastor Clark talking about Jesus taking our sins and wiping them away. *As far as the east is from the west.* That's how Pastor Clark had said it. That was one of the things that was so attractive about Christianity to Katherine: No matter how many mistakes we've made, Jesus just forgets about them. And so should I, Katherine thought. After talking with Jennifer, Katherine was convinced that the right course of action was to end things with Cowboy Jack and pretend it never happened.

Still, there was this nagging guilt telling her she couldn't just make a mistake and be forgiven for it. Maybe she'd misunderstood. Maybe the Christian thing to do was to wallow in her guilt. But she decided to push those feelings away, she decided to side with Jesus and forget about her past mistakes even though siding with Jesus probably wasn't the Christian thing to do.

She drove to Wal-Mart with Cowboy Jack, focusing only on the task at hand of getting chairs for the Sunday service. Cowboy Jack thought that this would be their chance to talk again, but whenever he tried to get Katherine to open up and tell him how she was feeling, Katherine always quickly changed the topic. The affair was in the past. That was exactly where she was going to keep it. And once they got the chairs, they arrived back at the Chuck E. Cheese parking lot, where they saw a herd of hundreds of people standing around, unsure of exactly what they were supposed to be doing.

Fifteen minutes earlier Ryan had been left to make the transition from the dining room to the parking lot. He'd made the announcement, telling everyone in the dining room that they were having church in the parking lot, saying it coolly and confidently, as if this were the plan all along. But no one seemed very pleased about it. Ryan could see the questions on their faces. What kind of church is this? Service in the parking lot, really?

Still, Ryan felt the key here was not to show any doubt. If he showed doubt, insecurity, everyone would jump ship. The service would spiral into chaos. No one was going to follow that kind of leader. But if he acted like he believed in the plan, as if he were completely convicted about it, at least some of the folks here would follow him. Because people want in a leader and a hero what they can't find in themselves — total conviction. Most people can't decide what to eat for dinner, where to send their kids to college, which politician to trust. Most people feel like they are being swallowed by quicksand when they have to face a difficult decision, or even an easy one. So when they see someone confident, they will follow him to the ends of the earth. They will think, he must know something I don't know.

And Ryan was planning to lead with that sort of confidence. He instructed the congregation to grab chairs from the dining room and take them into the parking lot. However, the dining room was so overcrowded that it was difficult for someone to pick up a chair without knocking their neighbor onto the ground.

Nancy, the manager with a golden nametag, was busy prepping the restaurant for the day's business when she heard one chair snap in half. She ran into the dining room and was horrified to see that people were grabbing chairs and taking them outside.

"Pastor Ryan, this is not allowed," Nancy shouted. "If the GM hears about this, I am so busted."

"It'll be fine," Ryan said. "We'll just be out there for a little bit."

"But Pastor Ryan," Nancy said, and then her voice trailed off. She couldn't think of anything else to say. She just saw the group of people, looking more like disgruntled cattle, grabbing chairs and heading outside. They were following Ryan's orders but with little care of what happened to the dining room. Chairs were breaking and tables were getting knocked over. Nancy's assistant manger had been trying on the new Chuck E. Cheese suit that corporate had sent when he heard all of the commotion. He ran out into the lobby and saw everyone grabbing chairs. He tried to scream, "Stop!" but his voice was muffled by the Chuck E. suit. There was nothing he could do but flail his arms in protest, and that ended when an elderly woman pushed by the Chuck E. mascot knocking him to the ground. After that, he looked more like a beetle who had been placed on his back with his arms and legs kicking and waving.

Ryan ran past Chuck E., the elderly woman, and all the other cattle so he could get outside to see how things were progressing.

They were not progressing well.

No one was sure where to set up their chairs, so people had split into several clumps and placed the seats in disorganized ovals. Others had gone straight to their cars. They were leaving. They were fools for having thought this church could be different.

Ryan thought for a moment. This was bad, but did it have to end this way? It was like one of those sitcoms where things start out bad—everyone is snowed into a log cabin, or a group of angry people are stuck in an elevator with a pregnant woman who's due the next day. But those sitcoms always turn out well. The people in the log cabin admit how much they love each other, while the people in the elevator put their differences aside and realize that they are all human beings with feelings. Then the really mean guy on the elevator delivers the baby, and he smiles the warmest smile imaginable when he sees the new baby girl. There are always sitcom episodes like this because when people get placed into unusual and difficult circumstances, they either unravel or grow very close together.

Ryan already had a few people who believed in him and they sprung into action. Sheriff Somersby found an open section of the parking lot and ordered people to help him organize the chairs into tight rows. Cammy Miller started talking about how exciting and refreshing it was to have church outside and some agreed — this was fun. They were expecting a regular church service with hymns and preaching, and this was nothing like they expected. Jimmy Buckley drove his pickup in front of the chairs, pulled the tailgate down, found Ryan's pulpit, and placed it into the bed of the truck. They might not have had a microphone outside, but if Ryan and Cowboy Jack led the service from high up on the pickup truck, the congregation would be able to see and hear much more clearly.

The members of The People's Church were taking the service and turning it from a debacle to something special, and this would become a memory. This was becoming a legendary Sunday morning. Months from now people would ask each other, "Were you at the service where the Chuck E. Cheese was so packed out that we had to meet in the parking lot?" The People's Church was growing together as they all worked in unison to produce a makeshift service.

Ryan took note of the present dynamic and months later he would occasionally create a chaotic situation for The People's

Church to fix. When he was scheming a chaotic situation he would tell Katherine they were going to have a "Community Sunday." On one Community Sunday he paid a school bus driver to take a bus (full of high school girl volleyball players) and get it stuck in the mud. Then, right in the middle of service, the driver would run in and say, "Help! I need help! We were on our way to the regional tournament, but the bus got stuck." Without being asked, the men in the congregation would run outside, roll up their sleeves, plant their feet, and push together until the bus got unstuck. Many would ruin their suits, but when the women of the church cheered as the bus sprang out of the mud and onto the highway, it would make it all worth it. The men would walk back to their wives as soldiers returning from victory, they would receive hugs and kisses on the cheeks. The children would look at their fathers as if they were heroes. Ryan would say, "I don't see how we could continue with the service now. Let's just start the potluck early." And everyone would cheer again. Ryan usually created a Community Sunday when he couldn't think of anything to preach about.

But this morning he had something to say. Once everything was set, once the Sheriff's crew had set up all the chairs, including all the lawn chairs and kitchen chairs that Katherine and Cowboy Jack had brought back from Wal-Mart, Ryan stepped up to the pulpit. Suddenly, the parking lot was pin-drop silent. Their leader was standing in front of them, and the congregation was listening.

"Other churches already have a building and pews and stained glass windows. Other churches don't have to have its members help them set up a sanctuary outside, don't have to meet in a children's restaurant. Other churches are a lot more safe," Ryan said.

No one said a word. They just thought to themselves, where's he going with this?

"So I say there must be something wrong with other churches.

There must be something that we have here that is right. Because look around you, look how many people have come here when they could have gone to any other church this morning. They must be looking for something that you're also looking for, something that's exciting, something that's not safe."

"Amen," the elderly woman that knocked down Chuck E. shouted.

"That's right, sister. You are at The People's Church. You are at a place that isn't about buildings and programs and pipe organs. You are at a place that's about a community. You see friends, I've been a pastor for nine years, I've seen a lot of churches that become so focused on self-preservation that they forget what the church is really there for. Churches are supposed to help people, to help the poor and the needy and the sick. And it makes me sad how so many churches have forgotten that. I'll be honest. I wish I would have come into Wilma Wilson's life a whole lot earlier, because maybe then it wouldn't have been too late. Maybe then we could have prayed some prayers while there was still time."

"Preach it," someone else shouted.

"But I'll tell you this, I will be here for this group of people. I will be your pastor when your kids get married and your loved ones pass away. I will be there on a dark and stormy night when it seems like you don't have any other friends.

"But I am not enough. You must do the same. You must be like Jesus and be friends to each other, support each other, and most of all you must give your lives to making this church succeed. Because this is not really a church at all. Look around you."

Everyone did as Ryan instructed. They looked to their right and to their left, but they were not sure what they were looking for.

"There are no walls, or pews, there is nothing. Well, there is nothing but people. You are our greatest commodity. You are the key to making this church thrive and grow. And if you fail, well, you're not failing me; you're failing your neighbor.

"And you want to know what?" Ryan leaned forward and paused. This was a trick he'd learned by going online and watching the best speakers in the country. The best speakers always asked a dramatic question, and then would pause right before giving the home run statement.

"You're not going to fail. We are not going to fail. We can't. We won't. There is too much at stake here!"

The parking lot erupted with applause. Katherine looked at Ryan and smiled from ear to ear. This was what she wanted Ryan to become when she agreed to uproot her life from Denver.

Ryan glanced at Cowboy Jack, who jumped onto the truck and began to lead the congregation in "Amazing Grace." All of the first-time visitors were in awe of Cowboy Jack's voice. It was as if the archangel Gabriel himself had come down from heaven to lead them in song. People driving down the road heard the singing, pulled over, and joined the group in the parking lot. They weren't sure what they were joining, but they just sung the songs along with the rest of the crowd. After the service, they would learn that they had been at Bartlesville's largest church. And they would be invited to come the next Sunday. Many would accept the invitation.

One person driving down the road was Andy, the karaoke host at the Greasy Spork and the beat writer for the *Bartlesville Post*. He took a picture and flipped open his notebook and began to write notes about what he was seeing. This was the type of exciting thing he'd been waiting for. In the weeks and months ahead he would become the church's biggest fan. He'd often write stories about all of the great things The People's Church did. He made the church appear in the paper so many times that soon people outside of Bartlesville couldn't help but notice. And the coverage of The People's Church started the next day when the story of this upstart church with an out-of-town pastor was on the front page of the Lifestyle section.

After Cowboy Jack finished the last song, Ryan prayed and dismissed the service. And people stayed in the parking lot for hours. Some went home, changed, grabbed a bucket of chicken from KFC, and then came back until the sun set. There was no place they would rather be. This was the hippest place in town. And Ryan mingled around for hours; he mingled with every person he could, encouraging them to come back next Sunday, telling them they were vital to the church's success.

15

The First Lady

Katherine sat in the car and gazed at her husband. It was a loving gaze, a passionate gaze, the type of gaze that Katherine used to give to Coen Jackson when she watched him play at the Coffee Pot. Feeling this way about her husband brought back old memories. It made her feel young. Katherine wasn't sure if she'd ever loved Ryan as much as she loved him right now. And looking at him, with that glow he had, made her appreciate him so much.

He was a hero. A rockstar.

Katherine felt something completely new and unexpected about Ryan at The People's Church service—she felt proud. Not proud that he had done something good necessarily, although there was that too, but today Katherine was proud that Ryan belonged to her. She used to feel the same way about Coen. After they'd been dating for a few months, Katherine would go to the Coffee Pot and help him set up. Then she would sit there all night acting like she was doing homework, but she was really watching the other girls stare at him, having a crush on him just like she used to. It would make her smile. He's mine, she thought. She liked him, sure, that was a part of it, but she also liked that other girls wanted him—they were jealous of what she had. He could have chosen any of those other girls. But he chose her.

Shortly before Coen dumped Katherine, he joined a band called the Saltines. Katherine got involved in the business side of things. She started by helping them get gigs, but she would also handle the band's schedule and negotiate how much they were supposed to get paid. They started playing all over campus. They were getting popular. Katherine created T-shirts and an album cover for their new CD.

She felt a high, the rush of success, after their CD release party was such a hit. It was her idea. She made it happen, and the band loved her for it. Coen told her how psyched the other guys were that the release party was so killer.

But when she went to ask Coen if he could take her home after the party—it was late and she had a huge English paper due in six hours—she saw Coen with his hands all over Sarah Michaels. Coen and Sarah looked up at Katherine, not with remorse, but as if she was the intruder.

"Coen, what's going on?" Katherine asked.

"Right, um, I probably should have told you, Sarah and I have been hanging out."

Hanging out? I'm not sure what this is, but I would not call it hanging out, Katherine thought. But all she said was, "Oh. Okay." And she didn't say this in a furious or cold or nasty way. She said it the only way she could—helplessly.

"Listen, I've been thinking, maybe we should take a break for awhile," Coen said.

"Yeah, maybe so," she said. Then she waited for Coen to elaborate. He didn't. So she said, "I'll talk to you later."

"Yeah, I'll give you a call."

Katherine didn't ask Coen for a ride home. She didn't ask anyone. She walked for an hour and a half and she cried every step of the way. When she got home she stared at the phone. She stared at it for the next three days.

Coen never called.

And when she thinks back on it today, what hurt her so much was that she was dumped right when she was getting involved with something bigger than herself—something important.

Maybe that's why the church service in the parking lot was so special to her. Because at church today was the first time since she'd been the manager of the Saltines that she was an integral part of something bigger than her. Something important. Everyone said that they couldn't ever remember a church service or an event that felt so good and seemed so right in Bartlesville. And the buzz was all about Ryan: How they were lucky to have such a successful pastor, such a great God-ordained leader come to their town.

And all day long people were so happy to meet Katherine. "You're married to Pastor Ryan?" they asked. "You're a lucky woman. He's a great man." Katherine would just smile and thank them for coming to the church. And at the end of the conversation many people would often giggle, saying how honored they felt to be talking with the "First Lady" of The People's Church.

First Lady, Katherine thought. I'm royalty. He's a king and I'm his queen.

Katherine wished Jennifer Anderson could be here to see the people say that. Jennifer was just married to one of the *assistant* pastors and everyone treated her like she was Jesus' sister or something. Katherine felt silly for ever looking up to Jennifer so much. Ryan wasn't some lowly assistant: he was the main man, the leader, the *creator* of the church. If Katherine was still in Denver, she was sure that all of the girls at Bible study would have cherished every word she had to say. How could they not when she was married to someone so important?

When they got home Ryan placed his keys on the table. His thoughts were spilling over with what to do about church the next week. He was happy with how the service went that day. Happy was an understatement; he was thrilled, overwhelmed, vindicated. He always knew this church was going to work, that he had all of the God-given skills to become a pastor, but today was the first day that everyone else could see that. What happened in the parking lot was a minor miracle, it was special and magical, but there was next Sunday to think about, and Ryan felt he could go only get away with the parking lot magic once. Maybe he'd be able to recreate it later on, but for next Sunday he would need to—

Ryan suddenly couldn't think about church anymore.

His wife was standing in the doorway to their bedroom. She was wearing something frilly and lacy and she had a sexy grin on her face. She was breathtaking. He couldn't remember the last time she wore something like this for him. She said to him, "Church was amazing today."

"Katherine, wow," Ryan said reflexively.

"These people love you."

"You think so?"

"I know so."

"They did follow me a little bit, didn't they?"

"Of course they did sweetheart," Katherine said as she stroked her fingers across Ryan's face.

"We're going to make a difference here."

"This church is going to change everyone's lives."

And then there was no more talking. There was only kissing. It was passionate and sensual, it rivaled the kiss Ross gave to

Rachel while the rain pounded on the windows of Central Perk, or the one Han Solo gave to Princess Leia right before Darth Vader froze him in carbonite. It was the kiss of two people who are madly in love with each other, the type of kiss where someone forgets that there is, or ever was, anyone else on the planet. And for the first time in a long time there were no ovulation kits, no thermometers, no timers and watches. There was no planning.

For the first time in a long time, Ryan and Katherine made love.

At sunrise the next morning Ryan sprung out of bed with a mission—he had to find somewhere new for The People's Church to conduct services. They had clearly outgrown the capacity of Chuck E.'s; people wanted to be comfortable at church, not feel overcrowded and suffocated.

They had taken an offering on Sunday and come away with nearly twenty thousand dollars, a nice lump of money, but clearly not enough to buy a church. Besides, he couldn't spend it all on a church, could he? He had to keep some of it. But how much? Half? What do churches do with all of the money they make? Should he create a budget? What do churches spend their budget on? These questions would have to wait.

They could be answered once he found a place to meet.

But there weren't a lot of options. Ryan wanted something that could seat at least three hundred people, and the only things of that size in Bartlesville were the auditorium in Jefferson High (553 people) and the performing arts center (337 people). Even if Ryan could get one of those auditoriums—and he may have been able to with the growing influence he was getting in the town—he didn't really want them. He wanted something that was his own. A place where he could decide what it looked like and felt like when people entered for services, somewhere he could manipulate the environment. He could understand now why Pastor Clark and the staff at Fellowship Christian Church wanted things to feel a certain way, why they were intentional about everything: the lighting, the music, the announcement bulletins, the nametags the greeters wore. Every detail that people may or may not have even noticed added up to something greater. Giving the people one unified brand helped Fellowship Christian Church grow into one of Denver's most successful churches. And if a first-time visitor entered The People's Church and saw lockers, or posters for the springtime performance of *Macbeth*, or skeeball machines, that would weaken the brand.

Ryan had been thinking through his problems in the Greasy Spork. That came to an end when the large man in the John Deere hat (the man who had insisted he could pay for his own breakfast) stood over him, glaring.

"You always planning on having a church in the parking lot?"

"No, I'm actually looking for somewhere new to have services."

"Well I own a big field near that Chuck E. Cheese restaurant."

"Isn't a field just a parking lot with grass?"

"You could put a tent on the field. That's what the Miracle Man used to do. There was nowhere big enough to hold the revivals so he met in a tent. I'd let you use the field for free. You know, if you wanted to."

This could be it, Ryan thought. It's April; it's getting warm and will just keep getting warmer for the next couple of months. We could meet in this field at least until the fall. It would be like a big concert in a park. There could be a stage, a large truss packed with colored lights, speakers blasting out music and preaching, and they could even surround the tent with flame heaters, just like they have on the outdoor patios of restaurants. A tent—it works on so many levels. A tent signifies a big occasion and that is exactly what Sundays at The People's Church need to be. An event. A celebration.

"I'd love to use your field," Ryan said.

Still, it would take an army to put a service like this together. And fortunately — or maybe by the grace of God — an army seemed to be exactly what Ryan had. All morning long he'd been talking with one person after another who'd been "blessed" by the service and asked if there was any way to help. Ryan knew he needed lots of help but he didn't know how anyone could help him. He didn't have a plan. Until now.

"Excuse me, everybody. I know some of you were just asking for a way to help The People's Church, and I think I have a way now. For everyone else, um, please enjoy your breakfast."

Ryan had a group of ten volunteers around his booth and he painted a picture for them of church in a field, just like a concert. There was excitement in the room as he finished. Everyone wanted to help. And then one person after the next had their cell phones out. They were calling Oklahoma City, Tulsa, Denver, and St. Louis for light rigs, stages, and concert tents. Many of the church members claimed they had a brother, or cousin, or old college buddy who could hook them up. Some in the Spork hadn't even gone to Ryan's church, but they wanted to chip in because it seemed fun.

A man named Dean Parker (an insurance agent) soon organized the effort. Dean was perfect for the job because he was the type of guy who created every ensemble he would wear for the week on Sunday night. He would spend hours toiling over which tie went best with which pair of slacks. He color coordinated his groceries, always wore matching socks, and in his den he had a large collection of unwrapped *Star Wars* action figures organized alphabetically by home planet.

Today, Dean had a clipboard and checklists; he was totally in his element and Ryan marveled watching Dean work because he could never be as organized as Dean was. By that afternoon Dean had contacts for everything they needed to create a makeshift auditorium in a tent. They could get a stage, a large tent, speakers, chairs, and lights, and if something couldn't be delivered, Dean had a volunteer to drive somewhere to pick it up. Ryan had quickly maxed out the $20K offering, and he took out three new lines of credit to pay for the equipment.

You've got to spend money to make money, he thought. Not that he was trying to make money, necessarily, but still it took money to grow a business, or a church, or really anything for that matter.

Ryan was so grateful to Dean that he made him an elder on the spot. Ryan wasn't sure what an elder did, but he was sure that Dean deserved to be one. And Dean Parker was so honored to be the first-ever elder in The People's Church, that he told Ryan he would personally make sure all of the equipment was set up in the field by Sunday morning.

— 16 —

LETTERMAN
OR LENO?

Of course, there was still the service to plan.

And the next service had been nagging at Ryan. What should it be? Should he preach a regular sermon and have Cowboy Jack just lead a couple of songs? Was that enough to make the service feel special and tent-worthy? No, it wasn't, but Ryan didn't have any better ideas. People had been doing church for a long time, and it seemed to Ryan that no one had really reinvented the wheel. Church was singing and sermons, simple as that.

Still, Ryan couldn't sleep. He felt that if he and Cowboy Jack did what they'd always done, the church would eventually wither back to its normal size. They were going to have a new venue and Ryan had to do something worthy of that new venue if he wanted to keep the church growing.

Ryan got out of bed, punched a button on the remote, and *Nightline* popped onto the screen. He felt a moment of nostalgia.

This was where it all began.

His last late-night viewing of *Nightline* was the moment he decided to join the Christian world. Ryan had a moment of hope. Maybe tonight's story would be the second part of the revelation. Maybe *Nightline* was about to drop a nugget of wisdom into his lap that would make everything click. He ran into the kitchen and grabbed a pen and a note pad, put on his reading glasses, and waited for God to speak to him.

This evening's *Nightline* story was about how the bubonic plague had gotten into a crop of tomatoes in Florida. That crop had made its way into numerous Ralph's and Albertson's throughout the West Coast. Hundreds of thousands of tomatoes were being sacrificed, needlessly thrown away; the price of tomatoes had quadrupled, but it was a small price to pay when the bubonic plague was involved, Sam Donaldson said.

This was not the revelation Ryan was hoping for.

Ryan changed the channel and Jay Leno was reading headlines with typos. "Most of the time people go out to buy pork and beans," Jay Leno said. He held a newspaper clipping up to the camera. "But this store is offering something special: 'Porn and beans.'" The audience cackled and Jay Leno grinned proudly knowing he just made a funny.

Ryan rolled his eyes. For four years of marriage Katherine had always made Ryan watch *The Tonight Show*. When they were first married Ryan protested; he was a *Late Show* man and wanted to know why Katherine preferred Leno over Letterman. Katherine said, "Because Leno's sweet. He's so much nicer to his guests. It's like he genuinely cares about them. Letterman's too sarcastic. He's just waiting for a chance to pounce, to make a joke about whatever the guest says." That's what Ryan loved about Letterman. Leno was such a brownnoser—he was too nice to his guests, like the insecure kid at the cool table wanting everyone else to think that he belonged. But Letterman, he was the outsider, the nerd, this was his show, and he was going to run things his way, and he didn't really care if he offended George Clooney.

Then Ryan realized Katherine was asleep. He could watch whatever he wanted. He punched a button and smiled as Letterman appeared on the TV.

And then he had the epiphany he'd been waiting for.

His previous line of thinking about how to have a successful church had been misguided. Elementary. How could he have thought slick websites, killer graphics, and catchy ads would make his church grow? Maybe they could help but they weren't the key. He needed to stop looking at his church as a business. That was wrong. Sinful. Inaccurate. The key to success was right in front of him: He needed to start looking at his church as a late-night talk show.

Most households have a type of show they prefer. Some prefer a host with a top-ten list; others prefer a host who does game show sketches. Some want their host to be kind and cheesy, others want someone that's a little more edgy. But the key is that the entire show is built around the personality of the host. The graphics, sketches, opening monologues, everything about the talk show from start to finish reflects the personality of the host. And then it's up to the viewer to decide if they prefer Carson or Leno or Letterman or Arsenio or Conan or Kimmel.

Ryan lay swaddled in a blanket on his couch, the blue flicker of the TV bouncing off his face, and he started thinking: yes, churches pretty much do the same things, but that doesn't mean they're all the same. They can't be. It's the pastor who defines the personality of the church.

Three months later, Ryan would teach at a large ministers' conference on this very topic. He called his workshop, "Leno or Letterman: What Type of Church Are You Building?" He would speak to a room full of ministers and tell them, "Churches are built on two things: The personality of the pastor and the denomination. The denomination is like the format of your show. Different formats come with different expectations. There are countless formats for talk shows: daytime issue-oriented shows (Montel Williams or Maury Pauvich), shows for women (*The View* and *Oprah*), freak shows (Jerry Springer or Ricki Lake), and late night (Leno or Letterman). Those shows come with expectations, and you better believe the host completely understands these expectations. If a viewer turned on Jerry Springer and his show was filled with monologues and celebrity interviews, the viewer would be furious. Just like if you had a Baptist church and someone visited and saw that it was filled with dancing."

This would get a huge laugh from the crowd. He had delivered what was called a "preacher joke." All professions have them. Teachers, doctors, lawyers, and dentists all have jokes about themselves, but whenever Ryan would successfully deliver a preacher joke, he would feel especially proud, like he belonged.

He would continue, "But the key is, once you have your format, you must decide what kind of host you're going to be. And you should only try to be one type of host. Don't have your churches aim at every audience. It will confuse the people of your city. That's what I tried to do when I first became a pastor. Tried to get everyone to come to my church. I posted fliers that proclaimed, 'Everyone's Invited.' I failed miserably. It wasn't until I started aiming at just one type of person that my church grew in ways I could have never dreamed."

Ryan would take a drink of water from his Nalgene bottle, and he would make his voice get wispy (another trick he would learn as he'd mastered sermon delivery).

"Pastors, I want you to understand this, if you want to be successful, if you want your church to grow and have influence in your city, find one thing that you do, and do it better than everyone else. Decide, are you funny or do you talk about the issues? Are you great at teaching, or are you compassionate? Once you answer this question, start building your church around your strength, and God will bless your church in ways you thought possible only in your wildest prayers."

The pastors in this room would give Ryan huge applause. He'd given this talk seven times now and always gotten the same response. Ryan would just stand there, humbly, with a sheepish grin on his face, because one time after giving this talk, Ryan got a standing ovation and responded by pumping his hands in the air to "raise the roof" and blowing kisses to the audience, which prompted the organizer of the conference to say, "Pastor Fisher, we appreciate your enthusiasm, but at this conference we prefer for our pastors to act with a certain air of humility."

On the night of the Jay Leno revelation, Ryan didn't know any of that would happen. He just laid on the couch, eyes wide open, with his mind racing in a hundred different directions as to what type of talk show host he was. Was his church Leno or Letterman?

Ryan told his plan to Katherine as they were in the express lane at Safeway. Normally Katherine would be uncomfortable being in the express lane because they clearly had twelve items in their cart, two more than the maximum allowed. Ryan always told Katherine that "ten items or less" was just a guideline, but that didn't stop Katherine from feeling uncomfortable about the icy glares she got from everyone in line who had learned to count to twelve.

Today, she wasn't thinking about the items because she was listening to her husband's new idea. And Katherine felt about this idea the same as she felt about all of his ideas — she couldn't decide if he was a genius or insane.

"So I just can't decide if I'm Leno or Letterman. Or heck, I don't know, maybe I'm Conan or someone old-school like Johnny Carson," Ryan said.

"So you're going to run The People's Church like a talk show?"

"Listen, I'm just saying if the church is going to grow, it should have its own look and feel and personality like all the talk shows. And it'd be a lot easier if I could find a model."

"If you're going to model the church after something, you don't want to model it after the late-night guys," Katherine said.

"But the late-night guys are the kings. Who's more important than them?"

"Oprah," she said.

"Oprah," Ryan echoed. She was famous—extremely famous. She was bigger than all of those other late-night guys combined. But still there were problems with being Oprah Winfrey. "Oprah's famous for giving people cars. How am I going to give cars and toasters and George Foreman grills away every Sunday?" Ryan asked.

"Oprah's famous for more than giving people stuff. She's the most adored person in America. If all you had to do to become powerful and influential was give stuff away, then Pat Sajack and Bob Barker could run for president."

"That's different. Oprah just gives stuff away. People on game shows earn their prizes."

"A person can win a car by guessing the price of Swiss Cake Rolls, and you call that earning it?" Katherine asked.

"Listen, all I'm saying is on *The Price Is Right* people expect prizes, and on *Oprah* people expect prizes."

"They didn't use to. Oprah built her show on compassion and caring for people. That's what she's famous for, Ryan. She's maybe the most Christian person in America. When Oprah was in her prime, she and Dr. Phil would tag-team to fight child obesity and spousal abuse, they would do anything they could to help soccer moms who ate Milk Duds and cried every afternoon for no reason at all. They were about the people," Katherine said as she inched the shopping cart forward.

"You're right."

"You really think so?" Katherine asked, smiling from one ear to the other.

"Yes, absolutely. Oprah had the talk show Jesus would have had if he were alive today."

"Well, that's probably going a little far," Katherine said.

"It's brilliant. Every Sunday we have a guest. It's kind of like 'Meet the People of The People's Church.'" (Ryan still cringed every time he said the segment's full title.) "Except instead of a little segment, I would build my whole sermon around the interview. And it couldn't just be a get-to-know-you segment; the person would have to have a problem. Something interesting. Something like the problems the people on *Oprah* have. Then I could teach some biblical life lesson around what is actually going on in one of our members' lives."

"Ryan, I love this. We can work together. I mean we can *really* help people. No problem will be too big for us, and for sure no problem will be too big with all of the resources of the church."

Ryan and Katherine tried to continue their conversation but the kids in front of them were screaming. Ryan was annoyed at the kids and even more annoyed that somehow he and his wife always seemed to find themselves in their most meaningful conversations at awkward times, like being in the express lane of the supermarket at rush hour. Ryan couldn't stay focused on his conversation with Katherine, so he watched as the children's mother tried to calm them down, but they couldn't be bargained with. Nothing would buy their silence other than ice cream and toys.

"Dad would buy us ice cream," they said.

"We don't need ice cream. We just need some milk and butter so I can cook us supper."

The cashier handed her the card back saying, "Thank you very much, Mrs. Buckley."

"Wait, are you Megan Buckley?" Ryan asked as he approached the mother and cashier.

"Yes, I am, Pastor," Megan said.

"Are you married to Jimmy Buckley?"

"That's my dad's name," the little girl said.

"We're separated at the moment," Megan said.

"I'm sorry to hear that. Can you tell me why?"

"Ryan, that's a little personal," Katherine said.

"I know, but that's our job. To get personal. I'm a pastor, and this is my wife. We help people, and we help marriages that are in trouble. So, Megan, let me help. Tell me what's going on."

"Well, Jimmy has a problem."

"Go on."

Megan grabbed Ryan's arm and pulled him aside, out of earshot of her children. "He gambles," she said.

"How much?"

"Anything he can get his hands on."

"How long's this been going on?"

"I don't know, I just know he lost thousands of dollars a few months ago. I haven't been living with him."

"Okay Megan, let me ask you this, if I can fix Jimmy, would you be willing to go back to him?"

"I don't think you can; it's really bad."

"I know it is. But what I need to know is, if I can fix him would you be willing to give him another chance?"

"I still love him, Pastor Ryan," Megan said.

17

SUNDAY MORNING MIRACLE

Ryan was in his car, flying down the interstate. He'd called a friend of Jimmy's and learned that Jimmy usually spent his Tuesday nights at the Gold River Casino out on the reservation. Ryan had to find Jimmy, to convince him to be the subject matter for Sunday's sermon. Jimmy's situation was perfect for Ryan's sermon: a husband who'd lost his wife because he was being controlled by a wicked sin, a man in desperate need of redemption.

That would preach.

If Ryan could convince Jimmy to be in the sermon on Sunday, then the first service in the tent really would be memorable; it would be the event he had promised. It would also show the congregation that The People's Church is a place where lives are changed. And Ryan had the ace up his sleeve to convince Jimmy to play along.

He could get Jimmy his family back.

As Ryan walked through the revolving door of the casino, he was greeted by a thick cloud of cigarette smoke. He couldn't think of a more depressing place. Lights flashed and machines made happy blipping noises that seemed to scream, *"Look how much fun it is in here!"*

But the looks on everyone's faces did not make it seem like this was a party. There were elderly people camped in front of slot machines, feeding it dollar tokens as if it were their job, looking as excited as workers on an assembly line. Ryan walked by one woman who'd hit the jackpot — she'd gotten three lemons in a row, and she didn't even smile. She just waited for the machine to finish paying her the 308 dollars in tokens so she could start playing again.

Ryan found Jimmy at the blackjack table, alone, staring at his fifteen while the dealer was showing six, debating whether or not to take another card.

Ryan told Jimmy, "You should stick. He doesn't have another face card in there. He'll have to hit and he'll bust."

"Hit," Jimmy said. The dealer flipped over a seven. He took Jimmy's chips, and like that, Jimmy had lost twenty bucks. Jimmy didn't care. He put three more chips on the table and waited another hand.

"Sir, if you're going to sit here, you have to play," the dealer said.

"Sure," Ryan said. He threw two twenty-dollar bills on the table.

Then Jimmy asked, "How can I help you, Pastor?"

"I wanted to say thanks for letting me use your truck on Sunday."

"You came all the way down here to say that? Or do you just normally come here and you happened to see me?"

"Um, no, I've actually never been here before. But this place is great," Ryan said. Ryan looked all around. Nobody was smiling.

Not a soul. Everyone's eyes were glazed over and their faces were sour.

"Honestly, Pastor Ryan. I don't care why you're here. Do whatever you want. I won't tell anyone at church. I'm not going to go anymore anyway."

"No?"

"No, I don't even like church. It's not my thing. I only went because I thought I could get my wife back."

"And that didn't work."

"She didn't care. She just thinks of me as a gambler. And I only gambled one time, Pastor Ryan."

Ryan looked around the casino, befuddled. "I hate to break it to you Jimmy, but you're gambling right now."

"Of course I'm gambling right now. But I wasn't before, and then Megan told me, 'All you are is a gambler.' So I figured if I'm being accused of gambling I might as well gamble."

"Jimmy, do you realize how destructive gambling is?"

"And the new player gets blackjack," the dealer said.

"What? Really, wow! This is awesome," Ryan said. He'd never played blackjack at an actual casino. He'd only played on his computer at home. And even then he never won.

"Congratulations," Jimmy said as he sipped a bit more of his scotch.

"Jimmy, listen to me, I'm going to make things real simple for you: Do you want your wife back? Do you want your family back?"

"It doesn't matter what I want. We don't always get what we want, Pastor."

"But that doesn't mean that we can't always fight for what we want. Jimmy, we can fight for you to be back with your family. I'm not promising you'll get them back, but isn't it at least worth trying for?"

"I don't know what more I can do."

"I know, Jimmy, that's why I'm here," Ryan said, and won another hand.

Before service Sunday morning, families were walking around eating cotton candy and funnel cakes while children played with balloons and visited the petting zoo. It felt like the Oklahoma State Fair. This was exactly what Ryan wanted. He'd had Dean call vendors to bring the types of things that were at the State Fair to church on Sunday morning. Dean hadn't got everything—Ferris wheels were a lot more difficult to track down than one would think—but he'd gotten close. And the morning felt like an event. It was electric outside, and the doors to the tent were guarded, no one was allowed in until 10:55. So people had no choice but to fellowship and build community, to get reacquainted much like they had in the parking lot of the Chuck E. Cheese's just a week ago.

When the curtains finally opened and the crowd of nearly five hundred rushed inside the auditorium, there was a collective gasp of awe. Inside the tent looked like something that should be at the Academy Awards or Golden Globes; something this spectacular didn't belong in Bartlesville. There was a huge oval screen in the center of the stage that said, "Welcome to The People's Church," there were ten-foot-tall speakers, smoke, and colored lights. The crowd pointed at all of the incredible technical gadgets in the tent, and even though there were a few people who grumbled and commented that things like this didn't belong in church, they couldn't really believe what they were saying. This was all too breathtaking to do anything but marvel.

At eleven sharp, Cowboy Jack sauntered onto the stage like a sexy country music rock star. And with Jack was his new band. During the week, while Ryan had been busy getting the tent and Jimmy Buckley, Katherine had been helping Cowboy Jack put a band together (but before she even started to help, she made sure that Cowboy Jack knew this was just business, the affair was over, never to begin again). She even helped Cowboy Jack run the first practice.

As Cowboy Jack and his band came up on stage, the whole audience cheered. They still couldn't believe that the karaoke cowboy from The Greasy Spork was leading worship at a Sunday morning church service. When the cheers died down, the lead guitarist began to play and Jack led the whole crowd in "Here God Is, He Rocks Me Like a Hurricane." Everyone sang along with Cowboy Jack. It was easy to, now; the words were right in front of them on the fat oval screen.

The band only performed three songs—that was all they had time to learn. Even that was a stretch. Katherine had been managing the band all week and she was scared they would fall flat on their face once they were put in front of the crowd, but that didn't happen. They performed brilliantly, each song better and punchier than the one before, and The People's Church loved them. They held their hands in the air and belted out every syllable to the song right along with Cowboy Jack. When worship was over Cowboy Jack said a short simple prayer, thanking God for being with them this morning, and then he walked off stage.

The congregation sat down without even being told to, as if it were second nature, a reflex. A video played on the oval screen. Jimmy Buckley appeared on the oval, he was wearing a blue shirt with a yellow tie, and he told the audience, "My name is Jimmy and I have a problem." Jimmy held up a picture; it was of him and his family from their vacation at Lake Tahoe last summer. They looked beautiful, happy; they looked all-American.

"I can't see my family anymore," Jimmy said as a shot of cards and poker chips appeared on the screen.

"A few months ago I gambled away everything in our checking

account on online poker. I lost thousands. We couldn't afford to pay our bills. Our heat and water got shut off because I couldn't pay our utility bill.

"My wife left me. She took the kids and I don't blame her. I asked her to forgive me, but she couldn't even bring herself to talk to me. It hurt too much. I wasn't the person that she married. I have a sickness, sin in my life, and it has robbed me of my family, my friends, and my happiness. I deserve everything that's happened to me." A tear then rolled down Jimmy's face, and many in the audience wept right along with him. "I just wish there was a way I could get my family back. But I don't know how. So, I thought maybe Pastor Ryan, The People's Church, and most of all, my Lord and Savior Jesus, can help me get my life right."

The video faded to black.

Lights came up on Pastor Ryan standing in a black suit holding a Bible. He looked serious, but also warm and compassionate. "Today we are going to talk about sin," Ryan told the congregation. "And the Bible is very clear about sin. It says when it gets into our lives it takes everything that it wants to, it destroys whatever it pleases, and sometimes all we can do is sit back and watch."

As Ryan said this, the congregation noticed that he, too, seemed different on that first morning in the tent. What they didn't know was how much time Ryan had spent watching, studying, and reading the best Christian speakers in the country. His studies were paying off. He was getting more and more confident mimicking the best preachers. He was starting to fully understand how to command a service.

"So this morning I want you to welcome Jimmy Buckley."

The audience clapped for Jimmy as he walked onstage. Ryan sat in his interview chair while Jimmy sat on the couch. Jimmy rubbed his hands together, looked around, and squinted beneath the bright stage lights.

"Jimmy, how are you today?"

"I'm nervous, Pastor."

"That's okay, we're all here for you. Aren't we church?" Everyone responded by giving Jimmy warm supporting applause. One person even shouted, "We believe in you Jimmy!" Then the audience laughed, much like a family does when a small child says something warm and innocent while they are all sitting around in the living room.

"That's good, 'cause I really need everyone's help," Jimmy said.

"Why don't you tell us what's been going on?"

"Okay. Well, it's not like I wanted to lose money gambling. I thought I could win. I'd seen the players on TV, and I thought 'this doesn't look so hard.'"

"The Enemy* had you deceived," Ryan said.

"Yes, that was the problem. It was pride. I thought I could do it. I wanted to win money to take care of our family. I wanted to buy us the stuff that I could never afford. Instead, I've lost everything. And I've lost something that's worth so much more than money. I've lost my family."

Everyone in the audience made an "aww" sound. Jimmy was the sweetest man on the planet.

"Jimmy, we want to help you. We want you to get your family back. But you have to be willing to work for them. Are you willing to do that Jimmy?"

"I'll do anything to get my family back, Pastor," Jimmy said.

"Okay, well you need to get some professional help, so we are going to pay for you to have a weekend at the Gambler's Anonymous clinic."

Everyone clapped at this. Ryan was so generous.

---

*Katherine was a little startled to hear Ryan say this because she was pretty sure that he still didn't believe in God, and she was positive he didn't believe in Satan.

"And then you have to promise to stay away from all forms of gambling: websites, casinos, you can't get near any of that stuff. Don't give the Enemy a chance to get his claws on you again."

"I can do that, Pastor."

"I'm glad to hear that, Jimmy."

"Do you think if I do all of that, Megan will take me back?"

"I don't know, why don't you ask her yourself?"

The audience gasped as Megan walked out onstage.

When Jimmy saw her, he broke down crying. Somehow he managed to say, "I'm so sorry, baby." And Megan stood there for a moment while the audience sat on the edge of their seats, feeling worried and excited about how Megan would respond. She ran across the stage, flung her arms around Jimmy, and began to kiss him. The kiss was a little more PG than would normally be acceptable for church—Jimmy and Megan were like a groom and bride who took a little too much liberty with their chance to kiss after the vows—but no one in the audience seemed to mind one bit. They just cheered. They cheered for Jimmy and Megan, and for love and redemption and for second chances.

They cheered for what a wonderful place The People's Church was becoming.

18

PASTOR
JOSEPH SAMPSON

The People's Church enjoyed a full month of successful Sundays, and by month's end the church had ballooned to over a thousand members.

This was a huge problem for the other churches in town.

Pastor Walton (Baptist), Pastor Fitzgerald (Lutheran), Father Skip (Catholic), Pastor Mason (Presbyterian), and Reverend Stockton (Assemblies of God) had been meeting every Tuesday for breakfast for the last couple of years. They did this because they felt it was the right thing to do; they should be promoting harmony and unity between the clergy of Bartlesville. And you would think they had a lot in common, because they were all leaders of churches, hence, they must all have similar hopes and dreams and passions.

But you would be wrong.

The ministers had something in common the way that Yankees and Red Sox fans have something in common. Yes, both fans are passionate about the sport of baseball, but the traditions, the culture, the experience, even the way the sport itself is viewed greatly differs between the fans of both teams. The same was true here. They were all devoted to God and Jesus, but the theology, culture, and doctrine greatly differed between all of the faiths.

A conversation about God always led into heated debates between these ministers. They would argue about what the Bible *really* meant in certain spots. For instance, the Bible says when a person accepts Jesus Christ as Lord that they are saved, but can salvation be lost? Or is belief in Jesus enough to get us into heaven? Is one prayer enough to do the trick? Or is it even up to us? Did God handpick us from the beginning? Or have some been chosen for heaven, while others have been predestined to hell?

They could spend days talking about this topic alone.

For years these men had been meeting for breakfast, trying to keep the conversation civil. But if they weren't debating doctrine, they often found there was nothing else to talk about. All they could do was stare at their charcoal toast while they tried to think of something to say.

Today, silence wasn't a problem. Today, they all had something in common worth talking about: There was an enemy, a man who'd brought a circus act to town, complete with cotton candy and a petting zoo. And this new church—if you could even call it that—was emptying their pews and draining their offerings.

Something had to be done. This had to be stopped.

"He doesn't even use the Bible in his sermons," the Baptist said.

"Yes, he does. What else could he teach about?" the Lutheran said.

"He teaches heresy. He's a David Koresh. He's starting a cult. He's stockpiling guns and cooking up a giant vat of Kool-Aid," the Baptist exclaimed.

"We don't know that," the Father argued.

"We don't know anything," the Lutheran added.

"Yes, we do. We know our congregations are leaving to go to the circus," the Presbyterian said.

"Maybe it's just a good church. Isn't our goal here to teach people about Christ? He could be helping people in our effort," the Lutheran said.

"He's reckless. He never even came and talked to us," the Baptist said.

"Perhaps because we wouldn't talk to him," the Lutheran countered.

"But why here?" the Presbyterian asked. "Why is he trying to create a giant church *here?* If he wanted to do this, why not in a large city?"

"Because these cult leaders love to prey on small-town folks," the Baptist said.

"You can't just call him that. We don't know he's a cult leader," the Father said.

"Well, we need to find out. We need answers. Where did he come from? What's his training? Why is he here? What is he trying to do to the good Christian people of our town?" the Baptist asked.

Ryan had never been to a ministers' luncheon before. He was excited about the prospect. Surely he'd be the belle of the ball, the popular, respected pastor everyone wanted to talk to—he had the largest church in town. However, what really excited Ryan about the luncheon was a chance to make friends. He'd discovered that being a pastor was quite lonely; there were so many needy people, so many problems and situations, and on top of all that it took so much effort to create a church. Ryan looked forward to meeting other pastors because he needed a place where he could share his problems and get advice. He needed a place where he could be understood.

The luncheon was at the Bartlesville community center, and as Ryan entered the room he instantly felt uncomfortable. The room was as inviting as an abandoned warehouse. In the middle there was a single dark brown table, with folding legs and fake wood on top. That was all of the color in the room. The ceilings were made of white popcorn asbestos, the floors were filthy speckled tile, the walls dingy beige bricks, and there were no windows; the only lights in the room were florescent ones that emitted a quiet drone. The centerpiece of the room was the five ministers sitting down with their hands folded — they looked as if they'd always been in this room waiting for Ryan.

"Welcome, Pastor Fisher. I'm Pastor Walton," the Baptist said.

"Hello," Ryan said, suddenly feeling young and awkward. He hadn't felt this way since his senior prom when Kelly Mayhew's father interrogated him when he came to pick her up. He remembered sitting in her living room, feeling powerless and naive, and he wondered why today all of those feelings came flooding back to him.

"We are so glad you accepted our invitation. We've wanted to meet you for a long time," said the Lutheran.

"Well, that's good. So, tell me about your churches," Ryan said, trying to get the topic of conversation off himself.

"Our churches are doing alright," the Assemblies pastor said.

"Though, some of our congregants have been checking out The People's Church," the Presbyterian said. The other ministers went quiet: some were silently thinking that this was the first time one of them had called The People's Church by name. Usually they just referred to it as "that place," or "the circus," or "the mockery of all things holy."

"And some of my people have been checking out your churches," Ryan said. "Isn't that what's so great about church? I mean, we're all teaching about Jesus, aren't we?"

"I don't know, are we?" the Baptist asked.

"Of course we are," the priest said.

"Listen, I'm all about having a church where people are getting fed," Ryan said. *Getting fed* is shorthand for receiving grounded spiritual guidance, and Ryan was trying to show that he fit in by using that term.

"That's good," the Assemblies pastor said. "So, tell us, what denomination is The People's Church?"

"We're nondenominational," Ryan said. He knew this would not be a popular answer, but it would be a perfectly acceptable one. He'd wondered if The People's Church was going to need to belong to some larger denomination, and he was pleased to learn that there were lots of large and small churches all over America just like The People's Church; they'd sprung up out of nowhere and weren't connected to anything.

"Then where did you go to seminary?" the Presbyterian asked.

"I didn't," Ryan answered.

"And do you feel capable of leading a congregation of this size?" the Baptist asked.

"I'm as capable as anyone in this room," Ryan answered.

These were the types of questions Ryan had been waiting for, ever since his church started to really grow. As long as his church was small and met in a children's restaurant no one would care what he did. But the second it grew into a force to be reckoned with, someone was bound to ask, why you? Who are you to be leading something like this?

Luckily for Ryan he'd been planning for this, and he'd mentally rehearsed a response to every sort of opposition. It was something he'd learned to do as a realtor. When someone got close to closing on a house, they'd always think of all sorts of reasons to back out of the deal. But a good real estate agent has an answer for any sort of reluctance. A good real estate agent squelches all doubt.

"How can you be so confident without any training?" the Lutheran asked.

"I didn't say I hadn't received any training. I said I hadn't gone to seminary. Perhaps you should read Matthew 7; I think there's a passage about a plank in your eye," Ryan said.

"What are you saying, Pastor Fisher?" the Lutheran asked.

"I'm saying that you're a—"

"Okay, let's calm down. No one's trying to accuse you, Pastor Fisher. We apologize if we're coming off that way. But you have to understand, what you're doing in our town is really remarkable. We're all a little confused by it. I'll be honest, we all feel a little threatened by it. But we don't want to. All we really want is to get to know you better," the Father said.

"I can appreciate that," Ryan said.

"So, if you did not get your training from seminary, where did you get it from?" the Baptist asked.

"Pastor Joseph Sampson," Ryan blurted.

"And who is Pastor Sampson exactly?" the Presbyterian asked.

"He has his master's in theology from Fuller Theological Seminary, he's been a nondenominational minister for twenty-five years, and I trained under him as an associate pastor for nine years before he sent me to Bartlesville to plant The People's Church," Ryan said.

It may seem like Ryan was incredibly quick on his feet. But this wasn't the case. Truthfully, Ryan had been working on Pastor Joseph's bio for quite awhile. Ryan felt that he needed to have some sort of training to be leading all of these people. He'd already told

Cammy that he'd been a pastor for nine years, and when word spread, everyone in town assumed he was a seasoned minister. But Ryan knew that he didn't have any theological training, and it's difficult to lie about having graduated from seminary. So he invented Pastor Joseph Sampson by cutting and pasting bios from Pastor Clark and other successful megachurch pastors. If he gave Pastor Joseph an impressive enough pedigree then every one would assume that Ryan was the beneficiary of that training. This was all very simple.

"What church did you come from, Pastor Ryan?"

"The Lord's Church."

For a long time Ryan had been thinking about the name of Pastor Joseph's church. He would call it "The Lord's Church," because it sounded like Jesus was the pastor. And who would dare question Pastor Jesus?

Then Ryan added, "They commissioned me to plant this church, and I still talk to Pastor Joseph weekly. As a matter of fact, I talked to him on the car ride over and told him how I was excited to be meeting with other pastors in this city. I told him Bartlesville is a place where there is no competition; a place where the only thing people care about is winning souls. Now, I hope I'm not going to have to call my pastor back and tell him that I was lying about all of you. Please, don't make me tell him that I made all of that up, because everyone here is vindictive and competitive. I'd hate to discover that all the pastors in this town really care about is padding their own pews and wallets. That people and souls are just a commodity."

"I know that's not the case with us," the Assemblies pastor said.

"Okay, what is this, then? I didn't know we were here to talk about me or my church."

"Well, we are. So, let's cut to the chase, Pastor: Why are you really here? If you wanted a big church, why move to a small town?"

"I didn't want a big church. Pastor Sampson thought that this might be a nice place to plant a church — any size church. I had no idea that we would be so blessed, that it would grow so quickly."

"But all the gimmicks, the cotton candy — "

"An excuse to build community — I wanted it to feel like an event so people got to know one another. I don't think that's against the Bible," Ryan said, confident, but not absolutely positive that there were no Bible verses prohibiting the consumption of cotton candy at church.

"You know, maybe my church has grown not because of what I'm doing right, but because of what you all are doing wrong," Ryan said. "Now, if you'll excuse me, I think I've had about all of the questions I can handle for one day." Then he grabbed his belongings and left the room. No one said another word until he was gone.

Someone, sometime, was bound to check up on Pastor Joseph Sampson. Maybe it would be one of the clergy that he met with today, or maybe someone from the media. It was possible, after all; Ryan had received invitations to be on some talk radio shows and *Good Morning OKC* (imagine *Today*, only small budget, cheesy hosts, and in Oklahoma City) wanted Ryan to be a guest sometime in the next week. Any of them could ask about Ryan's past, and they could possibly check up on Pastor Joseph Sampson and the church that he had preached at for the last twenty-five years. The problem, of course, was that neither the pastor nor the church existed. So Ryan would have to make it look like they did.

He had to invent something, so in case anyone went digging, they could find some information, some proof and evidence that there was a Pastor Joseph Sampson. No one would look maliciously; no one would have any reason to believe that Ryan was lying, would they? After all, who in their right mind would invent a pastor and a church just to give himself a credible background? Ryan decided that he could take a couple of simple steps to create his mentor, so that anyone who went digging would have something to discover. He wouldn't have to do anything too elaborate; after all, it wasn't like Pastor Sampson actually existed, it wasn't like he had a mother and sister who would be looking for him. There just needed to be a couple of things to validate Ryan's story and prove that he did have training and the appropriate background to be leading such a large church.

The first thing Ryan did was create a website for Pastor Sampson's church. He bought thelordschurch.tv (.com and .org were already taken and .biz just didn't seem very classy) and then created a website much like that of The People's Church — he figured most churches in America have the same basic buttons on their websites: Mission Statement, Service Times, Events, Youth Services, Contact Us, and About Our Pastor.

Under the About Our Pastor section, Ryan wrote a brief bio for his mentor, including all of the information that he told the other pastors at the luncheon. Ryan also got a cell phone with a Denver area code and made that the contact number on the website. He figured he would periodically check messages on the phone and that way he could see if media members or the other pastors in town were really checking up on him.

Finally, Ryan got a P.O. box and put Pastor Sampson on six or seven mailing lists, and subscribed him to magazines like *Christianity Today* and *Newsweek*. It took Ryan nearly a day and a half to create Pastor Sampson and his church, but once he had finished, he felt proud. Ryan was also happy once he learned the first and last name of his fictitious pastor were prominent characters in the Old Testament.

That made Pastor Joseph Sampson seem extra spiritual.

At the end of the process Ryan thought about the amazing thing he had done. He had created a pastor out of thin air; he'd made his mentor and his home church, and Ryan was starting to feel like there was nothing that he couldn't do. He was starting to love being a minister and running a church because there was so much authority and respect. And if he was determined enough, he could accomplish anything he wanted.

When Ryan set up the cell phone number for The Lord's Church, he couldn't leave the message himself, so he wrote for the voice mail: "Thank you for calling The Lord's Church, we're out of the office right now but if you leave your name and number we'd be happy to call you back. God bless."

When Ryan tried convincing Katherine to create the phony voice mail recording for The Lord's Church, he didn't want to give her a reason why, because that would require too much explanation. He was hoping he could just give Katherine a piece of paper, a phone, and ask her to read what was on the paper for a voice mailbox. But inevitably Katherine asked why, and Ryan wouldn't answer; he simply said it would only take thirty seconds.

"That's not a reason," Katherine said.

"Pastors need proper training, and this will help me prove to people that I have the proper training."

"But you don't have any training."

"Exactly. I don't have any training and the church is doing great. I don't need any training, but I need people to think that I have training," Ryan said.

"I'm not sure I'm following you," Katherine said.

"The other pastors at lunch today asked me if I went to seminary. And so I was completely honest when I said I didn't go to seminary, but instead I trained under a pastor named Joseph Sampson for nine years."

"How is that completely honest?"

"Because I didn't go to seminary."

"But you didn't train under a Pastor Sampson."

"I practically did."

"How?"

"I trained under Pastor Clark at Fellowship, in a way. I've also been studying every successful pastor in the country. I've been watching them preach, I've been listening to their sermons while I drive, I've been reading all of their books. Everything I've learned I've learned from those guys, and that's why I know how to preach the right way and create church services to move the masses. So, for all of that great training I have, I've just given it a code name. I've called my training 'Pastor Joseph Sampson from The Lord's Church,' but it's mostly a metaphor."

"You're not presenting him as a code name or metaphor, honey. You're presenting him as an actual pastor," Katherine said.

"Just please read the message, sweetheart."

"It's a lie."

"It's not a lie; it's presenting the truth in a different light. Listen, church is all about trust, all about making people feel okay. People need to feel like God answers their prayers, they need to feel like their loved ones are going to a better place, and they need to feel like their pastor has jumped through all of the preordained hoops so he can lead a church. It doesn't matter what the reality is. The only thing that matters is how things appear to be."

He was right. Or at least, he was sort of right.

Katherine took the slip of paper from her husband and agreed to read the message. Partially, she did so because her husband had made a compelling argument; people did need to trust him, and if this helped to gain people's trust, then it was for the greater good. But when she was honest, she knew this wasn't the real reason she agreed to read the message. In the end, she did so only because she had to, because her husband had lied, and his tracks had to be covered. If those pastors did go snooping around to check out Ryan's story, they'd have a good chance of uncovering a fabricated church, and they could prove Ryan a liar and potentially destroy The People's Church.

And wouldn't that be the real tragedy in all of this? Katherine knew they were really helping people, that The People's Church was the greater good and she wouldn't let all those jealous pastors attack her and her husband. She even began to think, "God, isn't this the right thing to do? Shouldn't I be a good wife, shouldn't I be protecting The People's Church at all costs?"

And for some reason, at that moment, "No" popped into her thoughts and echoed around in her mind. If Katherine didn't know better, she would have thought God himself had spoken.

— 19 —

GOD'S
GARAGE BAND

Under normal circumstances the size of The People's Church was nothing to marvel at. It only had 1800 attendees on a Sunday morning. There were nineteen larger churches in Oklahoma alone, and hundreds of larger ones in the country. In a day where church membership reaches over twenty and thirty thousand human beings in some congregations, 1800 was miniscule and it would have been barely a blip on anyone's radar if it had been like any other church.

But these were not normal circumstances. The town only had twenty-three thousand people in it, so already, after three months, nearly one in every ten people in Bartlesville was attending The People's Church.

That was unheard of.

Everyone wanted to know why, what was it about The People's Church that made it so successful? Ryan had phone calls from local TV stations, magazines, newspapers, and talk shows. They all wanted interviews and statements, and they wanted to know what made his brand of Christianity so popular. But that wasn't all. They also wanted him to argue about the state of things in Palestine, they wanted him to talk about gay marriage, abortion, and ultimately they wanted any quote they could get from the man who clearly understood the spiritual pulse of the country.

Ryan had to hire Sally (a forty-six-year-old waitress from the Spork) as his full-time secretary to filter phone calls, book interviews, and manage his schedule. Quickly, his schedule was booked with appointments and interviews from morning till night for the next six months. He did lots of interviews because he figured all press is good press, and he told most of the media outlets the same thing, "I have no idea why the church has grown so fast. I'm just grateful to God for all of his blessings."

In the few interviews where he came off as a business tycoon, the press didn't respond well, and his inbox was flooded with angry emails. They all said something to the effect of: "You came off really arrogant in that interview, Pastor Ryan. It appeared almost as if you think it was *you* and not God who has made this church grow."

Ryan quickly understood that the press and everybody else was most comfortable with a pastor who appeared happy and simple, and as he watched interviews with other megachurch pastors they seemed to come off in the same way. He realized that in America we want our CEO's to appear shrewd, our politicians two-faced, and our pastors to act as if they've just walked off the set of the *Andy Griffith Show*.

Ryan, of course, had lots of thoughts on why his church was so successful and everything that he was doing right, but he wasn't going to tell that to the press. Instead he wanted to paint himself simple as a caveman, a well-meaning person who was just following the will of God.

"Okay, we really need a big Sunday this week," Ryan told his staff.

That's right, his staff. With such an explosion in growth, it took a whole staff to run The People's Church: Cowboy Jack to lead worship, Dean Parker to be the administrator-accountant, Katherine to run the women's ministry, Cammy to run the children's ministry,* and Dave Fitzgerald had stepped down as the senior pastor of the Lutheran church to become Ryan's associate pastor.

This move was met with little reluctance: Dave's congregation had dwindled and there were already rumors that he was going to be removed from leadership. That's what sometimes happens in churches when things start shrinking—the pastor gets removed. It's nothing personal, it's more like firing the head coach of an NFL team that fails to make the playoffs.

Their loss was Ryan's gain. He was excited to have Dave on board because it would give him an experienced church leader who could serve as a guide; an Obi-Wan Kenobi who'd let him know if his church was going off course.

The other ministers in town were furious that Pastor Fitzgerald joined the circus, but Dave didn't care; he loved The People's Church. He'd never been part of a nondenominational church and he immediately decided that he'd been missing out. It was so free here. They didn't have a bunch of rules and red tape and committee meetings—they could focus on the important things like taking care of people and spreading the gospel.

"How about we do a series on Leviticus?" Dave said.

"Who's Leviticus?" Ryan said.

Dave cackled and slapped his knee, "See that's what I love about this place, we can joke around. We can be free."

---

*Cammy recruited a team of volunteers, and since she didn't have children of her own, she actually enjoyed every Sunday when she was up to her neck with screaming toddlers and bratty eight-year-olds.

"That's one of our strengths," Ryan said, not quite understanding the joke. He really had no idea who Leviticus was. Maybe he was one of the kings in the Old Testament.

"I was just kidding anyway," Dave said. This was his first staff meeting, and Ryan was curious about how he would jell. Ryan hoped Dave would get along with the team because he and Dave had been getting along great since he'd been hired. Dave was there to coach Ryan on what he should preach about, how he should counsel church members, and how to keep The People's Church looking and acting as if it were an actual church.

Dave didn't know why Ryan was asking so many questions; he just thought they were collaborating on how to better run a ministry—but still, at times, Dave was shocked by how little Ryan knew about church, theology, and Scripture. Dave assumed Ryan must be holding back much of what he knew, like he was simple and even naïve, so he could keep an air of humility about him.

"Dave, we try to build our Sunday mornings around here on core human needs," Ryan said. "We want church to be a place where people can improve themselves. So we talk about marriages, parenting, finances, diet and exercise—the everyday stuff. We strive to present practical *Who Moved My Cheese* types of sermons."

"So what'd you have in mind for Sunday, boss?" Cowboy Jack asked.

"Well, I got this idea the other day after my prayer time," Ryan said. Ryan had learned if he came up with an idea on his own, it could be accepted or it could be tossed away. But if the idea came after prayer time, if God gave him the idea, that was different, that had to be respected and carefully considered.

"What is the idea, Pastor?" Cammy Miller asked.

"Has anyone seen *Fight Club*?"

Silence.

"Well, there's this scene where Brad Pitt tells everyone that they have to pick a fight. It could be anyone, a mechanic, a real estate agent, or maybe your best friend—"

"This sounds like my kind of sermon," Cowboy Jack said.

"Wait, you're going to have people pick fights?" Katherine asked.

"I don't think the Sheriff will be too happy about this," Cammy said.

"No, listen, I'm not going to have them pick fights. I'm going to have them commit random acts of kindness," Ryan said.

"Random acts?" Dave asked.

"Sure, you know, like pay for someone's dinner at a restaurant, wash your neighbor's car, read to the elderly, babysit the kids for some couple who badly needs a night out on the town. Everyone can have fun with it—they can be creative."

"This isn't a bad idea," Dave said.

"It's a great idea. It gives us an opportunity to do all of the stuff Jesus talked about," Ryan said.

"What stuff?" Katherine asked, curious how Ryan would answer.

"The 'love your neighbor as yourself' kind of stuff. Kindness is contagious," Ryan said. "And I think our church should spread the message of Jesus through being kind. And there's just one catch."

"Which is?" Katherine asked.

"You have to commit your act of kindness toward someone who has never been to The People's Church," Ryan said.

That week Ryan spent his nights crafting a sermon to convince his church of the importance of kindness, while Katherine spent her nights in a garage with Cowboy Jack. Recently, her favorite pastime had become managing Cowboy Jack and his worship band, and they practiced tirelessly on Tuesdays and Thursdays. While the band practiced, Katherine would pace back and forth like a lioness, watching every member of the band to make sure they were singing and playing to their full potential. If Katherine saw someone slacking she would not hesitate to say something like—

"Lindsey, what was that?"

"What? I was singing," Lindsey, the backup singer would answer. Lindsey always thought that Katherine was a little jealous—Katherine wished she could sing and be in the band and that's why she always cracked down so hard on her.

"Just because you say words with a little melody and harmony in your voice does not mean you are singing," Katherine would say.

"Well, what am I doing then?"

"You are acting like a person who wants to be kicked out of the band."

"I don't want that, Mrs. Fisher."

"Neither do I, but everybody, we've got to play with some urgency. Devin, don't just wave those drumsticks around like a couple of wet noodles; crash those bad girls against the toms. And Tracey, you're playing the guitar like you're scared of it. Don't be scared because there is nothing to be scared of. The guitar is the tool and you are the master blacksmith so start acting like it." Katherine didn't really know what she was saying in such speeches, she just knew she needed to crack the whip from time to time to bring the band into focus.

Cowboy Jack was grateful for it. Years ago he'd been the lead singer of a couple of bands, and they had talked about great things: becoming famous and touring across the country and making millions, but then the bass player couldn't make a practice and the drummer couldn't make a show because he had to work. The bands would always scatter, leaving the members feeling silly for ever even thinking they could make something of themselves. But with Katherine it was different. She was the leader. She kept everything in order so all Cowboy Jack had to worry about was singing. That was all he really loved to do anyway.

And Katherine was making the band better. After talking with a couple of members from the church she learned there were worship leaders that wrote songs specifically for God and church. A lot of the music had a British pop feel as if they were watered down, simple versions of U2 or Coldplay. And almost all of the songs were essentially about three things. The first: How great-awesome-incredible-powerful-majestic Jesus/God is/was/and forever will be. The second: How much we love-thank-adore-worship-bow down to Jesus/God. The third: How happy-touched-amazed and pumped up we were that Jesus/God saved us. That was pretty much it. There were thousands of these types of songs, yet so many of the lyrics were nearly identical. It was almost as if a songwriter could take one song, change five or six words, and then have an all-new song.

That's not to say the songs didn't work. They were moving and profound and when Katherine brought these songs into the Sunday morning set, worship was noticeably better. The congregation embraced these songs, and it was instantly clear that they seemed to carry an inexplicable power. There were stories around the church of people breaking down into tears during worship because they truly understood the love of God for the first time. Other stories had people falling to their knees and confessing their sins in the presence of the almighty God.

Katherine could relate. Worship was always the time when she could fathom God and His goodness. It was in those moments that she felt His love while simultaneously feeling dirty and ashamed for how sinful she was. She and Ryan had lied about everything to get here. And they may have been fooling Bartlesville, but they would not fool God.

He knew everything.

But there was no way Ryan could believe that God actually knew everything. Ryan wouldn't be manipulating the facts about his past and the church if he thought God knew what he was really doing. Would he? Ryan had always thought God was just a nice idea — he'd always told Katherine God is a fairytale. God is something invented long ago to explain things science could not. God helps us deal with the fact that we only have an average of sixty-seven years on planet Earth. Man created God, and in return for the favor, God made man immortal.

Still, there were moments when Katherine thought Ryan was wrong. There were moments in the dingy garage amidst the fiberglass, tools, and the smell of burnt oil where she suspected she'd completely misunderstood God. In those moments, as the lyrics and worship music swirled around Katherine, there were endless possibilities of who God was and what He wanted. In those moments Katherine felt surrounded by God's everlasting love. And she felt in awe of the lyrics of the songs.

Then practice would end, the music would stop, and everyone would begin to unplug their instruments and pack things away. Katherine would always snap out of her trance and wonder if she imagined all of those feelings, if she'd just placed herself under a spell of her own creation.

God wasn't really here. The mind can make me feel a lot of things that aren't real. It makes me feel sympathetic and elated for characters in movies that I've never met, or it can make me fear for monsters under the bed, or serial killers downstairs late at night when I'm in bed and weak and vulnerable.

Katherine even remembered a story in Psych 101 of an experiment where a girl was put under a hypnotic trance. The hypnotist told the girl that he was about to put a burning coal into her hand, and even though he put an ice cube in her hand she still screamed about how it was scorching hot and dropped the ice cube. Seconds later, burn marks appeared on her hand.

"Night Katherine, night Cowboy Jack," the band members said to them as they left Jasper's garage. Jasper, Cowboy Jack's buddy, was the only person with a garage large enough to practice in when the band started. It was right across from the horse stable where the mess with Katherine and Cowboy Jack started. And Katherine thought it was good that she was near the stables. It was a reminder of what an awkward mess her seductive, dangerous, exciting affair was. It was a reminder of how she didn't want to get caught up in something like that again.

"Night everybody. Great practice. And remember 7:45 Sunday morning. We need to be there on time. We have lots to get done at sound check," Katherine said. And then she and Jack were alone.

"That was a good practice tonight, Kate" Cowboy Jack said.

"Yeah, a little rough in the middle, but towards the end we were making progress."

When Katherine first broke off her lunch dates with Cowboy Jack she promised herself that she would not be alone with him. She understood her own weaknesses, her ability to be tempted, and she resolved to not leave any room for feelings to resurface. Lately, she felt that occasionally being alone with Cowboy Jack wasn't that big of a deal. After all, she'd resolved that she and Cowboy Jack were like a brother and sister; sure, she admired his musical ability but that didn't mean there was anything romantic. They were Greg and Marsha. There weren't any feelings between them. None whatsoever.

"Listen, thanks for helping out with the band. I know you don't get any of the credit on Sunday mornings, but we really wouldn't be the same without you," Jack said.

Kate liked when Jack looked at her like this. His gaze felt like a hot bath, it was so warm and steamy and safe. And before she knew it, Katherine began to miss Jack. She missed their talks and lunch dates — she missed spending time alone with him in their own little universe.

If Jennifer Anderson were here, she would have warned Katherine about this situation. She would have told Katherine that once Satan gets his hands on you he doesn't easily let go. He will find your weak spot and he will attack it. You can think he's gone, that he's no longer tempting you, but he can place a desire that lays dormant deep within your soul only to manifest itself when you least want it to. Unfortunately, Jennifer Anderson taught this lesson at Bible study the week after Katherine moved to Bartlesville.

"It's been my

(you need to leave. Right now. You're starting to feel that way for him again, and the church is too big and too important. Ryan is too big and too important for you to start acting like the naïve college girl who's flattered by the cute curly-haired boy with the guitar. Now, shake Jack's hand and tell him good-night)

pleasure," Katherine said.

"Can I tell you something, Kate?" Jack said as he grabbed Katherine's hand.

"Yes."

(And by yes, you mean no. What are you doing, Katherine?)

"You can tell me anything."

HONK!

Katherine and Cowboy Jack spun around to see Ryan in his new Hummer coming up the driveway. Cowboy Jack jumped away from Katherine as if he were a teenager on a couch with his girlfriend when his parents came home.

Ryan hopped out of the car and slammed the door shut. He stared at his wife and his worship leader.

"Hey guys," Ryan said.

Ryan hadn't seen Cowboy Jack holding Katherine's hand. He hadn't seen the way that she was looking at him thirty seconds ago. He didn't need to. He could *feel* that something wasn't right here; there was something between them that he'd never suspected and he'd certainly never seen.

"What are you guys doing?" Ryan asked.

"Nothing, really," Cowboy Jack said.

"Worship practice just ended," Katherine said.

"Oh."

"What are you doing here?" Katherine said.

"I came to inspire the troops."

That really was his plan. He'd never stopped by before; he'd never even paid that much attention to the band. They just kind of did their thing, and as long as they played well on Sunday mornings, Ryan didn't care how they did it. But lately, Ryan had noticed how popular the band was. Singing along with the Worship Wranglers was a highlight of the service—some members even said it was their favorite part. Some liked the band *more* than Ryan. So Ryan decided he'd better start paying more attention to the band; he'd better keep them happy and inspired so his church could continue to grow.

And tonight Ryan suddenly felt there were other reasons to keep his eye on the band.

"Do you guys always hang out like this after practice?"

"No."

"Never," Katherine added.

"Listen boss, I know this looks bad—"

"Why would this look bad? You're a grown man and woman alone sharing a moment on a starlit night. No harm in that, is there?" Ryan said.

"Pastor, everyone just left, they were here thirty seconds ago," Cowboy Jack said.

"Really, thirty seconds? That's just a little odd because when I was driving up the road I didn't see any other cars."

"Well, maybe it was more like a minute," Cowboy Jack said.

"Sure, a minute," Ryan said.

"Honey, I was about to leave. Why don't you come with me? We can ride home together and pick up the other car tomorrow."

And for a moment no one said a word. It seemed as if Ryan was planning his next move, as if this was a western and Clint Eastwood was staring at the villain waiting for the moment when he would draw his gun and fill the villain full of holes.

But Ryan never made a move. He just said, "Yeah, that's a good idea."

Katherine didn't look at Jack; she walked to the Hummer and sat in the passenger seat. After a moment Ryan followed Katherine. He started the car and they drove away.

On the ride home Katherine explained everything, "Jack and I are almost never alone like that, and there is nothing going on between us at all. We were just talking about band business."

"Jack?" Ryan said.

"You know, I mean Cowboy Jack."

"Oh."

"Do you want to know the truth?"

"Sure. That'd be nice."

"When we first got to Bartlesville I had some feelings for Cowboy Jack. I was just confused and lonely. I mean, Ryan, we left all of our friends and I was here in this new town by myself. But it's different now. I'm so happy here. I'm so happy with you. I love you, I love this church, and I would never do anything to hurt our lives here."

Ryan pulled the Hummer into the garage. It was a huge

garage. They now had the fifth biggest home in all of Bartlesville, a house much larger than their home in Denver. In fact, over the last month or so, as The People's Church grew, Ryan's salary increased significantly. The Fishers now had nice cars, nice clothes, and a huge house. Katherine was able to quit her job, since money was no longer an object. They were quite well off considering things were so inexpensive in this small Oklahoma town. No one in Bartlesville said a thing about all of the nice stuff Ryan was suddenly buying. And if they did say something, they would say "well done" because they thought that Pastor Ryan deserved everything he was getting.

As Ryan took the keys out of the ignition he said, "Good-night, honey."

Then he went upstairs and crawled into bed. He didn't do any of his normal bedtime rituals, he didn't watch *Sportscenter*, didn't kiss Katherine good-night, he didn't even brush his teeth. But when Katherine crawled into bed she didn't know that his eyes were wide open. She had no idea how long he lay in bed staring at the wall—or how long it really took him to fall asleep.

20

THE GOOD SAMARITANS

By eight a.m. every Sunday, volunteers were busy outside the tent of The People's Church getting ready for the service. Dean Parker had a clipboard and a headset to make sure everyone was doing their job. He had some volunteers firing up the cotton candy machine, some popping popcorn, some bringing in livestock for the petting zoo, and some setting up tables in the first-time visitor tent.

They'd created the "welcome experience" outside of the tent a few weeks ago because Ryan wanted first-timers to enjoy The People's Church from start to finish. He remembered how awkward it was walking through Fellowship Christian Church's parking lot on his first Sunday and he didn't want anyone visiting his church to have the same experience. So he spared no expense. When visitors arrived they were treated to a first-class breakfast. The church hired short order cooks to scramble bacon, mushroom, and spinach omelets, and then they made freshly squeezed orange juice. Everyone raved about the breakfast. Afterwards, ushers would escort visitors to their seats, which were the best in the house.

It took nearly 150 volunteers to set up The People's Church on Sunday mornings, and every volunteer did their job with a smile—they loved the satisfaction of being a crucial part of the success of the church, and they loved the personalized laminated name badges they were given. It was like having a backstage pass at a rock concert. Except the passes didn't get you backstage, and it wasn't technically a rock concert.

While the setup crew was getting everything ready, Ryan met with his staff to go over the order of service. The meeting was normally fairly pedestrian: the soundman and lighting engineer would just make sure they were on the same page for all of the transition cues and Ryan would tell his team how long he wanted the service to go.

However, this morning's meeting was a little more interesting:

"Then after my sermon you roll the *Oprah* clip on acts of kindness. You got that, Jeff?" Ryan asked.

"Yes sir," Jeff the soundman/video operator said.

"Okay, great. I think that's about it. Oh, except there's one other thing, um Lindsey, I thought it would be great if you led worship this morning."

"Really?" Lindsey asked, a little excited.

"Ryan, we didn't practice with Lindsey leading worship," Katherine said, her voice coated in disbelief.

"Yeah, sure, I know, but Lindsey, you know all the songs, don't you?"

"Yes, I do, Pastor Ryan," Lindsey said.

"Why are you changing this all of a sudden?" Katherine asked, even though she knew the answer.

"I just thought we've had Cowboy Jack leading every week since this church started, so it might be nice to hear a woman's voice up there. You know, a little change of pace. Is that okay, Jack?"

"Anything you say, boss," Cowboy Jack answered, though he was clearly startled by being yanked so effortlessly.

"See, Katherine, anything I say," Ryan stated.

The morning's service began like usual—with opening credits. Like the ones on *Saturday Night Live* or *The Tonight Show* where an announcer introduces all of the cast members. Only instead of cast members, the announcer introduced the staff members, and instead of being somewhere cool like New York City, the video was shot on a farm where all of the volunteers were doing things like feeding pigs and tossing hay bales. Ryan thought that this would make everyone seem personable and friendly.

At the end of the video the announcer shouted, "And now, will you please welcome Cowboy Jack and the Worship Wranglers!" The crowd had learned that this was the time where they sprung to their feet and began to worship.

But they sprang to their feet a little slower and worshiped a little softer when they saw that Lindsey was up there to lead worship instead of Cowboy Jack. And during the first verse and chorus of the first song, the crowd seemed confused. But soon they began to forget about Cowboy Jack because the music was too good, Lindsey's voice was too soothing, and before anyone knew it they were in the trance of worship singing about their love for Jesus Christ. After service, few even mentioned Cowboy Jack's absence.

Cowboy Jack couldn't believe this. He thought he was irreplaceable—a pillar of Sunday mornings. The place would crumble without him. Wouldn't it? He was one of the celebrities of the church. Everyone around town knew him for worship. One member of the church even told Cowboy Jack once that he should go to

Nashville. The member said his cousin was a big time agent. But he couldn't just leave Ryan and Katherine and the church high and dry. And besides, everybody has some cousin that has a connection—but Cowboy Jack knew that when he got to Nashville the connection would fizzle somehow.

But still, if Katherine was being so weird, and the church could discard him so easily, maybe this would be the time to go out for a couple of weeks. Maybe worship music was the first step to being a breakout country music star. That was how other country greats like Johnny Cash and Dolly Parton got their start—wasn't it?

After worship, Ryan walked on stage and began his sermon. He cracked open the book of Luke and read the story of the good Samaritan.

A few days ago he'd never heard of the story.

It was Dave who had recommended that Ryan use the illustration for his sermon, but Ryan didn't even know there was an actual story, he just figured "the Good Samaritan" was an idiom like, "let the cat out of the bag." But sure enough, there was a parable in Luke involving a man who was robbed and left for dead. A priest and Levite each passed the man, and also left him for dead because they had other places to be. Only the Samaritan helped the man—he got the man medical treatment and a place to stay.

Ryan was excited to discover this story because it perfectly illustrated his point on kindness. He was learning what a wonderful thing the Bible was, it was almost better than *Chicken Soup for the Soul* (Ryan's other favorite sermon resource) because there were so many insightful stories and ideas within its sixty-six chapters.

Perhaps there was even a story that explained what it really meant to let the cat out of the bag. Why was the cat even in the bag in the first place? He would have to read his Bible to find out.

When Ryan finished reading the story, he said, "The priest is the person that we expect to stop for the robbed man. Isn't he the one with the responsibility to care for the man? Shouldn't he have stopped whatever 'ministry' he was doing to take care of the injured man? I mean, church, this man is dying on the side of the road, and this 'priest' has somewhere better to be?"

Throughout the congregation people shouted things like, "That ain't right pastor," and "He's no real priest."

"But you see, that's how you and I are today. There are a lot of hurting people out there, and you know what we do? We walk on by, just like that priest. We say, 'Sorry starving children in Africa, I can't give you money for food; I need a bigger TV.' We say, 'I'm sorry homeless person, I can't volunteer at the shelter; I have better things to do with my time.' "

"That's true! Preach!" various members of the congregation said.

"And do you know who ended up helping this robbed man, this man who was on the edge of his death bed? A Samaritan, that's who. That would be like a Blood helping out a Crip, or Batman helping out the Joker, a Republican helping out a Democrat!"

Laughter.

"And Jesus told this story, because he knew we often get help from the least likely of places. And do you know what I think? I think we have a church full of Samaritans, I think we have a church that's interested in showing people the love of Jesus rather than just talking about it!"

Huge applause.

"Look around, church. Look how quickly we mobilized, how quickly we've changed our little town. Everybody's talking about us now, because we're *doing* the Christian thing and not just *talking* about it. And I think the next step for us is to start giving tangible evidence of Jesus' love. But we can't just talk about the love of Christ to each other. That's what the *priest* would do.

"So, I'm going to give us a simple task: This next week is Good

Samaritan week, and you must find someone who has never been to The People's Church, someone who needs to experience the love of Jesus, and do a Good Samaritan act for them. You see, I'm the pastor of this church. But this week, I want you to all become pastors. I mean, we're all supposed to be pastors right? So it's time to act like it. I want you all to buy someone's groceries, wash their car, fix their plumbing; you all have skills and talents, find a way to utilize them so you can love your neighbor as yourself. So *you* can be a Good Samaritan. So you can be a pastor!"

After Ryan said this, The People's Church gave him a standing ovation. Not that this was a big deal. He was getting used to it.

Then Ryan added, "And when someone asks you why you've done what you've done, just tell them 'God loves you. And so do the people of The People's Church.'"

Throughout the week, stories of random acts of kindness quickly spread throughout the town. It was like that moment in *Ghostbusters* where the EPA shuts down the containment system even though Peter Venkman and Egon strictly warned them not to. Immediately ghosts and slimers are swooshing around Manhattan terrorizing everyone. Except Bartlesville wasn't terrorized with ghosts but rather with kindness. The town became one giant Hallmark card—the syrup of kindness was seeping into every crevasse of the city.

For instance there was one story about a man who spent two days trying to fix a rusty Oldsmobile for a single mother. When the car couldn't be fixed he bought the woman a new car and volunteered to take over the payments until the woman could get on her feet.

A group of teenagers grabbed buckets of paint and covered every spot of graffiti that the eye could see. By the time they were done, the water tower, street signs, ditches, and bathroom stalls no longer had gang signs and dirty limericks—they were bland and calm like they were intended to be.

Clive Wilson knew of a woman in town who'd lost her husband to cancer, so he gathered a group of contractors and their wives and completely remodeled this woman's home. Before it was rusty and rundown, but by the time Clive and his crew were finished, the widow's home had the hippest bathroom in town. Later on, Clive even started meeting her for breakfast every morning at The Greasy Spork. And in the evenings, after *Jeopardy*, they would take long walks and talk about sunsets and lost love and the future.

One man paid for the groceries of every customer in the express lane for two straight hours. No one knew that the groceries had been paid for until the checker told them. And as people found out they would cry or laugh or just walk away with their jaws dropped in disbelief that they didn't owe a dime. And the man would just whisper, "I paid for your groceries, but Jesus paid for your sins."

If kindness was contagious, the town of Bartlesville had leprosy.

There was one kind act after another and soon the members of the town who hated The People's Church couldn't help but be impressed or at least curious. They assumed that the church was evil, that this pastor was doing something corrupt to ruin their town. Some had even formed groups to protest the church. But how could they hate the church now? How could they protest something that was doing so much good?

Soon the reluctant residents of Bartlesville were being persuaded one act of kindness at a time that they had to at least visit The People's Church. And even the most reluctant souls were being convinced of the age-old axiom, "If you can't beat 'em, join 'em."

21

The Boy Who Was Coated in Vegetable Oil

The other pastors in town had given up on worrying about Ryan and his church. They'd gotten used to him. They still didn't like him, but he was starting to seem like part of the landscape. It was as if he were a forever-stalled construction project on a busy street. He was annoying but there was nothing they could do.

Pastor Mark, the Baptist, had the most difficult time letting go of his grudge against Ryan. He couldn't stop thinking about how much he disliked him. One Sunday, Mark even had his associate speak so he could see The People's Church for himself. He was aghast at what he saw: dancing in the aisles, smoke, lights, and a sound system that pumped music with the decibels of an airplane engine.

But the worst was Pastor Ryan Fisher, looking so smug and all-knowing with the church hanging on his every word as if he were JFK or Gandhi. Mark was determined to catch Ryan in a lie or deception. He was sure that Ryan had just invented Pastor Joseph Sampson, but with a little bit of research, it appeared that Pastor Joseph checked out, and Ryan's home church in fact existed.

Mark was still sure Ryan was pulling the proverbial wool over everyone's eyes. But there was no way to prove it. Even worse, there was no way he could get Ryan out of his thoughts. He was everywhere.

Every time he turned on the TV, Pastor Ryan was on some show talking about the miracle of The People's Church. He was even on *Good Morning America* a week ago, and Diane Sawyer asked him, "How could a church grow this large in a town this small?"

"You know, Diane, our church has four thousand members in a town of around twenty thousand. That means nearly one out of every five people in town is a member of our little church. Few, if any, other churches in America can claim something like that."

"So then what's your secret? Are you a cult?"

Ryan unleashed his charming smile, leaned forward, and said, "Far from it, Diane. We're just a simple group of believers who love and take care of each other—"

About then, Mark violently pounded the remote and clicked off the TV. Ryan had been giving interviews locally for the last month. He said the same thing every time. Now he was giving his line of garbage on national television. *Good Morning America* was profiling prominent churches in America every morning because they wanted to hear what different pastors were thinking about the upcoming presidential election. Mark could not believe they chose Ryan Fisher, and in his introduction they named The People's Church "the most powerful small-town church in America."

Mark's focus on Ryan had sent him spiraling into depression, and if he didn't have such a deep sense of duty he would have skipped his Tuesday night leadership meeting. This was the meeting where the leaders of his church were supposed to get together and pray, followed by Mark casting vision for the church. After an utterly uninspired and stale prayer time, Mark had to rally his troops. But he couldn't. There was nothing left in the tank.

Then one leader had the gall to ask, "What's the plan for this week?"

"The plan is for our church to go down in flames," Mark said. He could no longer put on a happy face and pretend everything was going to be okay. Ryan was going to destroy his church. Why fight it? He should accept the facts. It would be easier that way.

"Not true. We will battle. We will be victorious," a man named Clovis said.

Clovis was the newest member of the leadership team. He had coke-bottle glasses, curly hair, a patchy beard, and kind of creeped everyone out. He'd just recently joined the leadership team—a few months ago Mark wouldn't have let him come within ten miles of the church, let alone the leadership team, but these days he had to take all the help he could get.

Clovis glared at Mark with a vigilant stare, but everyone else looked at him with worry and concern. They'd been part of this church for years, and Mark had always seemed so optimistic and fun-loving. But not lately. Over the last month he was getting bitter and distant and they wanted to know why.

"What's wrong, Pastor?" one leader asked.

"It's Ryan Fisher. He comes into our town with this circus act and it's killing us. He's a liar and a manipulator," Mark said.

"How do you know that?"

"How do you not? Just look at him. He's teaching heresy."

"From what I heard he just talks about kindness, loving your neighbor, and the importance of having a balanced diet."

"Exactly. Where is the Scripture in that?" Mark asked.

"He uses Scripture to support his ideas."

"But he doesn't break down the Scripture. There's no meat* in his talks," Mark said.

"Well, maybe we can be the church of substance. Maybe he can have the church with all of the frills, but we can be the church where people learn the deeper truths of Scripture."

"It won't matter if nobody comes. Do you realize that one out of every five people in town go to his church? That means 20 percent of our town is at The People's Church every Sunday," Mark said.

"Which means 80 percent of our town isn't."

Mark was suddenly ashamed and embarrassed. His leadership team was right—they had the answers of how to respond to Ryan if he would just listen. But Mark had let Ryan turn him into Jan Brady—he had become insanely jealous of Ryan's success just like Jan was of Marsha. He might as well have been telling his church leadership team, "Ryan, Ryan, Ryan" in a whiny voice. But Ryan didn't matter, God had not placed him in charge of Ryan Fisher; God had placed him in charge of the Bartlesville Baptist Church. It was time to start acting like it.

He spent the next hour admitting all of this to his leadership team, and it worked. To this day the church enjoys a thriving and healthy existence. Sure, over the upcoming months there were times when Pastor Mark again would find himself getting jealous of Ryan Fisher. There were times when he would find himself thinking it wasn't fair that a charlatan like Ryan got whatever he wanted and enjoyed unstoppable success. But whenever Mark started feeling this way, he learned to talk about his feelings with a trusted friend. And they would always tell him the same thing.

---

* "Meat in your talks" often refers to the use of Scripture in sermons. Having meatless talks is a shameful thing for a pastor, although Ryan could never understand how much Scripture (meat) he was supposed to have. He tried to use just enough to make his sermons seem substantive so he could get on to talking about more practical everyday things.

"Ryan isn't your problem. Take care of what God has put in front of you." Pastor Mark would listen to his friends' advice and from that time foward, everyone could tell there was a difference in him. Everyone was proud to see how Mark had overcome his envy so he could continue to be their pastor.

Everyone that is, except for Clovis. The last thing Clovis heard was how Ryan Fisher was teaching heresy.

Clovis Whitman thought he had to do something about Ryan Fisher because he was sure Jesus was coming back in his lifetime. He'd known this ever since he'd been born. Maybe even before he was born. Jesus was coming back and Clovis had to do everything in his power to make sure everyone knew about it. To make sure they were warned. He loved other people (even the ones who weren't very warm to him) because he wanted to make sure they didn't burn. That was not allowed. Even the people who said they wanted to burn really didn't know what they were asking for.

His mother prepared him for this assignment at a young age as she read him the book of Revelation every Friday night when he was a child. As she read he'd lie on his back and soak in all of the frightening imagery: snakes and dragons, flaming swords and flying horsemen — it was all so wonderful. Clovis was a huge sci-fi fan, but after the age of eight, his mother did not allow him to watch television. "The devil's box," that's what she called it. She'd gone to a revival and come back saying the television was no longer to be watched. She'd learned how evil it was. However, there was still a television in the basement, but it was *only* to be used for watching VHS tapes of James Robinson revivals.

So Clovis had to get his science fiction fix from the book of Revelation, which was by far his favorite book in the Bible. All of the other books were so boring. Nothing (especially in Paul's letters) ever happened.

But Clovis's mother couldn't keep him from hearing about all of the amazing shows on TV. He wanted to check them out for himself. Late one night, long after his mother was asleep, he crept to the basement and discovered a show called *Battlestar Galactica.* There were ships, aliens, lasers, robots, and a hero named Starbuck.

Battlestar Galactica was way better than the Bible.

When the credits rolled Clovis turned around and saw that his mother was staring at him as the blue light from the TV bounced off her face.

"You're not supposed to be watching this," Clovis's mother said.

She ran upstairs, picked up the phone, and within fifteen minutes Clovis was coated in vegetable oil, while people from his mother's prayer group were screaming for the demons to come out of him.

Clovis didn't think he had demons, but they were all so sure. So they must be there, he thought.

Three hours later, they were all gone and Clovis's mother was tucking him in. And as his mother kissed him on the forehead, Clovis said, "Thank you for freeing me from the demons Mommy."

Clovis didn't disobey his mother for another eight years.

But then, when he was sixteen, he was invited to an all night D & D (Dungeons and Dragons) party. D & D was far worse than *Battlestar Galactica.* His mother would never approve. So he told her he was going to a prayer group. He snuck over to the party and felt like part of the club. Everyone at school probably saw these kids as nerds, but Clovis didn't feel like a nerd. He was eating pizza and laughing; he was one the guys.

He was normal.

Then the impossible happened: Clovis had the perfect roll with three twenty-sided dice, and his level-7 elf was about to slay Matthew Bailey's level-16 wizard. It was going to be the greatest moment of his life.

Until his mother appeared in the basement and said, "Rebellion is like witchcraft, Clovis."

Clovis looked so guilty, he might as well have been playing with a Ouija board or sacrificing a virgin. "Mother, it's not what you think," Clovis managed to blurt.

"Dude, your mom is scary looking," Matthew Bailey said.

"Yeah, man, is she going to kill us or something?" another boy asked.

Mrs. Whitman had heard enough. She could not tolerate her son being corrupted by these horrible boys for one second longer. She grabbed Clovis by the earlobe and dragged him out of the basement.

When they got home, she told him, "I can forgive you son, but not tonight. Tonight, you're sleeping with Max." She went inside and locked the door behind her.

And Clovis quite literally spent the night in the doghouse.

The next morning she made chocolate chip pancakes and strawberry milk—his favorite breakfast—and they ate together.

Neither of them ever mentioned the previous night's events.

They didn't have to. Clovis's mother had taught him what was at stake. He now understood how trivial things like Dungeons and Dragons parties were. He understood how trivial *friends* were. There was a battle for the planet, for souls, for eternity in the balance. He couldn't be distracted by temporal things. He had to make a stand. He lived in a world where people were cruel and sinful and selfish—

Selfish.

That was the word. Selfishness is the root of so many of the problems in this country. We buy flat-screen televisions even though that money could feed an African family of eighteen for a year. America's motto was once "In God we trust" and now it might as well be "If it feels good, do it." So we satisfy any and every selfish urge while our families and marriages crumble, while our schools decay, while the moral fiber of the country's core rots away.

Clovis had been waiting his whole life for a moment to take a stand against this vanity. And finally there was someone to stand up to: Pastor Ryan Fisher. It was so clear now. Clovis was so grateful to Pastor Mark for helping him understand that his whole life had been leading up to one thing—doing whatever it took to show what a false prophet and heretic Pastor Ryan really was.

22

H. E. Double
Hockey Sticks

Pastor Clark stood over the Fishers' bed. He was dressed like the pope—wearing a silk robe and a pointy hat—and he was holding a trident. His eyes were mustard yellow, glowing, nearly mechanical like an android's. Ryan was waiting for Pastor Clark to speak. And when Ryan looked at the trident again he realized it wasn't a trident at all—it was a sickle, and Pastor Clark wasn't dressed like the pope, he was dressed more like a priest, cloaked in black with a white collar.

Not that it really mattered what Pastor Clark was wearing. Ryan was just shocked to see him. He hadn't seen him in nearly six months, and all of a sudden he was standing over his bed at three in the morning wearing some sort of Halloween costume.

"Pastor Clark, how did you find me?" Ryan asked.

Pastor Clark continued to stare at Ryan for a moment, then he put his finger over his lips, and when Ryan looked around he realized he was no longer in his bedroom—he was in heaven.

At least this was the way heaven looked in all the TV

commercials. There were billowing white clouds, bright blue and gold beams of light, and there were angels with harps.

Ryan was standing in a line, but not just any line. It was so long that if you combined every person waiting for a ride at every amusement park across the planet on a hot summer day, you would only have a small fraction of the people in this line. And no one said a word. Every soul just stared straight ahead, looking at the front of the line where there were large pearly gates stretching up as far as the eye could see. It would take an eternity to get to the front of this line. And an eternity is what everyone seemed to have.

When someone got to the front of the line he would talk to a man with a feather quill pen checking the names in a large book. Suddenly Ryan was next in line, and the man was looking for his name.

Ryan had thought maybe it had been St. Peter who had been checking the names, but he could now clearly see that it was not a man at all; it was Wilma Wilson looking young and healthy and happy. She looked as if she'd never even heard the word *cancer*.

"Wilma, it's me, Ryan!"

"I know your name, Pastor Ryan."

And then Wilma was silent. Ryan hadn't really thought much about if he would get into heaven because he didn't really believe there was a heaven to get into. But now that he was here he thought surely he deserved to make it through the pearly gates. He'd introduced kindness and hope and love to an entire community. He'd done more good in the few months than most could muster in several lifetimes. If he couldn't get into heaven, then the standards were just too high.

Still, looking at this woman whom he failed to heal, he thought there might be a chance he wouldn't make it in. Was it possible? Was he lacking in some way? Would he be denied a chance for clouds and harps and whatever other goodies heaven had to offer?

Of course not.

"Welcome to heaven," Wilma said.

Ryan walked through the pearly gates and discovered heaven was even better than advertised. Beach Boys songs played, there were round-the-clock bocce ball tournaments, and every so often, ruby red, buttercream, and royal purple rose petals would fall from the sky just because they looked nice. All around Ryan there were steak and lobster and shrimp buffets. And everyone Ryan had ever known was in heaven: his friends and family members were skinny and had full heads of hair; they all smiled and laughed about nothing and everything. Then Ryan saw Katherine there in a skimpy toga that was being toussled by a heavenly wind. Next to Katherine was Cowboy Jack. He grabbed Katherine's hand and Ryan watched as their fingers interlocked.

"Um, hey sweetheart. What are you doing?" Ryan asked. But Katherine didn't answer—she just walked away into the cloudy distance with Cowboy Jack. She never even turned back to look at Ryan.

Ryan turned around to see Pastor Clark standing next to him. "Ryan, I'm sorry, this is really awkward," Pastor Clark said.

"What's really awkward?"

"There's been a mistake."

Then, suddenly, it was very cold.

Ryan and Pastor Clark were alone. There was nothing but pointed rocks and ice. Pastor Clark's sickle began to glow and Ryan could see millions of faces amidst the rocks and ice. And when Ryan looked closely, the faces were the members of The People's Church. The Buckleys, Smiths, Campbells, and Johnsons were there staring at Ryan. Cowboy Jack and Katherine were staring at him as well, but when Ryan looked into their eyes, it was like nothing was there—their souls were as thin and hollow as an eggshell.

"Where are we?" Ryan asked Pastor Clark.

"You see, there was a mistake in the paperwork, and you're really supposed to be here, in the place of forgotten souls," Pastor Clark said as his voiced echoed across the rocks.

"Why?"

"Because this is where you wanted to go."

"I did not want to go here. I want Beach Boys songs and bocce ball," Ryan said.

"Yeah, I hear you. But this is where you belong," Pastor Clark said. "And unfortunately, you're taking all of them with you."

Pastor Clark waved his sickle and bright blue flames grew all around them. These weren't natural flames like the ones at a campfire—these were the flames of a chemistry lab or a factory when foul-smelling chemicals are ignited. Then everything and everyone around Ryan began to melt. He tried to scream, but he no longer had a voice. He tried to move but he was no longer in control of his body, and he tried to shut his eyes but they would not blink. There was nothing he could do but watch the people that he loved most burn.

Ryan sprang out of bed, relieved that Katherine was lying next to him, beautiful as ever and sleeping peacefully. The sheets were drenched with his cold sweat, and the room was lit with moonlight so Ryan could see that Wilma Wilson and Pastor Clark were no longer there. Why would they be? It was a dream.

What was he supposed to do? Wake up from this and become Ebenezer Scrooge, change his life and his practices and the way he was living? That didn't make sense.

Scrooge robbed people and hated Christmas. Ryan was teaching people to love and be kind to one another. The problem was that he'd spent so much time reading about the powers of God and about heaven and hell that he was actually starting to believe what he was reading. It would be no different than reading twelve Stephen King books in a row and then going to bed. Of course you would have nightmares after that. Ryan realized that perhaps his life had become too consumed with church. Perhaps he'd spent too much time thinking and reading about supernatural beings and powers. Maybe he needed to get away for a couple of days so he could clear his head and get God out of his thoughts.

Then he could go back to being a pastor.

For the next month Ryan spent his weeks making sure the machine known as The People's Church was running at full steam. He always had fifteen voice mails and a to-do list a mile long. There were potlucks, deacon meetings, budget issues, Sunday morning planning committees, counseling appointments, and Billy Finn was always pestering Ryan to pray over his sick cattle. Ryan was now the most popular and powerful man in town, which sounds nice, though what it actually boiled down to was everyone needing or wanting something from him. Ryan had to handle every request with care and consideration, because even though the church was gaining influence, there were plenty of fires to put out, and any fire left to burn long enough could torch his dream.

Today was another day full of work and chores and meetings, and at the moment he was in his Hummer, driving toward a lunch meeting with the church's deacons and elders at the Spork. As he drove he mulled over the one raging inferno: services were growing stale.

He'd known it since the night he caught Katherine talking with Cowboy Jack. Not that Cowboy Jack was really even the problem.

As a matter of fact, he wasn't even in the picture anymore. Last Sunday after the service Cowboy Jack had told Ryan, "Hey boss, I need to go to Nashville for a couple of weeks. Buddy of mine's got a great music opportunity that I have to at least check out."

And Ryan said, "Okay."

Ryan knew the real reason Katherine was talking with Cowboy Jack had absolutely nothing to do with Cowboy Jack. Rather, she was talking with him because she was getting bored with the church and she needed some sort of new adventure. Now, this was not a huge shock to Ryan. For their entire relationship Katherine always had to be impressed and won over; he'd always had to find a way to show off so he could earn her love.

This may sound dysfunctional, but Ryan didn't see it that way. Nobody loves someone simply because they're *supposed* to. If this were the case there would never be a divorce; couples would stay together because it was the right and proper thing to do. But couples break up all the time. Relationships quickly grow stale when the husband stops proving his worth to his wife (or vice versa). Ryan knew that once a couple stops trying to impress and wow one another, their marriage is doomed. He even taught this principle to couples during marriage counseling sessions.

So Ryan didn't resent his wife for highlighting the fact that his church services were getting stale with her threat of infidelity; rather he was grateful to her for pointing it out. She was just a little more perceptive than everyone else, and to save his marriage and his church he'd have to fix his services.

The root of the problem was that his sermons and *Oprah* segments used to be so dramatic and breathtaking. That's why the church grew so much initially, because while other churches were focusing on dogma, his congregation was focusing on the human element. Yet, lately, the segments were extremely lackluster. For instance, one story revolved around the Parkers who swore their dog could pray, and another involved a man who got a long-awaited promotion, and who could forget the riveting tale of Thursday night prayer poets? These stories were as flavorful as white bread dipped in milk.

And even though the church was still going strong, it wasn't thriving, not like it was a few months ago when it was the only thing anyone talked about. Back then there were powerful stories of Wilma's cancer, Jimmy's separation, and there was the story of the underground crystal meth ring that Ryan, Sheriff Somersby, and the prayer poets helped bring down.

But those stories had seemed to dry out. All the drama was used up. Now, there were only stories of good lives getting better, of happy things turning to wonderfully happy things, the town of Bartlesville suddenly seemed as safe and cuddly as a Precious Moments calendar.

There may have been other dark, dramatic stories, but they took a lot of work to uncover because people didn't want their dirty laundry aired. And Ryan felt that if he couldn't begin to find better stories soon, the church would get bored (just like Katherine had) and then things would begin to dwindle.

As Ryan pulled up to the Greasy Spork he realized something horrible was happening: he was getting complacent. Settling for good enough. He was not trying to be the best anymore, and neither was the church. For the last month they'd been coasting. And the whole town no longer seemed amazed, but they were okay; they were content with everything that was happening. So, couldn't they be equally content if one day the church just went away? The church grew so quickly, couldn't it dissipate just as fast? Something better, or someone hipper and cooler could stroll into town and next thing you know, Ryan would have an empty tent and unpaid bills.

If he were lucky, maybe Chuck E. Cheese would take him back.

That night Ryan tossed socks, boxers, slacks, T-shirts, and shoes into his suitcase. He was determined but not fervent—it wasn't as if his house were on fire or aliens were coming to abduct him—but still he was a man with a mission. The church had to be fixed.

"What are you doing, honey bear?" Katherine said, surprised to come home to her husband packing up. "Do you have an interview to fly out to?"

"I need to get away for a couple of days. And I need you to run things here."

"Where are you going?"

"Let me ask you this: Don't you think the church has gotten a little static?"

"It's been fine."

"Fine," Ryan said, his tone coated with disgust, "is exactly the problem."

"It is?"

"Yes; this church used to be marvelous. It used to blow people away."

"It still does."

"We're coasting. And every business book will tell you that once you get too comfortable with *fine*, once you settle for *good enough*, that's when the competition blows you away."

"I think you're overanalyzing."

"I probably am. But I still need to get away for a couple of days."

"Can't you just work here?"

"Wish I could, but there's always something I have to do here. Katherine, when we first started the church I would just sit around and think stuff up because I didn't have anything better to do. That's where I got all my good ideas. There's no time for that around here anymore."

"When will you be back?"

"By Thursday. It's just two days. Make sure everything stays okay while I'm gone," Ryan said, kissed Katherine on the cheek, and left.

23

Everything That Happened Before Lunch

Emerald Lake was a hundred miles southeast of Bartlesville. By the time Ryan arrived at his rented cabin, the sun was setting and orange beams of light bounced across the lake's surface, illuminating the gnats and dragonflies dancing above the water. It was almost as if they were daring the catfish to spring out of the water and end them.

This is where I need to be, Ryan thought.

Ryan cooked some stew for supper; it was his father's recipe, and it seemed like the manly, hearty sort of Jacob-and-Esau meal that he should be enjoying in his log cabin. After supper, he cracked his laptop open and pounded his fingers against the keyboard, imagining all of the places his church could and should go next. He was planning on taking a moonlit walk through the forest after he finished, just to get the blood pumping and a little bit of exercise. But his writing took too long, and after he typed the last idea, he used the only strength he had left to crawl into his bed.

It was probably for the best anyway, because if Ryan had taken a walk, he may have run into a rusty brown station wagon parked amidst the trees. Inside was a man Ryan had never met; someone named Clovis Whitman, who was sitting in the cold and the dark and doing a little brainstorming of his own.

If Clovis knew what Ryan was doing, he would have cackled and laughed. There was no need to plan for the future. There was no point in mapping out where Ryan would take The People's Church next. Clovis had decided to make sure Ryan would never pastor again.

Clovis made this decision because it was no coincidence that he'd ended up here. After he had his revelation at the prayer meeting, he'd spent the next day following Ryan around. Clovis waited in his car as Ryan did whatever business he needed to do for the day. Clovis waited while Ryan met with the deacons at The Greasy Spork, he waited outside the tent of The People's Church as Ryan told the setup team how to position the banners and advertising for his next sermon series. And Clovis waited outside Ryan's house as he packed his things for his getaway to Emerald Lake.

A heathen would say it was dumb luck that led Clovis to waiting outside Ryan's cabin, it was pure chance that Clovis should find himself in a secluded place with Ryan, but Clovis knew better. He knew God had provided him this opportunity. He knew that it was here that he would make his stand and put an end to Ryan's lies and manipulation.

The only question was how.

Clovis could hire a woman to tempt Ryan and take compromising pictures. Nothing tore a church apart quicker then a sex scandal, nothing would send the congregants running away from his church like mice from a burning sewer.

Or maybe Clovis could just make it so that Ryan never left Emerald Lake. Clovis could dismember Ryan and bury different parts of him around the forest, or he could wrap him in heavy chains and send him to the bottom of the lake. Ryan hadn't told anyone where he was going. No one would know where to look. In fact, they might not ever find him. Ryan Fisher would just become another unsolved missing persons case.

When Clovis saw the lights click off inside Ryan's cabin, he decided it was time to go to bed as well. He laid his face against the cool glass window. And as he drifted to sleep, his mind swam through all of the different fates Ryan Fisher could meet. There were so many ways he could torment Pastor Fisher, so many ways he could destroy his life. Clovis just wished he could try them all.

In the morning, it was so cold in the station wagon, Clovis could see his breath. He woke up with a crick in his neck and lines from the leather seat creased across his face. It was worse than waking up on the wrong side of the bed. He was waking up without any bed at all.

He would not spend another night like this. Something had to be done about Ryan today. He had been telling himself that he was waiting for the perfect moment, the ideal situation to do away with Ryan. But when he was honest with himself, he knew that wasn't the truth. He knew he hadn't done anything because he was scared.

He'd never broken any laws, never stolen a thing, cheated, lied, or hurt anyone else. But today he would hurt Ryan for the greater good. It was as his mother always told him, "We live by God's laws, not man's laws."

And the simple fact was, Ryan was bad for Bartlesville, bad for this country, and bad for Christians. He'd always thought so, but when Pastor Mark said, "Ryan is teaching heresy," Clovis knew what he had to do. We live in a world where marriage is distorted and life is not sacred. We live in a world where Jesus could come back at any moment.

And pastors like Ryan Fisher just focus on marshmallow feel-good nonsense. Finding your inner happiness, being kind and friendly, Ryan's sermons had as much nutrition as a bag of gummy bears.

This has to stop. We are soldiers. We must fight for righteousness, Clovis thought.

Pastor Ryan's death would be a wakeup call to passive Christians everywhere.

Clovis wasn't scared anymore. And for the second time in as many months, Ryan Fisher woke up to discover a strange man hovering over his bed.

Wonder what this dream is going to be about, Ryan thought.

And as Ryan waited for something to happen, he suddenly felt very afraid of the beady eyes glaring at him through the coke-bottle glasses. In this dream there were no Halloween costumes, no heaven and no hell, the only thing unusual at all was that this man was holding a sawed off shotgun. And in the moments before the stranger lifted the shotgun and bashed the butt of it against Ryan's face, Ryan couldn't help but think, maybe this isn't a dream at all.

Maybe this is really happening.

Katherine was already stressed out about the long day that stretched out before her, stressed out that she had to take so many counseling appointments, stressed out that later this afternoon she would have to explain where Ryan was to all of the deacons and elders.

Then there was no more time to be stressed out because her first appointment arrived: a couple named Miles and Paige White. And after Katherine asked what she could do for them, she sat back and listened as they told her their story.

Miles and Paige always knew that they wanted to have kids—six of them to be exact. They even had names that they joked about: Zack, Kelly, Slater, Jessie, Lisa, and Screech. They planned to start trying as soon as they were married. They assumed they'd get pregnant right away.

Two years after they were married, no kids.

They went to a fertility doctor and were willing to try anything: drugs, in vitro, surrogate mother, yoga, whatever it took. And they tried everything they could.

Two more years passed; still no kids.

Then they realized why they hadn't been able to get pregnant. God had something greater, something much more rewarding in store for them: adoption. They would find a mother who was unable to afford the emotional and financial price it took to raise a child. They would raise and love this baby as if he were their own, maybe even more because they'd know what a gift he would be.

Jodi King, mother to be, had interviewed countless couples but she instantly fell in love with the Whites. She felt so comfortable with the Whites that she invited Paige to be in the delivery room. And Paige stood by Jodi's side, and they both cried as she gave birth to that little baby boy.

A day and a half later the Whites took the baby home, and they named him Isaac because they felt like Abraham and Sarah, the couple that no one else thought could have a child. No one except God. That night Isaac slept in bed with them, and Paige thought the sound of his little lungs breathing was the most miraculous thing she'd ever heard.

But it all fell apart the next morning. The adoption agent appeared at the Whites' door and told them, "I have to take Isaac back. Jodi's changed her mind."

"She can't do that, can she?" Paige asked.

"She has seventy-two hours to change her mind with no

questions asked. But she's probably just a little emotional. I'm going to make sure this is what she really wants to do," the agent said right before she left with Isaac.

"God's testing us," Miles said. "Just like Abraham had to be willing to sacrifice Isaac, we have to be willing to give up our little baby for the moment, and God will return him. You just wait and see." And they did wait. But two years later, they still hadn't heard from Jodi or seen their little baby Isaac.

Katherine was sure you're not supposed to cry during counseling appointments, but she couldn't help herself.

"We actually stopped going to church after all of that happened. But your church has renewed our faith. Still, we want to know why God won't give us something we want so much. What have we done wrong?"

Katherine sat across from them and didn't say a word.

It was dried blood.

That had to be the substance all over his shirt. Ryan didn't know how long he'd been out. All he knew was that he was tied to a wooden kitchen chair and there was a man he'd never met with a double-barreled shotgun pressed against his cheek.

Ryan wasn't sure if this man was going to say something, or if he'd just pull the trigger and take his life. He wasn't going to wait to find out.

"I think you have the wrong guy," Ryan said.

"I know *exactly* who you are, Pastor Fisher," the man said.

"And who am I?"

"You are Prozac. You are the drug that dulls the pain, the person who dopes up Christians so they can smile and nod, so they can ignore the real problems our country has."

"Wow, you really *do* know me," Ryan said. Charm would get

him nowhere; the man didn't even grin. But Ryan thought he should keep this man talking so he could figure out exactly what was going on. He asked, "What's your name?"

"Clovis."

Ryan looked at his kidnapper in his dingy white button-up shirt, with his patchy beard and fluffy hair. Ryan couldn't quite decide if Clovis was intimidating or cuddly looking. "What do you want from me, Clovis?"

"I want to help you. I'm going to make an example out of you. Your death will ignite the godly warriors of this country."

"My death?"

"Will be the great wakeup call of our generation!"

"Okay, Clovis, I don't really know if you've thought this through."

"I've done nothing but think about this. You are an example of everything wrong with the church. You manipulate people into feeling good about sitting idly by while two guys named Tom can get married, while old people and babies can be disposed of when they get inconvenient, and while everyone is satisfied with just *watching Extreme Home Makeover* instead of actually getting out there and helping people."

"And my death will stop this?"

"It will help."

Ryan's cell phone rang. It was a happy chime and felt highly inappropriate for the moment.

"Are you going to answer it?"

"My hands are kind of tied here, Clovis."

Clovis read the name off the cell phone's screen, "It's Sally."

"That's my secretary."

"What does she want?"

"I don't read minds, Clovis."

"I'm putting it on speaker phone," Clovis said. "But if you even *hint* at what's going on, this will be the last conversation you ever have."

"Good to know," Ryan said.

"Hello, Ryan!" Sally said.

"Yeah."

"I've been trying to get a hold of you all morning."

"I'm here now. What is it?"

"Oprah called," Sally said.

"I'm assuming that you don't mean the billionaire with her own talk show, magazine, and book club."

"Yeah, no. That's the one. Not her, but someone from her show. They want to have you on the show with a panel of different spiritual leaders. They're going to be discussing miracles."

"Miracles?"

"Yeah, like, do they really happen, and have you ever seen them. The producer described it as a 'town meeting' sort of episode."

"When do they want me?" Ryan asked.

"Well, that's just the thing. Rick Warren fell through, and they saw you on *Good Morning America*. They need you by tomorrow."

"Tell them I'll be there. Book me a flight; make all the arrangements. I'll call soon."

"Yes sir," Sally said and hung up.

Ryan was going to be on *Oprah*. He couldn't believe it. She was his hero, the person that he modeled his services after, and she called him. She wanted him on her show. How many pastors get to be on *Oprah*? Surely, this would catapult him into being one of the most influential, powerful ministers in the country.

Clovis did not seem as happy as Ryan did. "How are you planning on being there?" Clovis asked. "You're never going anywhere again."

Ryan's mind was racing. Some psychopath was not going to keep him from this career-making opportunity. A weaker pastor might let that happen, but not Ryan. There had to be a way to get on *Oprah*. What could he tell Clovis that would make him let him go?

There had to be something.

Think, Ryan.

And then he realized the perfect thing to tell Clovis: "Clovis, I'm going to be on *Oprah*. And you're coming with me."

"I'm what?"

"Think about it. It was God's perfect timing that Sally called when she did. You could kill me, but you know the American public. They could completely misunderstand the message. They could see me as a martyr; I could become the reason people *get passionate* about passive Christianity. I could be the poster child, the person who died to enable all Christians to sit idly by while America spirals toward darkness," Ryan said.

"Well, that might be true but—"

"But if you went on *Oprah*, you could say everything you want. You could give the battle cry for rising up against sin and evil on the most powerful television show in the world."

"You would let me do that?" Clovis asked.

"No, Clovis, I need you to do that," Ryan said.

Katherine's morning hadn't gotten any better.

After her appointment ended with the Whites, she was emotionally drained. But there wasn't time to be drained. Her next appointment involved a couple on the brink of divorce. He'd been cheating on her but felt "really sorry" and wanted to reconcile things. His wife wasn't sure she should, and she asked Katherine, "What do you think?" Katherine thought she should leave him right then and there, but she was somewhat sure the Bible was against divorce.

She told them, "You should go into marriage counseling."

They responded, "Isn't this marriage counseling?"

"Um, yes, it's a good start," Katherine said.

She spent the next hour trying to act like she knew what she was doing. She was so glad when they left.

Then her next appointment arrived. This one involved a man who'd been laid off six months ago, and he hadn't been able to land any real work since. Tomorrow his house was going into foreclosure. Katherine said a quick prayer and then wrote him a check for three thousand dollars from the church's account. She wasn't sure if this was allowed, or if Dean would get angry, but she didn't care. This man needed money.

The morning's final appointment involved concerned parents who told Katherine they were sure their daughter was having sex. Maybe even using drugs. They'd talked to their daughter about it, but she wouldn't even listen. "She's going to really hurt herself," her father said through deep heavy tears. "What can I do?" he asked.

Katherine replied, "Bring her in. Maybe we can talk to her."

They thanked Katherine and left, but they would come back, and they wanted someone qualified to talk with them. There's no one qualified here, she thought.

Katherine looked at Ryan's schedule. He had lunch with the deacons and then his afternoon was packed with more appointments. His next was with someone named Tina Monroe. Katherine punched the button on the intercom and asked, "Sally, who's Tina Monroe?"

"I'm not sure, but I think she just found out she has breast cancer."

"Wow," Katherine said.

"Did you hear Pastor Ryan's going on *Oprah*?"

"What?" Katherine said.

"Yeah, he's going to participate in a debate about miracles."

And that's when Katherine realized this had to stop. Ryan had no right to be telling people about miracles. Let alone should he be lecturing all of America on the subject. Even worse were all of these people's serious problems. Katherine had assumed everyone would just love God and be happy. But there were problems, lots of them, and they weren't coming to church to hear Ryan's great stories, or how great Cowboy Jack sang, or even to watch really touching *Oprah* segments.

They were coming to find God.

There was no way Ryan could ever show God to anyone. He didn't believe in God, and even if Ryan somehow decided to start believing in God, he certainly didn't understand him. At least not well enough to teach people how to follow him. Katherine suddenly had a new admiration

(you mean fear)

for how brilliant her husband was: He'd taken every step just right, played every card perfectly, and that's why this church had ballooned like it did. But she also suddenly realized that watching The People's Church sail along was like watching *Titanic*: it wasn't a question of *if* the ship would sink — it was only a question of *when*.

It was all so clear now why things would unravel: They had never gone to church, Ryan wasn't a pastor, he'd invented his mentor and their home church, he'd acted like he could heal people of cancer, he didn't know or understand the Bible, he passionately stood in front of thousands of people every Sunday and preached about a God that he didn't even believe in, and tomorrow he was going on *Oprah* to be the voice of Christianity in America.

Maybe the iceberg was closer than she thought.

It was her fault as much as Ryan's. Ever since that night at Bible study when she'd watched Kevin and Jennifer help the couple in trouble, Katherine knew what she wanted to do. She wanted to be a hero. She wanted to be grand and important, just like Jennifer Anderson or Coen Jackson. She'd been completely selfish, and she was affecting and manipulating thousands of lives, people who loved and trusted her. And she wasn't going to do it anymore.

She started to cry, and she asked out loud for God's forgiveness. "I'm so sorry," she said. "I just don't understand why you would let us do this. Why didn't you stop us? Because if you're not in control and we are, then God help us." She blushed. "You know what I mean.

"Please show me the way for Ryan and me to get out of this. Please tell me what to do next," she said.

But before she had time to sit and listen to Jesus' suggestions, Katherine ran off to the bathroom and threw up her breakfast, because she was so sick and troubled about all she'd gone through this morning.

24

Mott's Tomato Juice

"Now boarding flight 481, Oklahoma City to Chicago," the clerk at the United Airlines desk said.

"Come on, Clovis, let's go," Ryan said.

"Yes sir," Clovis said as he picked up his bags and followed Ryan through the gate.

Ryan wasn't sure exactly where or how he was going to ditch Clovis. He knew he had to take him to Chicago for a couple of reasons. One, it would have been hard to ditch him before the airport because on the ride from Emerald Lake to the OKC airport, Clovis had his shotgun nearby and threatened Ryan with it the whole ride. "If you go back on your word, Pastor Fisher, and I do not get on *Oprah*, it will not be pretty for you."

But Clovis had to leave his shotgun in the car because he and Ryan agreed it'd be a bad idea to try to check the shotgun. Clovis even recommended at one point that they just make the drive up to Chicago. He reasoned that it wasn't that much farther, but Ryan convinced Clovis there just wasn't time. "You'll just have to trust me," Ryan said. Once Clovis got into the airport and didn't have his shotgun, he seemed weak, timid, and scared. He even seemed likeable, or at least pathetic.

But being threatened on the drive up wasn't the only reason Ryan was taking Clovis with him. He could have probably ditched him in the airport if he'd really wanted to. Still, Ryan wanted to get Clovis to Chicago because of Katherine. If Clovis could find Ryan at a secluded cabin by the lake, couldn't he much more easily find their address, break into their house, and threaten *Katherine* with a shotgun?

Ryan couldn't stand the thought of that. He would get Clovis to Chicago, far away from Katherine, and then turn him in to the authorities. Maybe Katherine would never have to know what happened. Either way, from now on Ryan decided he would significantly upgrade the security at his house. Maybe he'd even hire some bodyguards.

"I can't believe we're really going to be on *Oprah*," Clovis said.

"Yeah, neither can I," Ryan said as he and Clovis walked through the gate and boarded the plane.

Clovis was asleep on Ryan's shoulder twenty minutes after the plane departed. Ryan couldn't believe when he arrived at the airport that Sally had booked them in coach; he tried to change the reservation but there was no room in first class. This trip is getting worse by the minute, he thought. So he sat in coach, surrounded by the sounds of the plane gliding through the air and Clovis's snoring.

Finally the trip was broken up when the stewardess came by with the beverage cart and asked, "What would you like to drink, sir?"

"Mott's Tomato Juice on ice," Ryan answered. Ryan hated tomato juice, hated to drink it, smell it, and he hated how it looked. But at thirty thousand feet above sea level, tomato juice was some sort of elixir. He'd watched someone next to him order it once, and it always looked weird and gross before—ordering tomato juice on ice made as much sense as ordering spaghetti sauce on the rocks—but for some reason Ryan felt compelled to try it. One drink was all it took. Now he never flew without drinking it—he always got a little sick and felt a little green after takeoff, and tomato juice helped. It wasn't that he was scared of the plane crashing necessarily, but the turbulence and rattling and motion all seemed a little much—it made Ryan worry that the airplane might just break apart. He felt the same way when he rode the Zipper at one of those carnivals that was just passing through town. Ryan would think, this ride wasn't even here yesterday, and some minimum wage mechanic just set it up today. What if he didn't screw something in right, what if this box that I'm soaring around in just flies off the track?

For drinking tomato juice squelched all of the fears of carnival rides and unstable airplanes. But as he took his first swig of tomato juice, he looked over to see Clovis smiling and staring right at him.

"You like Mott's Tomato Juice too?" Clovis asked.

"Yeah."

"Stewardess, make that two tomato juices. And give us an extra can."

"Okay," the stewardess said.

"I thought I was the only one who liked this stuff," Clovis said. Then he drank the entire plastic glass of tomato juice in one gulp. "It's good to know someone else likes this as much as I do. I knew there had to be other folks that drank tomato juice, otherwise the good people at Mott's wouldn't keep producing it. But I didn't know who it was, until now." Clovis drank another full glass.

"Yeah, I guess we have something in common," Ryan said.

"Seems like we have a lot in common. We both go to church, we're both Christians, we're both going to be on *Oprah*, and most importantly, we both like tomato juice. It's almost like we're friends," Clovis said.

We're both going to be on *Oprah*, Ryan thought.

He looked at Clovis and began to realize he had no idea what he was going to say on America's most important talk show. He knew nothing about miracles, he'd never seen one, never even heard of one—as far as Ryan was concerned they were all fabricated. Problem was, he was supposed to be making a case *for* miracles. And if he said the wrong thing on *Oprah*, it wouldn't catapult his career—it would obliterate it. Saying the wrong thing would make Ryan as obsolete as a tape deck.

Then Ryan began to think that maybe he was looking at this the wrong way. The question wasn't: What miracles are Christians are interested in? Rather, the important question was: What miracles is *Oprah* interested in? You do those miracles every Sunday, Ryan thought. Those miracles involved changes of the heart, involved taking a broken person and making them whole.

And who was more broken than Clovis Whitman?

Ryan and Clovis were in the greenroom sitting on a plush couch and staring at a fruit basket. They were completely silent and unsure of what to say. Clovis couldn't believe how fresh the fruit looked or how comfortable the couch was. It was easily the most comfortable couch he'd ever sat on. But he didn't feel comfortable. He was moments away from going on national television and telling Oprah Winfrey everything that was wrong with America.

Do people still call her Oprah Winfrey, or has she moved into the Cher and Madonna category? Maybe I should call her Ms. Winfrey, Clovis thought. He'd never seen an episode. He didn't know the appropriate way to act.

And even though he was about to tell every soul watching

that America was the most despicable nation on the planet (his plan was to walk on the show, interrupt whatever nonsense talk was going on, and proclaim that the only "miracle" God is going to perform is turning America into a third-world country. God'll bring famine, drought, and He'll rain down frogs and fire and brimstone if things don't change immediately) he still didn't want to be the disrespectful guest who was calling Oprah by the wrong name.

A production assistant, wearing black and holding a clipboard, burst into the room. "You're on in five, Pastor Fisher."

"Thank you," Ryan said as she left.

Earlier Ryan told Clovis his plan: "I'll go on the show first. We'll probably talk about miracles for a while, but then I'll tell Oprah I have someone she has to meet, someone who really understands miracles. And that's when you come on the show and tell America all about how it's going to hell in a hand basket. Is that good?"

"It's perfect," Clovis said.

But as Ryan was about to go on the show, fear began rise in Clovis's belly. *There's no way he's really going to do that. He's the enemy, the problem with this country that needs to be annihilated. How did you let him trick you into this? What makes you think you can trust him? Do something.*

But he didn't know what to do. All he knew was that you do not just surprise Oprah. Not on her own show. Clovis had come all this way for nothing. "You're not going to let me say what I've come here to say. Are you?"

"Of course I am," Ryan said, seeming shocked Clovis even brought it up.

"You're just going to go on the show, and after it's over you'll tell me there was never a right moment, that you never had the chance to bring me on. You're a snake-oil salesman."

"Where is this coming from, Clovis? Are we not minutes away from being on the *Oprah* show? Have I not done everything that I promised so far?"

"So you put me on a plane and took me to Chicago. Big whoop."

"If I didn't have a use for you, I wouldn't have brought you all this way. I would have told authorities how you assaulted me and kidnapped me yesterday. But I didn't because I believe in your message."

"You do?" Clovis said, like a child who'd just been validated.

The production assistant was back. She'd been in their room six times since they'd arrived and she always seemed incredibly frazzled. She must have the worst job in America, Clovis thought. Then Oprah herself appeared.

Oprah looked different in person. Ryan couldn't explain how exactly, but different. Still, she was powerful. Ryan was sure she was the most confident person he would ever meet.

"Hello Pastor Fisher. Thanks for coming," Oprah said.

"It's my pleasure. I really admire all the work you do," Ryan said.

"What happened to your eye?" Oprah asked.

Ryan touched the part of his face that Clovis had bashed with a shotgun. "Oh, it's nothing."

"Beth, see if makeup can do anything about that," Oprah said.

"Yes, Oprah," Beth said.

"All right, well, let's have a good show," Oprah said.

"I guarantee it," Ryan said as Oprah left.

"Come on, let's get you to makeup," Beth said.

"Sure thing." Ryan followed her, and as he shut the door he grinned and told Clovis, "See you in a couple of minutes."

25

THE MIRACLES
HE WILL PERFORM

"Are miracles real?" Oprah asked, looking into the camera. "We've all heard stories, myths, and urban legends about sight returning to the blind, the crippled walking, and the dead being raised. But are these just nice stories, or do they actually happen? We're going to find out on today's *Oprah*."

The lights went off Oprah, and the monitors showed a video segment chronicling three miraculous stories. The first involved a Tanzanian girl who'd been born with AIDS. Her case was hopeless; she had three years to live. The tribe's witch doctor wasn't a believer in Western medicine so he spread goat's blood all around her, prayed, danced, and instructed the whole village not to eat for three days. When her mother took her back to the clinic, the doctors couldn't find a trace of AIDS in her body.

Then there was a man in Iowa whose body had been ravaged by cancer. The doctors gave him six weeks to live. He flew down to Florida, went to a Christian revival meeting, and walked out completely healthy. His doctors were dumbfounded. "There is no *medical* explanation," they said.

Most amazing was the story of a woman in Mexico who died during childbirth. Three days later many of her family and friends came to pay their respects. As the priest closed the service, he asked for God to be with her, and she promptly rose from her coffin like a vampire coming to life. The woman seemed perfectly fine. She even drove herself home from the funeral.

"There are stories of miracles all over the world," Oprah's voice said as images of the African girl, Mexican woman, and the man from Iowa played on the monitors. "But are the stories real or myth? Do miracles actually happen or is this just some elaborate hoax?"

Lights faded up and the studio audience applauded.

"I'd like you to meet the distinguished panel that we have assembled to talk about miracles. We'll start with Pastor Jesse Lyle from the Church of Fire in Kentucky. Pastor Jesse's church is known for its charismatic revival meetings, complete with miraculous healings. The church claims to have documented over a thousand cases of healings.

"Next is Rabbi Jacob Davis from Los Angeles. Rabbi Davis is a noted scholar on the miraculous acts in the Old Testament. Also we have Jibril Najiar, founder of the Rainbow Muslims.* Then we have Naomi Fitzgerald, author of *The Religion Myth*. It's sold over a million copies and has sparked a national controversy. And finally, Pastor Ryan Fisher of The People's Church in Bartlesville, Oklahoma — *Good Morning America* has dubbed it America's largest small-town church."

The audience greeted all the guests with warm applause. Oprah seemed to know and like the guests; therefore they liked the guests.

---

*Jibril's sect is an offshoot of Islam, and his followers still study the teachings of the Koran, observe Ramadan, and follow the truths of Mohammed, but they do so without participating in Jihad or warfare. Jibril is a media darling. Still, most other Islamic leaders consider all Rainbow Muslims to be outcasts and heretics.

"So, let's get to it. What do you think when you see these stories?" Oprah asked.

"I think that they show the goodness of God," Pastor Jesse said.

"I think they are nice stories," Naomi added.

Ryan was happy, so far so good. He was scared that things might get intense with a firecracker subject like this, but thus far things were very civil. Everyone knew how to act—this wasn't *Jerry Springer* or some other daytime garbage—this was *Oprah*, the most important daytime television show in history.

Then Naomi said, "But that's all these are, Oprah—stories. Fairytales."

"Fairytales? Isn't that a little harsh?" Oprah asked. "What do you guys think? Are these just nice stories?"

"Absolutely not, Oprah. There are reports of miracles all over the world. There are documented cases," Pastor Jesse said.

"I've never seen a miracle. I've never seen a leg grow back into place, or someone rise from the dead. Have any you seen something like this?" Naomi asked the studio audience. A few people shook their heads no, one guy said yes, but most didn't move; they weren't sure if this was a rhetorical question or not.

"You know, that's interesting, Naomi, the closest thing to a miracle I've seen here in America is when they invented chocolate that actually helps you *lose* weight." Oprah paused as the audience belly laughed. "But honestly, as our team here has been researching miracles, it seems that most stories come from overseas. Why is that?" Oprah asked.

"Because our country is so godless. We have women in underwear on every billboard and drugs flow in the hallways of our schools," Jibril said.

"Then why doesn't God come and save this country?" Naomi asked.

"That's not his job," Jibril said.

"Or maybe it's because he can't any more than Santa Claus can deliver presents."

"I have to ask, Naomi, why so antagonistic toward religion?" Oprah asked.

"Because it's something politicians and clergymen have created to wage wars and brainwash their followers into submission."

"You have this all wrong," Jibril said.

"Really?"

"Yes, really. It is not our place to question Allah. Who are we to question him and the miracles he chooses to perform? He can do whatever he wants. He can rule however he wants. He owes us nothing," Jibril said.

"But why won't he just show himself? Prove once and for all that he's out there. He'd shut me up. See Oprah, I'd like to believe in miracles, but there's never any proof. I can't believe a person who claims to have seen a miracle any more than I can believe someone who's claimed to have seen Bigfoot or insists they've been abducted by aliens," Naomi said.

Oprah laughed. "God and Bigfoot are the same thing?"

"Lots of people claim to have seen Bigfoot. That doesn't mean he's really out there," Naomi said.

"This is such a skeptical and selfish line of thinking. It's so Western. We wait for God to find us, as if he should be seeking us out. That makes as much sense as a dog asking for his master to prove his worth," Jibril said.

"What do you think, Rabbi?" Oprah asked.

"My people have experienced many miracles. We have seen God part the Red Sea, he gave us quail and manna in the desert, and he caused the walls of Jericho to fall. But there is a problem with miracles. Sometimes we get so busy looking for them that we forget to look for the God who made them all possible," Rabbi Davis said.

"But Rabbi, God does use miracles to show us his faithfulness. I've seen many of them at my own church," Pastor Jesse said.

"Have you ever performed a miracle?" Oprah asked.

"Yes, I have."

The audience began to murmur.

"Well I'd love to see one," Naomi said.

"I can't just snap my fingers and perform. This isn't the circus," Jesse said.

"See, this is where the whole thing unravels. There can be miracles in remote mountains or church meetings packed with people who want to believe, but whenever it comes down to it, the religious person can never do a miracle in the plain light of day—they are as powerless as Oz without his curtain," Naomi said.

"I'll do a miracle right now!" Ryan blurted. "Right here in front of everyone, on the most popular talk show in America."

His whole sentence came out a little awkward; he was clearly the unknown man from small-town Oklahoma in this bunch. Everyone else here had been giving these arguments on *The O'Reilly Factor*, *Larry King*, and *Meet the Press* for years, but Ryan was the newbie and didn't quite understand how these arguments were supposed to work.

"You'll perform a miracle?" Oprah asked.

"Yes, right now. It should only take a minute or two. But I don't know if we have time to spare."

Silence.

All of the guests and panelists looked shocked, but Oprah smiled from ear to ear. This was great television. No one expected this timid pastor from Oklahoma to make such a bold claim. It seemed like a long time before anyone said a word. And then, finally, Oprah said, "We'll make time, Pastor Fisher." She looked into the camera, "So don't go anywhere, we may have daytime television's first-ever miracle when we come back."

The audience clapped and the show cut to a commercial break.

Clovis snacked on a pear in the greenroom. It was the juiciest pear he'd ever eaten, tasty as if it had been plucked off the Tree of the Knowledge of Good and Evil itself. Ryan and the others with Oprah were being shown on a monitor, but Clovis was too nervous to watch. Instead he turned the sound down, wiped the pear juice off his chin, and thought about how confusing Pastor Ryan's behavior was.

Ryan was unlike any pastor Clovis had ever known. And Clovis had been close to lots of pastors before. Thirty-six to be precise. He'd been on the leadership teams of churches all across the country.

And it always turned out the same way.

Initially, the pastor and church leadership team loved him. He'd come in willing to do anything; he was a workhorse. He'd set up for meetings, clean bathrooms, make phone calls, run errands, copy, cut, and paste any paperwork that needed it. Everyone was so grateful to have him around.

Then the pastor would smile, put his arm around Clovis, and tell him, "We are so lucky to have someone like you." That meant the world to Clovis. Especially after his mother died, the only validation Clovis got was from church leaders. But soon Clovis would notice that the pastor invited other people over to his house for dinner, other people would be treated like the pastor's friend, while Clovis always felt like an employee.

Clovis would ask the pastor why he never got invited over, and the pastor would say something like, "We work for God's love. Not for man's acceptance." Whatever that meant.

This made Clovis furious. He'd tell the pastor, "I have given so much to this church and this is how you treat me? I'm not your friend, am I? I'm just free labor!"

And after a few conversations like this, the pastor usually responded by saying, "Maybe it would be best if you attended a different church."

Pastor Ryan was different. Clovis had assaulted him with a shotgun, tied him up, and threatened to murder him. And how did Ryan react? By taking him to Chicago to be on the *Oprah Winfrey Show*.

It had been the most exciting day and a half of his life. On the plane ride they joked around, told stories, and Clovis learned that Ryan also adored Mott's Tomato Juice.

They were like Bert and Ernie.

Clovis took the final bite of the pear, and it was now picked clean with only the core left. He threw it into the garbage and smiled because he realized Pastor Ryan was his friend, and probably the best one he'd ever had.

Then the frizzy-haired girl in black was in the room again. She looked at Clovis and said, "Oprah wants you on stage in thirty seconds."

"What's going on here?" Rabbi Davis asked.

"He's going to do a miracle?" Naomi said. "This wasn't in the rundown."

"I'm as shocked as you all are. I was not expecting this, and very little that I don't expect happens on *my* show. The last person to surprise me was Tom Cruise, and we all know what happened to him," Oprah said. She added, "Now, I'm a little curious what Pastor Fisher has up his sleeve. So why don't you let us in on the secret."

"I can't," Ryan said. "You just have to let me perform this miracle."

"She doesn't have to let you do anything," Pastor Jesse said.

"Listen, this is my reputation, my career on the line. You all have nothing to do with it. With God's help, I'm going to perform a miracle, and somehow if it doesn't work, then I look like an idiot. My career and reputation could be destroyed, while everyone else walks home with a great story. Or a great TV show. All I'm asking for is a chance," Ryan said.

Oprah smiled, laughed, and grabbed Ryan's wrist. "How can I say no to that? I love this man. I think we have a lot in common."

"So do I," Ryan said. He then motioned to the girl with frazzled hair and asked her to get Clovis ready.

Ryan and Oprah talked while the crew got ready to come back from the commercial break. Cameras whipped around, boom mics hovered into place, the host got the studio audience clapping, and the floor director counted down, "Five, four, three —"

"We're back with our panel of religious leaders and today we're talking about miracles. Now, right before our last break, Pastor Fisher made quite a bold claim." Oprah turned to Ryan. They were sitting side by side now, while all the other guests were in the background, as if they'd been demoted because of their inability to perform miracles.

"Are you sure about this, Pastor Fisher?" Oprah said.

"Positive. And just call me Pastor Ryan. Okay, the first thing I need to do is call out a guest."

"By all means," Oprah said.

"Clovis Whitman. Can you come out here?"

The audience clapped, but it was clearly the least enthusiastic clap of the whole show. Clovis looked confused as a caveman under the hot lights. He sort of wandered in a figure eight with head swiveling like a scared puppy as he stared at the mics, cameras, and studio audience. And when he got to his seat, he forgot to sit. He just stood with his back to the audience, hovering over Ryan and Oprah.

"You can sit down," Oprah said.

Ryan was extremely nervous. He was crazy for bringing Clovis out here. But it was too late to back down now. "Clovis, why don't you tell everyone what you came to say?"

Clovis cleared his throat. "America is turning into a modern-day Sodom and Gomorrah. If things don't change, God will rain fire and brimstone down on everyone."

"Why is that?"

"Do you know the story of Sodom and Gomorrah, Pastor Ryan?"

"I do," Ryan said, even though he always thought Sodom and Gomorrah were from a Greek myth, "but I'm not sure if all of our viewers do."

"Abraham asked God to spare the city. And God said, 'Give me 50 righteous men.' Abraham said, 'I'll find 10.' But Abraham couldn't do it! And God had no choice but to destroy the city, to rain meteors from heaven and burn it to the ground."

"What does that have to do with anything?" Ryan asked.

"It's what's happening in our country! There are no righteous men left. I agree with my Christian brother over there who said this is a godless country!"

In thirty seconds Clovis had done what Naomi the atheist couldn't; he'd rattled Jibril, the cool, friendly Muslim.

"Oprah, really, is this going someplace?" Jibril asked.

"I hope so. We better see a miracle pretty quick here, Pastor Ryan," Oprah said.

"You will. Go on, Clovis."

"What I was saying is we have a country where everything is

permissible. We have a country where our politicians and pastors enable sin and debauchery because they don't want to rock the boat! Because they want to be kind and friendly and politically correct!"

"Oprah, earlier you asked what happened to my face. Ask Clovis," Ryan said.

"Clovis, what happened?" Oprah asked.

"I bashed Pastor Ryan's face with a shotgun."

"You what?!" Oprah said. "Pastor Ryan, I think—"

Ryan wouldn't let her stop Clovis. He was just starting to get somewhere. "Why did you bash my face?"

"Because I was going to murder you."

The audience gasped and murmured.

"And you were going to murder me because—"

"Because you were unrighteous, and you were leading your church to be kind and friendly instead of being righteous and set apart. You were part of the problem."

"I *was* part of the problem, or I *am* part of the problem?"

"You *was*. I mean, you *were*. You *are*." And then Clovis said, "I'm not exactly sure anymore."

"You seemed to know when you were trying to kill me yesterday. What's changed since then?" Ryan asked.

"Since then, you've treated me like we were friends. Are we friends, Pastor Ryan?"

"You don't have a lot of friends, do you, Clovis?"

"Not a lot of close ones. No."

"Why not?"

"People just use me for what they can get from me."

"Have you ever stopped to think, Clovis, maybe that's why you're so angry?"

"I don't—"

"Haven't you wanted to feel happy, safe, and loved?"

"Sure, I guess, but—"

"Maybe you wouldn't say the stuff that you're saying, maybe you wouldn't think America's such a dark place if someone in this country had treated you better. But no one ever has. I want to be your friend Clovis. And I think a lot of folks at The People's Church want to be your friend too."

"This isn't just about friends."

"What's it about?"

"Change. America needs to change."

"What's the best way to cause this country to change?"

"It's, um—"

"Is it to spew out this hate? Do you really think that helps?"

A few in the audience applauded.

"Clovis, maybe you're so angry with this country, with all of us, because you've been mistreated and abused," Ryan said.

"It's not that simple—"

"I mean, if people had treated me the way you've been treated, I'd want to bash someone's face in too. I'd want God to rain fire and brimstone on everyone to get them back."

"Pastor Ryan, that's not the only reason—"

"Maybe if people treated you like a friend, you wouldn't be acting this way. Maybe you'd rather see the world changed by loving your neighbor as yourself, rather than through famine and drought."

Clovis paused. "You might be right. I ... I don't want to see people suffer, Pastor Ryan, I really don't. I just want to see goodness and righteousness in this country again."

Ryan grabbed Clovis's hand. "I think we all want to see goodness in this country again."

"What is this Tony Robbins crap? I thought you said that you were doing a miracle!" Naomi sneered.

"I am. It's not a miracle that's going to happen overnight. But it's starting today right in front of your eyes."

"Oh, please," Naomi said. But Ryan could tell that the studio audience was starting to believe.

"Oprah, you wanted to know if I believe in miracles. And the answer is yes, I do. Sometimes God does miracles by healing bodies or raising the dead. I've never done miracles like those, and I'm not about to start acting like some televangelist who pretends like he can. You see, I don't think those are the really important miracles, because what God is most interested in is the heart. Think about it everybody. What good would it do for someone to be healed from cancer if their heart was still filled with hate and bigotry? Why cure someone of a disease if their soul is corrupt with deception? Should people feel better, live better, be cured? Absolutely. But the healing starts right here," Ryan said pointing to his heart. Tissues were popping up everywhere. Ryan was getting to them.

"You see, if we could really change hearts, we could start putting an end to bigotry and violence toward one another. Imagine a country where no one was judged, where husbands didn't abuse their wives, where people didn't lie and cheat one another. Imagine a country where we felt safe dropping our kids off at school. Wouldn't that be miraculous?" Ryan shouted.

The audience gave Ryan huge applause — and the applause sign wasn't even lit.

"Those are the types of miracles God wants me to perform! Those are the types of miracles I *will* perform!" Ryan proclaimed, as if he were William Wallace.

But it was hard to hear him. The audience was cheering too loudly.

Katherine sat curled up on the floor of her bathroom, in her purple robe, with mascara all over her face. It was a positive sign on all three tests. And they were three different kinds of tests from the most generic to the most costly. She even had Cammy Miller buy the tests, because Katherine felt that if she bought them herself it could cause a string of unwanted gossip. All three times she took the tests they gave a check mark or a plus sign or a smiley face, which all meant the same thing.

She didn't know how this was possible. She and Ryan hadn't been trying, they hadn't even thought about having kids since the church started. The People's Church was Ryan's baby

(and wife)

now. But she'd been feeling sick since yesterday afternoon and she was late. She expected to just take them so she could have peace of mind, so she could know for sure that she wasn't pregnant, that it was just the flu, and then she could down a shot of

Nyquil and take a nap. Instead, she was curled up in the corner of her bathroom, crying, alone, staring at these plastic sticks that unveiled a miracle.

She was going to be a mother.

But did she want to be a mother in the middle of all of this? In the middle of a church built on lies, in a flawed marriage, in the same town near the Cowboy with whom she'd had an affair? Did she want to bring her baby girl* into that?

"Katherine, honey, what's going on in there?" Cammy Miller said, knocking on the door.

Katherine grabbed all of the tests and jammed them into her pockets. She opened the door.

"Oh, sweetie, what is it? What did the tests say?"

"I'm not pregnant."

"It's okay, come here."

Cammy picked Katherine up and hugged her. It felt good to have such a kind friend comfort her. It gave her thoughts clarity. As soon as Ryan returned, things would change. He would realize that it had to stop, and he would do it, maybe not for her, but for little baby Julianna.† Pastor Dave would take over the church. And they would move away and start a new life. A real life.

God made me pregnant to free us from all of our horrible mistakes. This is our salvation. This baby is our miracle, like all of the miraculous babies in the Bible.

Then Katherine felt a cat curl up against her leg. But she didn't own a cat.

"Oh, sorry, that's Tangerine. She was running errands with me when you called. Maybe I should leave her with you until Ryan comes home. She could keep you company," Cammy said.

---

* She wasn't sure how, but she knew it was baby girl. It was some sort of sixth sense, like a psychic mother connection.
† She'd picked out a name too.

Katherine wiped tears from her eyes and mascara from her face. "Yeah, I'd like that."

Silence. And then, "Are you all right?"

"Yeah, I think we're going to be okay now," Katherine said.

RAPTURE

27

THE MAN
IN DOCKERS

The next day, the *Oprah* episode aired, much earlier than originally scheduled. Normally there is a week or two turnaround time,
but the producers decided the show had to air right away. That
afternoon, Ryan had hundreds of phone calls from media outlets
requesting that he come on their shows and perform "miracles of
the human heart." Ryan and Clovis did six interviews on Chicago
radio and television stations Friday. Everyone wanted a sound bite
from the miraculous duo.

By Saturday, Ryan had to take a day off from the press. It was
a long flight back. He was looking forward to spending time with
Katherine and relaxing. He was a hero now. He'd worked hard and
he deserved some time off.

Before Ryan went home, he took Clovis to his apartment near
the outskirts of east Bartlesville. Ryan stopped the car, popped the
trunk, and gave Clovis his knapsack. Ryan had no idea what was
in the knapsack because he'd never seen Clovis get anything out of
it — the only time Clovis had changed clothes in the last few days

was when he got into the outfit *The Oprah Winfrey Show* gave him. Clovis took the knapsack and the two stood staring at each other with only the sound of Ryan's car running breaking the silence.

"So, it's been interesting," Ryan said.

"It's been amazing, Pastor Ryan," Clovis said bubbling with enthusiasm. His eyes were glowing and his smile reached from one earlobe to the other. Clovis started to part his arms and Ryan knew what he was doing. He wanted to hug, but Ryan thought that seemed a little much. Ryan was glad it turned out okay, he wasn't going to press charges or anything, but he wasn't ready to call Clovis his best friend or start touring the nation with him. Clovis was just another man who'd helped Ryan out in his journey to the top. It was time to sever this relationship and move on to bigger things.

Ryan stuck out his hand. Clovis seemed a little hurt that there was no hug, but he shrugged it off, shook Ryan's hand, and smiled. "Thanks for everything, Pastor," Clovis said.

"See you around Clovis."

After Ryan dropped Clovis off, he headed home. It was good to be back in Bartlesville, but it looked different. Smaller. Maybe Ryan was getting too big for this town. Maybe he was ready to compete with the *real* churches now. It sure seemed like it on *Oprah*. He was the rookie and he still smoked everyone else there. He had talents and gifts that other people just didn't have. Few pastors in America had the gifts Ryan had. He understood that now. He understood how great he really was.

He walked up the steps feeling like a king. He'd step in the house and Katherine would wrap her arms around him. Then he'd see where things went from there.

But something was wrong. Clouds had been gathering all

day—Ryan had never seen clouds like this in Bartlesville. They looked like thick blankets dusted with charcoal and they covered the sky endlessly in every direction. And it was as Ryan looked up at the clouds, it was as he noticed them for the first time, that it started to rain. Just a few drops at first. But then it began to pour, flooding down from heaven.

Ryan ran inside, flung the door open, and saw Katherine sitting in the living room—with no lights on—methodically petting an orange colored cat. "Hello Ryan," Katherine said.

Ryan? Since when does she call me Ryan? And where did the cat come from? Ryan thought. I think she talked about buying a cat because I was going to be gone so much. Or maybe that's the neighbor's cat. I hope it's not ours. God, it's freaky looking, as if it just walked out of the pet sematary.

"Hey baby," Ryan smiled.

She wasn't happy to see him. There was no light on her face, but he didn't need light to see how she felt.

"Did you see *Oprah*?" Ryan asked.

"Of course," Katherine answered. "We need to talk."

"Okay," Ryan said.

What happened? he thought. A few days ago she's fine, and now she's sitting in the corner petting a cat like she's Dr. Evil.

Throughout their marriage this was how Katherine would initiate an argument. She would brood over things for days, weeks, months, and when she was finally ready bring it up she would react like a teakettle—it was as if she'd been holding onto the steam for so long that it came screaming out of her.

"We're going to get caught."

"Caught?"

"The church. Someone's going to find out about us."

"We haven't done anything wrong," Ryan said.

And then thunder cracked outside. It was just a coincidence.

Ryan was sure of it. Because, seriously, how lame would it be if thunder cracked because God was mad?

"We're lying to everyone."

"About?"

"We have no idea how to run a church."

"How can that be a crime? There are plenty of other pastors in America who have no idea how to run a church."

"We created a fake background for you."

"So a couple of angry ministers could feel better about me."

"You went on *Oprah*. You claimed to be the voice of Christianity for small town America."

"And?"

"And you're not even a Christian."

"But I'm what Christians need: I'm their new voice. And I can think so much more clearly than other pastors. I can be articulate and politically correct because I'm not encumbered by things like the Bible and Jesus. I'm making Christianity more palatable. Kabala, Buddhism, and Scientology all have A-list celebrities. Mormonism and Islam offer multiple wives and your own planet. What does Christianity have to offer? Its PR is horrible. And it's going to be obsolete pretty quick here if it doesn't have someone like me working for it."

"I'm leaving."

"You're leaving?"

"I'm going back to Denver. You should come with me."

"You're going to walk out on our church? Don't you care about them?"

"Of course I care about them. That's why I'm leaving."

"Okay, I'm really confused here, Katherine. What happened to you when I was gone?"

"I took your appointments. I had to talk to all of those people who were looking for help."

"And we're getting them help. That's the whole point of why were doing what we're doing."

"But they're not looking for *our* help Ryan. They're looking for God's help."

"What's the difference?"

"The difference is: you're not God!"

"I'm better than God. God can't help them. He just watches as they lose their homes and their marriages crumble. He doesn't do a thing while they destroy themselves. He just sits by with his arms crossed as they drink, gorge, and shoot chemicals into their veins. But I can actually help them. *I* can change their lives."

At that moment Ryan seemed less human than Katherine had ever seen him. His face was hollow and his eyes were clear. The last few months had stretched his soul so thin that it looked as if it were wax paper dipped in bacon grease.

It was suddenly clear to Katherine. The problem wasn't that he didn't *believe* in God. The problem was that he believed he *was* God. This was now the gospel according to Ryan Fisher. He was going to make Christianity whatever he thought it should be. And Katherine had been on his arm every step of the way, smiling and enabling him towards what he'd become.

Now he was unstoppable. Who knew what was next for The People's Church? Maybe Ryan would create franchises. The People's Church could be in every major city in the United States. What sort of acts of kindness could all of those churches pull off? Maybe they could pull their resources together to end hunger in Africa, rebuild New Orleans, cure cancer, and find a peaceful resolution to all of that senseless violence in the Middle East.

Or maybe things wouldn't turn out as well. Maybe Ryan would actually believe he was godlike and invincible. Maybe his delusion of grandeur would destroy Bartlesville. He could convince everyone to follow him to the afterlife, and like that, The People's

Church would end in a glorious battle with the FBI. There would be no survivors.

Anything was possible.

Katherine wasn't going to stick around to find out.

"I can't debate this with you anymore. You win every time. But you're wrong about this, Ryan. We have to stop. There are people who can take over the church—people who can help us. But we have to leave. This isn't right anymore."

And like that Katherine had created a fork in the road, and Ryan's life had once again become a Choose Your Own Adventure novel:

If you think Ryan should follow Katherine, turn to page 103.

Ryan would go back to Denver. He'd go back to being insignificant. No, worse than that: he would be a washup, a has-been, people would recognize him in restaurants and movie theaters and say, "Weren't you that famous pastor? Whatever happened to you?" Ryan Fisher would become Gary Coleman and Tonya Harding. He'd be yesterday's headline.

And the worst part: he would have to live his final forty years on planet earth knowing that his life had peaked, that things had become as good as they could possibly be. He'd have to wake up every morning knowing that from here on out, life was a downward spiral.

But then again, he'd have Katherine. She would love him with every ounce of her soul because of the decision he made. She would know what a sacrifice it was to leave The People's Church. She would know that he might not even agree with the decision, but he'd leave for her.

Part of him would be grateful. Part of him would realize that he really was in over his head. That things were bound to end badly—Clovis Whitman was only the beginning. Once you're that religiously famous, destruction is always around the corner.

He and Katherine would even realize some sort of great life lesson. Something like, "It's not what you do that's important, it's who you are." Or maybe, "A rotten apple spoils the bunch."

And they would have a greater and deeper love for one another. They would sail into the sunset, and sure, things would be tough at times, but every night they would drift asleep in each other's arms.

If you want Ryan to stay with the church, turn to page 106.

Ryan would tell Katherine, "I have built something here. You don't just walk out on something like this, that's insane."

"Ryan, I—"

"No, I'm done. I'm so sick of you doubting my every move. If you want to leave, fine. Maybe you don't have the nerve for this. Maybe it'd be best if you weren't a part of my church."

He would instantly regret his words as he watched them leap out of his mouth and smack Katherine across the face like a two-by-four.

She would be so hurt that she'd never even tell him what really brought on this conversation, the news she wanted so badly to share. But before she told him, she had to confront him about the church. She had realized she wanted him to make the right decision for her and for himself, and once he said the right things, the things he was *supposed* to say, she could tell him.

Her plan would have backfired. His words would sear her so badly that instead of telling her husband what she really wanted to, she would get into her car and speed off into the pouring rain.

And unfortunately, this is what actually happened.

As Katherine drove away Ryan screamed for her to come back. He begged her not to leave. He chased her down the road. She never slowed down, and one left turn later she was gone. Ryan stood in the middle of the road with the rain pounding against his face wondering if he'd really lost her.

He couldn't help but imagine what his life would look like if she were really gone. What would he tell everyone at church tomorrow morning? How was he going to cover this up? Pastors don't having failing marriages. How could The People's Church trust someone who can't even take care of his own marriage?

He'd just have to get through the morning. There had to be some sort of lie or spin or story he could tell everyone. By tomorrow afternoon Katherine would be back.

She's not really gone. She could never really leave me, Ryan thought.

And then, as if to prove his point, headlights reappeared. He knew it. She was sorry. She was turning around to ask for forgiveness. She wouldn't even say anything, she would just stop the car, jump out, and they would kiss passionately in the pouring rain.

Credits would roll and they would live happily ever after.

But oddly enough, it wasn't Katherine's Audi that pulled up in front of Ryan—it was an Acura with Colorado plates. The door opened, and Pastor Clark stepped out of the car and into the rain. He wasn't wearing a black cloak or holding a sickle; he was just wearing pleated khakis, a polo shirt, and his eyes were a dull brown. But Ryan still couldn't decide if he was actually standing there or if he was somehow imagining all of this.

"Hello, Ryan," Pastor Clark said.

Kind of a boring thing for an imaginary figure to say. So, Ryan came to the conclusion that this was all actually happening.

They sat in the living room. Ryan had changed his clothes and was towel-drying his hair. He'd made some Earl Grey and some sandwiches and Pastor Clark drank and ate as he talked.

"I saw you on *Oprah*."

"What'd you think?"

"I think you've lost your mind."

"That's a little harsh."

"It's the kindest I can put it. You were claiming to do miracles."

"You don't believe in miracles?"

"Nine months ago you were in my office telling me you'd just become a Christian."

"Is that what this is about? You're jealous? Pastor Clark, really, I thought you were above that."

"A few months ago you were asking me if God really healed people from cancer. And Jennifer Anderson told me that you started going to church fishing for real estate contacts. I checked around. Other people had the same story. This does not sound like the type of man who starts doing miracles," Pastor Clark said.

"God works in mysterious ways," Ryan said.

"Why are you doing this?" Pastor Clark asked.

"Doing what?"

"The church, *Oprah*, *Good Morning America*?"

"What do you want?"

"I want to help you," Pastor Clark said.

"I thought I was the only liar here."

"I can't let you invent a former life, a pastor, a church, and jump from talk show to talk show claiming to be the voice of Christianity. That would be irresponsible to say the least."

"Do you want money? Is that what you're after?" Ryan asked.

"Where's Katherine?"

"Don't do that. I hate it when people answer a question with a question."

"She's left, hasn't she?"

Ryan had to stop this line of questioning. There had to be something he could say. He was getting desperate. "I'll hire you to work with me, Pastor Clark. We can have the most influential church in the country. There's plenty of power to go around," Ryan said feeling a little like Darth Vader tempting Luke Skywalker. Who knew, maybe Pastor Clark would take Ryan up on his offer. Maybe Pastor Clark would realize Darth Vader had a point.

But all Pastor Clark said was, "I want to speak at your church first thing in the morning. We'll tell them you're taking a sabbatical effective immediately. Then, we'll figure out how to transition the church into different leadership."

It was quite the coincidence: Two people, very different, saying the same thing. Perhaps God himself was delivering a message. And for the second time in as many hours, Ryan Fisher was faced with a choice.

It was a choice he never got to make because that's when the phones began to ring. Almost instantaneously his cell phone and home phone rang. His BlackBerry blipped: he had eleven text messages in the last thirty seconds. And they all said something to the effect of:

Turn on CNN.

Ryan obeyed. He popped on the television. A reporter was standing in front of the Greasy Spork. Underneath her, a caption read, "Pastor Manipulates Oklahoma Town."

Ryan and Pastor Clark watched without making a sound as the reporter said, "—Pastor Joseph Sampson could not be contacted. But reports are now that Pastor Fisher's home church, The Lord's Church, does not exist, and some reports go as far as to claim that Ryan Fisher fabricated his home church and his pastor—creating a false website and phone number—to give himself credibility."

Clips of Ryan and Clovis on *Oprah* played as the reporter continued, "We have been unable to reach Pastor Fisher for comment. However, we have been able to contact several of the congregants from Fisher's church. Apparently, every Sunday at the church, Fisher tells the church stories of changed lives, much like the story on *Oprah* last Friday. And some congregants have gone so far as to suggest that the miraculous stories every Sunday are also invented."

Then Jimmy Buckley's face appeared on the television. Jimmy said, "I wasn't having any sort of marital problems, but Pastor Ryan said he'd pay me if I told the church my wife and I were fighting and then appear before the church to stage a 'reconciliation.' So I did. I wouldn't be surprised if he made the same arrangement with other folks. Even that fella on *Oprah*."

"That's not true!" Ryan yelled at the CNN anchor. She didn't hear him.

"The facts of this case are shocking and confusing. It's difficult to say what Pastor Ryan Fisher has been up to since he moved to this small town nine months ago. But needless to say, it should be interesting as we find out. Back to you, Jim."

Ryan wasn't listening anymore. The doorbell rang, and as Ryan and Pastor Clark peeked out the window, there were vans belonging to CNN, ABC, and Fox News parked across his front lawn. At the door were cameras, microphones, and reporters with a desire to be the first to report the most exciting news story in the last thirty-six hours. They weren't going to leave until Ryan gave them the answers they needed.

28

House of Cards

It was still raining when Katherine pulled up to the Greasy Spork. She wasn't sure exactly why she'd come here — when she'd sped away from her home she wasn't really planning on going anywhere; all that mattered was getting away from Ryan. She'd arrived at the Spork by default. But she couldn't go inside looking like this: her hair in a mess, makeup running down her face, her eyes puffy from all the crying. If she was going to go out in public, she had to look confident and happy, like a pastor's wife should. She'd learned over the last few months that it was the price of her celebrity — she always had to act like things were wonderful, always had to wear a smile, always had to be friendly and warm and loving, so she could be a shining beacon for every woman in town who wanted the perfect marriage. "Pastor Ryan and Katherine seem so in love, why can't we be more like that?" the other women would ask their husbands.

And even tonight, after the straw had finally broken the camel's back, after her marriage had finally come to an end, she still had to look and act as if things were going to be okay. She couldn't let those inside the Spork know that she was leaving Ryan. That wouldn't be fair. She had to give Ryan the room to spin this however he wanted to, to tell all in Bartlesville whatever he needed to tell them to make sure the church wouldn't skip a beat. That's what was important.

Once Katherine looked presentable, she walked inside the Greasy Spork. Her plan was to drink a hot cup of coffee, make some calls, and figure out what to do next, but it was pin-drop silent inside the Spork. Normally on Saturday night it was hopping. Tonight every soul in the room was glued to the lone 1970s television set (it didn't even have a remote, the television was so archaic you actually had to twist the knobs to change the channel) in the corner. It reminded Katherine of the day she had gone to work and everyone was huddled around the TV set learning the details about the planes that crashed into the World Trade Center. Katherine suddenly felt selfish. She was so focused on her own problems that she didn't even know there was a national tragedy going on.

Then she looked closely at the television and learned that her problems were the national tragedy. She saw the front door of her home with the words "Breaking News: Miraculous Pastor a Hoax."

As the story was breaking, all sorts of accusations were coming out. Jimmy Buckley stood in front of a trailer park and said, "Oh, yeah, Pastor Ryan came to the casino, won some money at blackjack, and *then* he told me he'd pay all of my gambling debts if I'd just make up some story about me and my wife to tell the church."

Next, Kevin Anderson was on a conference call with one of the networks. He said, "Well, I know Ryan Fisher has not been a pastor for nine years. He was at our church about a year ago, and back then he was just a real estate agent. It seemed like he'd never even been to church."

Pastor Mark, the Baptist, stood in front of his church and said, "I've been a pastor in this town for fifteen years. I have never seen something more suspicious than Ryan Fisher and his three-ring circus of a church. And that's saying a lot because I actually met David Koresh one time. Ryan Fisher has been manipulating and brainwashing this town since the moment he got here. I'm glad the news media is catching on. I was beginning to get afraid something horrible was going to happen."

Sheriff Somersby was the last on the screen. He was in full uniform in front of the station, with all of his deputies behind him. "Well, the first thing Ryan did when he got to town was bribe people to come to his church. It wasn't anything major, anything really that illegal, but looking back on it, I should have seen it. It was a bribe. I have to say that I'm startled because he seemed like a nice guy. But in my line of work, you learn that some of the worst lawbreakers, I mean, even serial killers and people like that, seem nice."

Katherine turned pale. Her stomach was in a free fall. Blood rushed from her face.

How is this happening? Katherine continued to watch as Ryan walked out onto their porch. Instantly he was swarmed—microphones were stuck in his face and cameras flashed.

Please don't make this worse, she thought.

"Pastor Fisher, is it true that you paid people to lie about the miracles that you allegedly performed?"

"Is it true that you fabricated your entire past, including your pastor and your church?"

"Is it true that this is a cult you have been starting, and you have been promising to take your followers to the mother planet?"

Ryan took a deep breath. Then he looked into the cameras,

confident. Who is this? Katherine thought. A year ago Ryan would have buckled under far less, no way he could have stood there confident and proud. She guessed she should have respected him for it. But it was too eerie, inhuman. It was as if he were a politician with no feelings—there was only spin, there was no time for emotions, all his energy had to be used to put out the next fire. The whole country was attacking Ryan, and he was looking how to use this to his *advantage*. And that's when Katherine realized Ryan was really gone—she'd lost her husband for good.

"Pastor Ryan, what do you have to say to America, to this town, to your own church?" a local reporter from channel 7 asked.

"I want to answer that, I really do, but you have to see things from my perspective. After all, do you know what the number one job of being a pastor is?" Ryan asked the reporters. "You might think it's teaching great lessons, or making sure the budget is in line, or casting a vision for the church. And yes, those are all part of it, but not the most important part. The most important thing a pastor does is to take care of his family, take care of the people God has placed in his care. So that's what I'm going to do tomorrow morning. We'll have a family conference to put all of these questions to rest. You can come if you want," Ryan said gesturing to the reporters and cameramen, "but I promise it won't be that interesting. You'll just see how ill-founded this story is."

"Pastor Ryan, could you just—"

"No, nothing more tonight. I'm sorry you came all this way for nothing." Ryan closed the door and turned off the porch light.

And then the broadcast went back to the studio so the news anchors could editorialize what they thought was really going on with Pastor Ryan.

"Turn it off," Katherine said, louder than she intended.

Everyone in the diner spun around, shocked to see Katherine standing there watching this with them. Ever since that first service in the parking lot of Chuck E. Cheese, Katherine couldn't go anywhere in town without being recognized and smiled at, but tonight there were no smiles, just blank stares that made her feel notorious and embarrassed. No one in the diner knew what to say.

"You heard Mrs. Fisher. Turn it off," Cowboy Jack said.

The bartender obeyed and shut off the TV, but nobody moved.

"There's nothing to look at here. Chuck, fire up the grills; Lucy, crank up the karaoke machine—it's Saturday night, we should be having fun, not watching the TV." Everyone complied, but at a molasses pace. They were watching Katherine out of the corners of their eyes. They all seemed to be saying, "Why aren't you with Ryan?"

Cowboy Jack took Katherine to a booth in the corner of the Spork. It felt right to have him there. She hadn't seen him, hadn't even heard from him, since he took off to Nashville weeks ago. Yet somehow here he was, just what she needed, heroic and kind with his snakeskin hat and warm smile.

"You okay?" Jack asked Katherine.

"Yeah, I'm fine."

"You sound fine."

"When'd you get back?" Katherine asked.

"A couple of days ago. Pastor Dave put me back on the rotation. I'm supposed to lead worship tomorrow."

"Yeah, of course," Katherine said. And then, "I'm pregnant, Jack."

"Oh. Okay. Wow."

"It's not yours."

"I know."

"I mean, it couldn't be because we never really—"

"I took health class in sixth grade. I learned all about the birds and the bees there—"

"I'm leaving Ryan," Katherine said. Cowboy Jack couldn't help but think that she wasn't really communicating—wasn't even really talking—she was just telling one thing after another as if they were the answers to trivia questions.

"Because of all of this," Jack said, gesturing to the TV.

"Because of everything," Katherine answered.

"Where are you going?"

"Anywhere but Bartlesville."

"Can I come with you?"

"No. I didn't even think I would see you here. I just came here, I don't know, I guess I was just hoping to find a little help from someone."

"Maybe you can stay at my place tonight."

Katherine didn't say a word.

"You know, you can stay on the foldout couch. Wait, you're pregnant. I can stay on my foldout couch. You can have the bed."

"I'm staying at a hotel tonight. But pick me up in the morning for church."

"Katherine, shouldn't you go with Ryan?"

"He won't even know I'm there," she said.

Ryan stepped back inside. Pastor Clark was watching CNN. The analysts were speculating on what was really going on with this Oklahoma minister: was he innocent, or was he the next James Bakker? What qualifies or disqualifies someone from being a minister in this country? If his church is happy with him and he's happy, shouldn't he just be left alone? Ryan's situation made great fodder for discussion about religion in America. "The Ryan Fisher story is so much bigger than Ryan Fisher," one analyst said. "It's about all of us. It's about religion and everything that's wrong with it in America."

"I don't even know why this is a story," another analyst responded.

Ryan and Pastor Clark watched the analysis for a minute; then Pastor Clark shut off the television.

"You don't need to watch that."

"Yeah, probably not."

"But you handled yourself well out there."

"Thanks."

"How did you get so good at that?"

"At what?"

"Sounding like a pastor."

"I am a pastor," Ryan said.

"Okay, but you're not. Why are you doing this?"

"Doing what?"

"Acting like a pastor."

"There's no acting here. I love being a pastor."

"You have no theological training. You have no church background. You have no accountability whatsoever. You can't just become a pastor and make up a church."

"But I did."

"And look what's happened. You're a national story. You're a black eye for the church."

"Maybe it would be best if you left."

"Listen, I'm not trying to be insensitive here, but this is a mess and it has to be handled the right way, for all of us. You need someone on your side—someone who can vouch for your character. Despite everything, I think you meant well. So, if you need someone to stand with you in the morning—"

"What, we're friends now?" Ryan asked.

"I can help you navigate this the right way. I can help you resign with dignity."

"You know, you pretty much don't have a leg to stand on

because the information you were just trying to blackmail me with has now been broadcast all over national television."

"I wasn't blackmailing you, Ryan."

"You can go out the back. That way you won't have to talk with any press."

"Ryan—"

"Good-night, Pastor Clark."

"Right," Pastor Clark said as he walked out the back and left Ryan's home.

And then Ryan was alone with nothing but questions. How had this happened? Was everything really falling apart? One bump in the road and was he really going to lose everything, his church, his marriage, his power?

He marched into his office and cracked open his laptop, determined to write the speech of his life, the speech that would save everything he had built. His fingers danced across the keyboard for a solid minute and a half, but then he sat for a moment staring off into space and thinking about what he would write next. And unfortunately, he was very tired. Ryan just didn't have much left in the tank after being kidnapped, threatened, and bashed in the face by one man; on national television, applauded, interviewed, praised—all by the same people who now questioned, accused, and lied about him; not to mention he'd just been left by his wife and accused of blasphemy and heresy by his former pastor who was one of the key men who inspired him onto this journey in the first place.

And as Ryan thought about the last few days, he closed his eyes wishing for darkness and sleep to wash over him, knowing that he was too exhausted to deal with all of these problems, that he was too weak and feeble to handle all of this. He was just a man. A mortal. A real estate agent who barely knew how to close a sale without Christians. He would crawl into bed. He would stay there for a long time, he would not go to church in the morning. He couldn't face all of those people. If they thought he was so evil, if they'd be better off without him, then fine. Great. He'd skip the service. They would flounder. They wouldn't know what to do. They would beg him to come back.

(Sleep. This is your heroic solution? You're going to sleep in? Wow, that is really impressive. You are really something.)

Okay, so he couldn't sleep. This was his moment to shine, this is what made him stronger than everyone, a leader; he would stand up against all odds, he would face the world and he would do something heroic. But what? He wished there was some idiot's or dummy's guide to being a hero. Why couldn't there be some sort of manual, a twelve-easy-steps program to go from average to heroic? Still, even though there was no manual, there were heroes to imitate. So the question was: what would Abraham Lincoln or Malcolm X or Mother Teresa or Captain Kirk do in a situation like this? He supposed he could watch episodes of *Star Trek* or all of his favorite Civil War movies, but he had a gut feeling that they wouldn't give him the answers he was looking for.

So instead, with visions of heroes dancing in his head, he went back to work typing up his Sunday morning sermon, typing the words that would make everything okay, the words that would win him back what mattered most.

29

A MAN OF FAITH

The day of the "family conference"* felt like a funeral, and not a good one like Wilma Wilson's. This morning felt gray and damp — the cotton candy machines were turned off, the chefs weren't making fresh omelets, and the petting zoo was closed. No one was in the mood for the usual friendly amenities of The People's Church.

Nonetheless, this morning would be, by far, the biggest service in the church's short history. The tent was overflowing with people who'd been going through the whole spectrum of thoughts and emotions. Some felt robbed of their innocence; some were suddenly skeptical to trust anyone or anything; others knew the church was a sham and a cult the whole time. But the faithful believers of The People's Church were trying to figure out what

---

*Ryan gave the morning's meeting the title "family conference" in a flash of inspiration. He had no idea where the term came from. If he rooted through his subconscious long enough, he would have discovered he got the title from *Full House* because Bob Saget always called a family conference after D. J. and Uncle Jesse had a particularly nasty fight.

had really gone wrong. Was God himself to blame for this mess? Or should they be angry with themselves for trusting Ryan in the first place? The fresh wound made some flash back to the past and they could see Ryan was a liar just like their father or mother or high school coach. Even worse for some, they realized Ryan was just like their old pastor. They came to The People's Church because Ryan seemed so *different*, but they were horrified to learn he was just like every other pastor, that they'd been lied to and hurt at church yet again.

Ryan couldn't believe how full the lot around the tent was. As he neared the church, he saw hundreds of cars and thousands of people everywhere. He didn't know it, but over eleven thousand would show up that morning; so many that the setup team had to open all of the sides of the tent. People were spilling out everywhere, thousands were standing in the field around the tent.

They've all come to hear me. The country is waiting to hear what I have to say this morning, Ryan thought; but not in a proud way, more in a "how is this happening" sort of way.

How did everything fall apart so fast?

Ryan drove down the road that led into the field and he could see many were waving pasteboards and signs that read things like, "WE HEART PASTOR RYAN" or "PASTOR LIAR" or "QUIT DRINKING THE KOOL-AID!"

Ryan pulled into the staff-only entrance. Even in the area that was supposed to be only for his staff and volunteers, there were still plenty of members around, and as he drove by he caught glimpses of their faces and could see their hurt and disgust and confusion. They needed answers.

Ryan pulled his car up to the tent's back entrance and walked toward the greenroom where his lapel microphone was usually ready for him. He was planning to put his microphone on, go over his notes, and clear his thoughts before he made the most important speech of his life. Except this morning, Pastor Dave, Pastor Clark, and several of the other pastors in town were in the greenroom waiting for Ryan.

"We've been trying to call you all morning," Pastor Dave said.

"I know. I didn't have anything to say to you."

"Well, I'm afraid we have something to say to you. We've been talking with your old pastor. He filled us in that it's all true," Dave said.

"What's all true?"

"You're an imposter. You fabricated your past," Dave said.

"I don't have time for this. I need Terry to get me my lapel mic, I've got a sermon to preach," Ryan said.

"That's what he's trying to say, Ryan. We're not letting you go up there," Pastor Clark said.

"You're not *letting* me go up there?"

"We don't want the congregation to get any more confused," Dave added.

"This is *my* church. I said on the news that I would explain what was going on—"

"We'll explain everything for you," Dave said.

The other pastors had made a decision of what must be done long before Ryan Fisher arrived. They would commandeer the church, Pastor Clark could explain Ryan's past, and then they would tell the crowd that Ryan was being placed on sabbatical for the next six months. They didn't want to say that he was being fired. Not right away. It would be some weeks before they announced that.

"And what happens to me?"

"We'll talk about that after church," David said.

"You think it's going to help just to sweep me under the rug? Pretend I was never here?"

"Ryan, we don't know what to do. You're the one who created this mess," Dave said.

"I need to go up there."

"What could you possibly say to them, Ryan? Are you going to go up there and say this was some big misunderstanding, or are you going to cry and tell them how sorry you are? Either way, you can't win. And if you say the wrong thing, you'll become Jimmy Swaggart, you'll be spoofed on *Saturday Night Live*, you'll be a punchline on *The Tonight Show*—the laughingstock of the country. Do you really want that?" Pastor Clark said.

Ryan thought about this for a moment. Then, after considering Pastor Clark's words, Ryan said, "What I want is to make things right."

The pastors all stood in silence, unsure of what to say. Unsure if they should trust Ryan to go up there. What if he said something to try to regain control of the church? Would he say something to embarrass them all on national television? It was tough to know.

"I'm sorry, Ryan. It's too late for that," Pastor Clark said.

Worship that morning was bizarre. Some sang passionately with their hands held higher than ever before, proclaiming God's ever-loving goodness. But there were also many onlookers and bystanders that morning; they were citizens of the town who'd never gone to The People's Church (or any church) before. They were standing with their hands sunk deep in their pockets watching everything around them. They'd come this morning because this may have been the biggest scandal in Bartlesville history—no one could remember national news networks ever visiting town, and they wanted to be there live and in person to watch things unfold.

The worship set lasted four songs. It felt eternal. This morning the Worship Wranglers were the opening band no one cared about. They were stalling for the main event: Pastor Ryan stepping onto the platform and telling the town of Bartlesville what was really going on, what he'd really been doing for the last nine months.

When worship finally ended, Pastor Dave stepped onto the platform. The whispers and murmurs turned into a hush as people waited for the church service to begin. Pastor Dave looked at the crowd and smiled. The press expected some official-sounding statement.

"Jesus is still Lord!" Pastor Dave cried.

A large percentage of the crowd cheered and shouted and whistled at this proclamation. They'd given their lives to Christ over the last few months or weeks or years, and the cheering people had something in common—they'd discovered (or rediscovered) how much they loved being a Christian and having a personal relationship with Jesus Christ.

The bystanders were completely confused by the cheering—what was there to cheer about? How could you cheer when you'd just learned that your pastor was an alleged fraud? How could you cheer when you had another piece of evidence that your faith was a sham?

"The sun rose this morning, and it will rise again tomorrow. This will not shake us," Pastor Dave said. More cheering. Dave was turning the atmosphere in the tent from a funeral to an Amway convention. He was surprised to hear himself being so positive; he hadn't necessarily planned on it, but he could sense the stares from the thousands and feel the cameras pointed right at him. He would not just get up there and be depressing or talk about how much this hurt—he would use this as an opportunity to defend his faith and its validity, despite the mistakes of one man.

"If you don't know me, my name's Pastor Dave. I've been on staff here for a little over two months now. But I'm just like you. I know many of you were confused by the stories that were appearing on the news last night, and I was confused myself. To be honest, a little bit of doubt began to creep into my soul. Until I asked myself, 'Dave, who are you going to trust? Your pastor, or your Lord?' And I decided right then and there that I will always first and foremost put my trust and my faith in God, because he is my rock and my salvation!" Dave didn't really understand how, but for the first time in his life, he was becoming a Pentecostal preacher. He was popular and powerful, and he felt more loved and admired than he ever dreamed possible.

But so what?

He was pumping up the crowd. He was making them feel great. He was supposed to tell them that they'd hit a bump, but not to worry, because they will march on. Ryan has troubles, but the team is working with him to make him back into the man God intended him to be. The whole thing was scripted out for him. All he had to do was execute the speech that was given to him by the other pastors.

But this speech was not what would help Ryan or the church. There was only one thing that had a chance of doing that.

"Still, I want to hear for myself what Pastor Ryan Fisher was really thinking this whole time. What was true and what was not true? And there's only one person who can answer that."

"What's he doing?" Pastor Mark said. Mark was standing off to the side with the clump of pastors who were there to ensure that Pastor Dave said what he was supposed to.

"He's going to put Ryan on stage," Pastor Clark said.

"We have to stop him," Mark said.

"We can't," Pastor Clark said. And then, "I don't even know if we should."

"Ladies and gentlemen, Ryan Fisher owes us an explanation. And I think he deserves the right to give us one." Dave locked eyes with Ryan, standing backstage, out of sight of everyone else. "Come on up here, Ryan. Say what you've got to say."

Ryan obeyed. He walked onstage. Not too fast and not too slow. He looked confident as ever, as confident as when he walked onstage at Wilma Wilson's funeral. You'd almost think the crowd was chanting his name in adoration.

But they were not chanting his name. A few clapped and cheered, but most watched in silence as their leader stepped behind the pulpit.

Katherine watched right along with them, in the back, wearing sunglasses and a floppy hat. She hoped her disguise would at least let those who recognized her realize that she was ashamed and embarrassed and did not want to be bothered.

Ryan noticed that when he walked up to the podium, the camera crews snapped to attention, their cameras and microphones were aimed right at him like sniper rifles, and reporters looked focused and ready to put their pencils to their notepads. They would form their stories around whatever he said next.

"We grow up being told that we can be whatever we want to be. We can be the president or an astronaut, a doctor, a lawyer, or a firefighter. The sky's the limit, we can be whatever we want; we just have to dream it up. But somewhere along the way this changes — we learn you have to be born into the right family to run for president, that medical schools are expensive, our test scores aren't high enough to study law, and we're too small to fight fires. And all of this makes us scared to follow our dreams. I know it frightened me, anyway. I had a wife and a career to think about, I couldn't follow my dreams. I needed to be stable and responsible and grown up. And I got stuck. My life got stale. I had to change things or lose my soul.

"The people of Bartlesville helped change my life. And so, for them, I'm here this morning to clear some things up. I never paid Jimmy Buckley to admit that a miracle was done in his life. The love that you saw between Jimmy and Megan on that Sunday morning was true. As a matter of fact, every story that you ever saw here on a Sunday morning was true. I never made any of it up, and never paid people to act like God was doing a miracle in their lives. If they were acting a certain way, it's because God really was doing something in them. And what happened to Clovis on *Oprah*," Ryan looked into the cameras, "where many of you were introduced to me for the first time, was also true. Clovis really did have a change of heart right before all of our eyes, and I was lucky enough to witness it.

"You may or may not believe me, but everything you saw on this stage for the last nine months was the real deal, it was truthful and authentic. Everything but *me*.

"I was a lie, a fake, a hoax. I am not a pastor. And I have no idea what it takes to officially be a pastor because I only started going to church last year. And when I decided to become a pastor I created a past, a church, and a mentor named Joseph Sampson — none of that is real. I invented it all to give myself credibility. So, here's the big question that I'm sure everyone really wants to know: Why would I do all of this?

"It's not because I'm the leader of a cult. I don't really know what a cult does, or why one would start a cult. Cult leaders seem to have some new vision from God that is going to take everyone to the promised land. I don't even believe in God."

This sent cameras flashing and the reporters scribbling furiously on their notepads. "Okay, let me rephrase that, I don't believe in a *false* God like other cult leaders do … Actually no, you know what, strike that. I'm going to stand by my statement. I don't believe in God. But for what it's worth, the people of this church have made me *want* to believe in God. You've made me wish I could have a faith as strong as you do. And I think that's why I played this charade for so long. Because I could see the good that was happening in people's lives and that seemed worth believing in.

"When I first started going to church last year, I could see how kind and generous the Christian community was. And I wanted to be a part of it. I thought I could even lead a group of Christians and maybe my faith would come later. And once I became a successful pastor, I loved everything about it so much that I made up whatever I had to in order to keep leading this church. I'm not proud of what I've done. I'm only telling you the truth.

"Katherine, my wife and the most amazing woman to ever walk on this earth, tried to talk sense into me every step of the way. She told me I couldn't just start a church or invent my past. She stayed with me only because she is so faithful and caring and wonderful. The only reason she went along with all of this was because she made the mistake of thinking the ends—which were all of the wonderful things that you good people were doing in each other's lives and in this community—justified the means—which was me and my wickedness and deception. Please don't blame her for what has happened, and for everyone else in the country, please don't look down on the good people of this town. They were trusting, and they worked hard at building a great community. They should be applauded for this. Not mocked.

"So, there it is. I needed to say this to all of you in person. You deserve that. I'm sorry, but I don't expect you to forgive me. I would be surprised if any of you did. I wouldn't, if I were you. You may even be wondering if I'm being honest right now. And I don't expect you to believe me, but I can tell you this is the truth.

I started this church because I wanted to feel important, and I've lied about everything since because I didn't want to lose it.

"But you don't need to worry about me anymore. This is my final speech to The People's Church. I'm turning in my resignation, effective immediately."

There were gasps, cameras flashing, and reporters scribbling notes and making phone calls.

"I'm turning this church over to Pastor Dave Summers because he is a good man, a man of faith, and he is worthy of leading this congregation. Thank you for all of your friendship and trust. I will miss you all."

And at that, with the buzz of confused, excited, hurt, and angry murmurs as his soundtrack, Ryan walked off the stage and out of The People's Church.

— 30 —

Aftershock

Before Ryan was married, he loved grocery shopping. It was an emotional journey for him, a cleansing, and a rite of passage. He would walk in confused and lost — the store was crammed full of countless aisles that stretched a mile high — there was food everywhere. And yet nothing to eat; there were only ingredients that had to be turned into food. He would wander around the aisles wondering what he should buy. When he first started grocery shopping it was unusual for him because bachelorhood was about going somewhere for a specific kind of food: Sonic for a burger, Panda Express for sweet and sour pork, Friday's for buffalo wings; rarely, outside of Denny's, could you find somewhere to get any type of food.

But at the grocery store the sky was the limit.

He could eat anything he wanted — if he could only figure out how to make it. With this in mind he'd go slowly down each aisle, carefully ensuring he got all of the right things: salsa and alfredo sauce in aisle seven, bow tie noodles and cilantro lime chips in aisle four. It was hard work, but he would tell himself, pretty soon these will be turned into nachos and pasta.

And when he finally got back to his one-bedroom apartment and cooked himself dinner, it tasted so good because it was something he had made. After dinner, he would start a load of laundry with the detergent and fabric softener he had just bought at the grocery store, and when finally he plopped down on the couch, he'd smile from ear to ear thinking—There's nothing I can't do.

Today was the first time Ryan had gone grocery shopping alone since he'd been a bachelor. His cart wasn't full of ingredients, only frozen foods in boxes. All he had to do to cook his meals was make sure he set his microwave to the proper amount of minutes and seconds. Even that seemed like a lot of work.

Ryan had one final item to buy, a frozen pizza, and he was faced with a difficult decision—sausage or pepperoni? He wanted to scream. He wanted to curl his fists into a ball and punch through the glass freezer case. This was what his life had come down to—a week ago he was running an empire and now pizza flavors were the most significant decision he had left to make. How did this happen? he thought, almost out loud, as his eyes turned bloodshot pink from all the anger and hurt and shame dancing around in his mind.

Ryan had left straight for Emerald Lake as soon as he'd resigned on that Sunday morning because he knew he couldn't go home and face the press or visitors or whatever else was there waiting for him. So he stayed at the cabin (the same cabin he'd been kidnapped at) for a week to let everything calm down.

Still, initially, he had a plan. When he followed Jesus' advice and told The People's Church the complete truth about everything he had been doing, he thought his sins were small enough that the church would take him back, maybe with a slap on the wrist, and he could go on being one of the most important church leaders in America. He would have learned his lesson, and now he would be a shining example of God's grace, a great story of the power of Jesus' blood to cover our sins. He would be the great story of tragedy turned to triumph.

It didn't play out that way.

There were many in town who still loved Ryan dearly, and probably would have welcomed him back with no questions asked. But the church leadership felt differently. When Ryan called home to Cowboy Jack to see how things were going, Cowboy Jack told him that the deacons and elders unanimously accepted his resignation. Additionally, they decided that it would be best if he did not visit for at least two years. It would give the people time to distance themselves from him; it would give them time to heal.

Like that, the door was slammed shut on his ministry career. Sure, he could have started over from scratch, but this time it would be even harder—most in town would mistrust everything he ever did. Or he could move to another town and start a church, but everyone in town would know him as the lying pastor from TV and that was too big a hole to dig out of.

So, after everything went down, Ryan spent his days sitting on the porch at Emerald Lake. He'd stare out at creation and think about what a senseless thing it was. Nature was so vicious and cutthroat, everything had to fight to stay alive. Spiders killed flies, birds killed spiders, cats killed birds, and everybody wanted to kill cats. Everything out there was hunting and being hunted. There was nothing but fear and loneliness and finally death, and Ryan wondered how a kind and loving God could have created this.

What were you thinking, God? You act like you're so caring, but you let everything suffer. You let me suffer. Where were you when I really needed you? And what about you, Jesus, you too busy to have a cup of coffee with your old friend Ryan?

In between being upset at God and nature, Ryan would try to call Katherine. He would call at every seventeen minutes past the hour because the seventeenth was their anniversary and it seemed like a romantic form of stalking. He'd been calling her at the same time every day for the last four days. She'd only answered once and said, "I can't talk to you right now."

"Where are you?"

"I'm safe."

"Safe where?"

"I can't tell you."

"Do you still love me?"

"I need to get my thoughts clear, Ryan. Just please, give me a little space for awhile."

"What's awhile? Three days? Three hours?"

Click. And Ryan was alone again.

For the next couple of days Ryan called just to hear the sound of Katherine's recorded voice. Every time she said, "Hi, this is Katherine. I missed you but not on purpose, so please leave me a message so I can call you back," Ryan started to wonder about how Katherine was feeling when she recorded that message. She sounded so happy; if you didn't know her, you'd think her life was perfect harmony, her voice mail sounded almost as if she'd been thinking about something really pleasant at the time, something like butterflies or ice cream.

But Ryan knew better. Back then everything wasn't okay. He now knew she'd been miserable toward the end. But why didn't he do something earlier? Other husbands would have done something when they saw there was a problem, but Ryan assumed she would be okay, and even if he'd wanted to help, there was always something more pressing to take care of.

Now, he realized how wrong he'd been. She was all that mattered.

He began to despise himself for not taking better care of her. It was bad enough that the rest of the world saw him as a liar and a fake, but he couldn't stand that his own wife thought of him that way. He sat alone on the porch, concentrating on his breathing and staring at the lake as sunbeams danced across the surface. It looked like a watery disco ball. He thought the lake might have the answers to his problems. Maybe all the answers were at the bottom. He could become Virginia Woolf, stuff his pockets with rocks, walk to the bottom of the lake, and stand there until he disappeared.

Ryan didn't have the energy for all of that, so he called his own voice mail to check his messages. Maybe Katherine called and he'd missed her. But as he called his line, he was shocked to hear how happy *he* sounded. He began to think about what an insidious lie voice mail was, how we all project ourselves to sound one way, when quite often we're feeling the opposite. He realized what a sham the human race was, and for the first time he understood that maybe we're all imposters. We all put up some sort of front and hope nobody calls our bluff.

So Ryan wondered, if we all do this, why am I being punished? Wasn't I just doing what it takes to survive?

On Ryan's sixth day at the lake, he started to worry about money. He didn't have an endless supply and at the moment he had no way of making more of it, so he'd have to ration everything he'd made over the last nine months at the church. Sure, eventually there'd be some other job, but that could take awhile — a long while. He had to take care of what he had. And that meant not throwing it away renting a depressing cabin in the woods. He had a nice home and he needed to be living there until he could figure out his next step.

So on the seventh day, he packed his suitcase, checked out of his cabin, and drove back to Bartlesville. He'd only lived at this house for a couple of months, but the place was loaded with memories of Katherine and of being a pastor. Both now seemed like distant things, left behind in another life. Now, he was Jonah, left under a withering plant with nothing but memories of his once exciting, productive past.

Inside the house it smelled like spoiled eggs and sulfur. It was the sandwich meat he left on the counter the night of Pastor Clark's visit. No one had been home for a week, and in all of the chaos of the CNN story breaking, things had been left out to rot.

So he spent his first hour home gutting out his fridge and coating every foul-stenched portion of his house with Lysol. By the time he finished there was nothing but ketchup and mustard and spicy hot mayo to eat—hardly a nutritious meal. Still, he needed food and he couldn't go out to eat because that would lead to seeing someone from The People's Church. Since it was after ten at night, he decided it was best to go to the grocery store now, when there was little chance of running into anyone.

Inside the store he crept down the freezer aisle and filled his cart with treats—pasta, stir fry, pot roast, and potatoes (not that it really mattered what he got; after a couple of days of eating nothing but processed, freezer-burnt food, everything would taste the same).

His last item was a frozen pizza, and as he stood between the sausage and the pepperoni pizzas, a man turned around the corner shopping for frozen treats of his own.

His name was Clovis Whitman.

When he saw Ryan, he turned frozen and stiff, his jaw dropped, and he stared at Ryan as if he were seeing a poltergeist. Ryan could understand Clovis's shock. Clovis was the first person to see Ryan since he'd returned from Emerald Lake.

"Pastor Ryan," Clovis said.

"You don't have to call me that. I'm technically not a pastor anymore."

"You are to me."

"That's kind of you to say."

"Well, the kindness you showed me changed my life."

Ryan couldn't respond to that.

"I'm proud of you," Clovis said.

"You are?" Ryan didn't know what that meant.

"You made a lot of stupid, bad decisions, but you made some good ones too."

"Yeah, I guess you're right." But was it possible he was right? Was it possible that this person who'd seemed so crazy and in-stable just a week or so ago, now had an endless wellspring of wisdom? Was it possible that it was always there and Ryan just never took the time to see it? No, probably not, Ryan thought. He was just desperate to talk to someone.

Clovis went on. "You know, you're not really that far away."

"I'm not?"

"No, I think there's still hope for you, Ryan Fisher."

"Who are you?"

"Do you not remember who I am? My name's Clovis and I tried to kidnap you — "

"No, of course I remember."

"Right, you were probably joking around. I always have a hard time telling when you're joking," Clovis said. "Listen, I know things have been hard, so if you ever need a friend to talk to, Pas-tor Ryan, I've got a six-pack of tomato juice in the fridge. We can knock some of those back and just hang out."

"Thank you, Clovis," Ryan said. These were the first kind words anyone had spoken to Ryan in a long time. He forgot what it felt like to have something like that said to him, to have a small act of kindness thrown his way. Ryan was so grateful that he walked up to Clovis and gave him a hug. And for a good while, maybe ten seconds, Ryan hugged the man with coke-bottle glasses and a patchy beard, the same man who'd tried to kill him just a week earlier. But Ryan was too caught up in the emotion of the moment to appreciate the irony of it all.

THE END

What's the best movie ending of all time?*

It could be *Citizen Kane* with Orson Wells laying on his bed crying out "Rosebud" (this was also the first line of the movie). Only now we've learned that "Rosebud" was his sled and the symbol for his lost childhood. Or *The Godfather* where Michael Corleone tells Kate that his family business will soon be clean, and she seems so relieved until moments later when all of the Mafia guys come in, kiss his hand, and call him "Godfather." That's when Kate realizes she's been had, that Michael has become the thing he once swore he hated.

All of those are great, but for Ryan's money, *Top Gun* has the best ending of all time. As the movie comes to a close, Maverick

---

* Sorry for all of these spoilers, but these are the best movies ever made and so there's no excuse not to have seen them. If you haven't seen them by now, you have only yourself to blame. After all, surely you're not one of those people who puts your hands over your ears anytime someone starts talking about the *Sixth Sense* or *The Usual Suspects*. If that's the case you should know that Verbal Kent really was Keyser Soze and Bruce Willis was dead the whole time.

has just defeated the bad guys (we know they were bad guys because they flew black planes, as opposed to the white Tomcats that Maverick and his buddies flew). When Maverick lands, Iceman, his old nemesis, tells him, "You can be my wingman any time." Maverick is a hero. There's only one problem—he's lost the girl. Or has he?

He sits in an old bar, reads the paper, and next thing he knows, a Righteous Brothers song starts to play on the jukebox. Maverick walks around the corner and sees Kelly McGillis in a bomber jacket looking blonde and foxy as ever. They just look at each other and smile while crisp golden sunbeams fight their way through the dusty windows. And as the chorus swells with, "You've Lost That Lovin' Feelin'," Kelly McGillis leans in to kiss Maverick and we think maybe there's hope for Maverick after all, maybe things are going to turn out all right.

Ryan was thinking about *Top Gun* as he drove to St. Louis.

A week after he'd come home from the lake, Katherine had finally called. She didn't say much—she just gave him an address and a time to meet her at some diner. Then she hung up.

When Ryan googled the address, he was surprised to discover it was in St. Louis. Had Katherine moved there? He wasn't sure and had no idea why she'd want to meet in St. Louis, but he wasn't in the position to ask questions. She wanted to meet him and it didn't matter where—could have been in Tibet or Antarctica—he would have found a way. So, a day later, he packed up and made the eight-hour trek up to the Mississippi River.

Katherine had indeed moved to St. Louis. The morning after Ryan resigned, she got in her car and began to drive north without any plan. Her only thoughts were: go north. Get out of Oklahoma. Don't look back. Just drive. She thought that if she did look back she might turn into a pillar of salt. As she drove she got an unexpected call from her college roommate. She'd seen the story on the news and called to ask if Katherine was doing okay. They hadn't talked for years but that didn't stop Katherine from telling her everything—the whole saga from the first Sunday at Fellowship Christian Church to where things were now. At the end of the conversation, Katherine's roommate simply said, "Why don't you come stay with me for awhile."

When Katherine first got to St. Louis she didn't go anywhere. She just sat on her old roommate's couch, ate Phish Food out of the carton, and watched the news. After Ryan resigned, there was a lot of news coverage; there were debates on *Larry King* and *The O'Reilly Factor* about what a church really was.

Some asked what Ryan really did wrong in the first place. Why was this even a story? Others thought Ryan should be burned at the stake. There was a growing mistrust of Catholic priests and evangelical ministers in this country, and the clergy needed to be purged of all liars and deceivers once and for all, because the institution of the church would soon collapse if no one could trust those who run it.

Then Katherine shut the TV off. She could no longer watch national news networks editorialize the last year of her life. However, if she would have kept watching the news, she would have seen how quickly Ryan went away because the next day there was a hurricane in Florida, and the day after that, one of the Rainbow Muslims defected and took an entire supermarket hostage. This caused lots of skepticism towards the Rainbow Muslims amidst the news pundits. They asked questions like, are all Rainbow Muslims fakes and hypocrites? Should they ever be trusted again? Was there any real substance to the Rainbow version of Islam in the first place?

But Katherine really didn't want to think about that either. It was time to think about new and exciting things. It was time to think about the future. She spent her time away from Ryan processing the past with her mother and old friends, even Jennifer Anderson—and with each person Katherine talked and processed through every piece and each moment of the past year. The talking made things better. The talking helped the past fade out of sight. Before long The People's Church and Bartlesville seemed far away, hazy and distant as a bad dream.

But the person who wouldn't fade from her thoughts was Ryan. There was still something there. Something between them that wouldn't just dissolve. She didn't really know if things could be reconciled, but she had to at least talk to him. It wasn't an act of charity, it wasn't for him—*she* needed it just as much. She didn't know what Ryan would do now that the church was gone, but that didn't really matter. She was sick of thinking about what he did; all she really wanted to know was who he was.

As Ryan drove into the city limits of St. Louis, Pastor Dave called. It was the first time he'd called since Ryan resigned. Ryan was surprised, but he answered.

This would be the last contact Ryan would ever have with The People's Church.

"Ryan. Um, hello, it's Dave."

"Hi Dave."

"Listen, you probably don't even want to talk to me, and if that's the case, you can just hang up the phone and I'll totally understand. You have every right."

Dave waited for a moment.

"I'm still here," Ryan said. Ryan thought Dave sounded the same way that he'd sounded when he started the church. Insecure, trying to be confident but second-guessing his every step.

"I want you to know we're moving forward with The People's Church. I'm trying to run things here. But there's a lot of hurt and division. So, I have a really weird question: What would you do if you were here?"

"What?"

"Well, the way you led this church was as dynamic as I've ever seen. So, I was wondering what would you do if you were handed a church that was split down the middle. I mean, some people want to keep everything exactly as it is and some people want to blow things up and start over. I can teach the Bible and counsel people on how to live their lives, but I have no experience with this sort of stuff. I need some advice. No one around here is much help, so I was wondering: what would you do?"

This was the deep sort of *Star Trek* question Ryan never thought he'd have to face. How would Ryan Fisher handle Ryan Fisher? If he were still leading the church, how would he deal with the mess that he'd made? What was the best way to go forward? Ryan didn't really have an answer to that. It was too hard to wrap his brain around this problem. He thought about it for a long time, and finally he told Dave, "You need to go forward with the church the way you think is right. You need to lead and make it the type of place *you* want it to be. Some will follow you. A lot of people won't. But it doesn't matter, because in the end you will have laid the type of foundation for a church that you're comfortable with. And they'll be comfortable with you."

Ryan couldn't tell if this was really great advice or maybe he was just setting Dave up to make the same mistakes he'd just made. He never called back to find out either way.

"Yeah, that makes a lot of sense," Dave said. "And listen, I'm sorry about how things went down that Sunday. I think we were all hurt and scared and a little confused."

"Yeah," Ryan said. "Good luck, Dave."

"Thanks, Pastor Ryan."

The diner was called Charlie's Grill. It was no Greasy Spork. Ryan was a little disappointed when he walked inside. It was the type of no-name place that wasn't proud about being a local joint, but rather embarrassed that it wasn't a chain. The decorations inside made it look like it wanted to be Applebee's or Friday's, but it was falling short. There were just too many cheap and cheesy things that made it seem flimsy and limp—if other chains were 'N Sync, this place was the Backstreet Boys.

Ryan thought that Maverick would have never come to a place like this. How was he supposed to have some sort of romantic reunion here? Then he realized this place didn't have a jukebox. Even worse, he realized that he and Katherine didn't have a song.

And that was the real problem. He'd always assumed things would fall into place for him and Katherine—he always thought that he deserved her. But he never took time to make sure they had *things*. He never even made sure they had their own song. And he certainly never ensured there were ongoing unbreakable romantic ties between them. Sure, he worked really hard when they'd first started dating, but once he proposed and she agreed, he'd acted like a man who'd just closed the sale.

He could just coast from there.

Now she had left him. She had not talked to him for two weeks. He would have to fight to get her back. And not just to get her back, but to keep her from this point forward.

But what if he never got a chance?

Ryan began to wonder why Katherine would bring him to a place like this. Why would she invite him here, somewhere that was so lame and plastic, if she wanted to get back

(she's going to leave you)

together? She was very cold and distant both times they'd talked on the phone. She was using her loan officer voice; she sounded much more like a woman who was making a necessary business transaction than someone who'd lost her husband. Why did she

(she doesn't want to form any emotional connection)

sound like that? This place was not ideal for a romantic encounter, but it was the perfect sort of place to end things. It was crowded; he couldn't yell or debate or cry, yet it wasn't a chain—if Katherine had ended things in a Starbucks, Ryan would have been reminded of his failed marriage on every corner in America, every person holding a coffee cup would be screaming, "Your wife doesn't love you anymore!" She had planned out everything. She would walk in, say it was over, and walk out.

And then she *did* walk in. Ryan started to sweat. He took a drink of water to calm down, but it wasn't working.

What's about to happen? he thought. My God, I'm not ready for this. Someone please help me.

He was sitting in a booth in the corner. She looked around for a moment, and then she locked eyes with him.

What's she going to do when she sees me? he thought. Will she grin, frown, burst into tears, how will she react?

She gave Ryan a little smile, but other than that, she was poker-faced.

Katherine sat down across from him. They were sitting face-to-face, and there was so much between them, all of the hurt and confusion of the last two weeks, all of the memories over their years of marriage; it made the space in the booth so full Ryan thought it was about to bust.

"I'm sorry," he said.

"So am I," Katherine said.

"How have you been?"

"It's been an interesting couple of weeks."

"Yeah," Ryan agreed. "Why did you pick this place?"

"It's the only place I know how to get to. I'm not really that familiar with things around here. I've been staying with Susan."

"From school?"

"Yeah, I needed a neutral place where I could just kind of decompress, you know?"

"That makes sense," Ryan said, and it did, but it told him nothing about her true motives for picking this place, or more specifically, what she really wanted.

"Listen, I didn't come here to talk about things. I mean, we can talk too, but I came here to give you something."

"Okay —

(give me something?)

what did you want to give me?"

Katherine slid a manila envelope across the table.

"What is this?"

(You know what this is. You know exactly what it is — divorce papers. This is it. She's leaving you. She's already drawn up the papers; that's how sick she is of you. That's how ready she is to end things. You're going to open this up, and it's going to destroy your life. I don't know if you'll ever recover. Things are over once and for all; ba-dee ba-dee ba-dee, that's all folks, forever and ever, the end, game over.)

"Just open it," Katherine said. She was using her business voice again.

Ryan opened the folder. There weren't divorce papers at all. Just images on slick photo paper. The background was black and there were white outlines all over, and in the corner there was typed information — dates and measurements and things like that. Ryan was at a complete loss; he had so been anticipating divorce papers that it was difficult to tell what this was supposed be.

"Um, what is this?" Ryan asked.

"That's our baby," Katherine said. She laughed—it was an odd laugh—it was the sound of joy only a new mother can have. With the laughter came a tear, and she smiled at Ryan. She wasn't just smiling because of the baby; she was smiling at *him*, and that was the best part of all. She had wanted to share this with him for so long.

"Our baby?"

Katherine nodded.

"Our baby!" Ryan said. And as he said this, as he uttered the words that he'd given up on long ago, it shattered his insides. He was so overwhelmed with joy that he, too, smiled and cried the way only a new father can. And this is such a lame thing to say—but it's God's honest truth, and it would be a lie not to put this in—it was the happiest moment of Ryan's life.

Ryan and Katherine just looked at each other for a long time. There were no words. They were two broken people, they were a complete mess and they couldn't have been happier about it. And when Ryan finally calmed down enough to talk, for the first time in a long time, maybe ever, he was going to open his mouth and tell Katherine the absolute truth, everything he was really thinking and feeling.

He could hardly wait to hear how it would sound.

ACKNOWLEDGMENTS

There are people whom I need to thank. People whose names aren't on the spine of this book. My name is on the spine. Not that it's a very cool name.* When we first started dating, my wife told me that Rob is a very eighties-sounding name. And I think she's right. Rob is the name of the guy with curly hair and straight teeth in all of the movies. Rob is the guy the girl should like, but she likes the bad boy or the nerd instead. So, if it were up to me, I would have given myself a cool name. Something slick like Jack Steele or literary like Thomas Hemingway.

Anyway.

There are people whom I need to thank, people who were instrumental or encouraging or whose thoughts helped shaped this book. Andy Meisenheimer is one of those people. If you ever write a book, I hope you can have an editor as wise as he is. His intuition is right 97 out of 100 times, and it's probably right 100 out of 100 times but I am just too proud to admit it. I'd like to thank Don

_____
* No offense Mr. Bell.

Pape for being this novel's champion and Marcy Schorsch for her marketing expertise. I'd like to thank Becky Shingledecker for thinking to ask the questions no one else did. I'd like to thank Patton Dodd and John Bolin: their friendship, encouragement, and insight along the way have been worth more than all the tea in China and that's a pantload of tea. I'd like to thank all who read different drafts and gave insight: Jared Anderson, Sarah Bolin, Ben Calmer, Whitney Davis, Owen and Bobbi Shifflet, Tia Stauffer, Rachel Stennett, and the Stinklets.

And for all of her love, support, and friendship, I'd like to thank Sarah Stennett, my smoking-hot amazing wife, who has never even looked at another Cowboy.

Z+
Insights,
Interviews,
& More

Contents

SELECTIONS
FROM SHERIFF SOMERSBY'S
CODE HANDBOOK

Sheriff Somersby would have never needed his own color-code system if it weren't for rap music. But those rap songs ruined everything. Guys whom the Sheriff had never even heard of—artists with menacing names like Dr. Dre, Tupac, Biggie Smalls, and Snoop Doggy Dogg—cracked the time honored police codes in their rap lyrics.

Sheriff Somersby first noticed it on a starless summer night when he was talking with a particularly rambunctious member of the criminal element. He could tell this kid was up to no good. So he picked up his police radio and said, "We've got a 415 in progress. I might need some backup. Over."

And the criminal element—it was this seventeen-year-old kid with corn rows and a red bandanna—told the Sheriff, "Shoot, playa, I knows what a four-one-five is. It stands for public disturbance. It was in a Biggie song."

The Sheriff dropped the receiver of the police radio. He was horrified. At that moment he knew a number oriented system just wasn't good enough anymore. It was too public. Anyone could crack it. He needed something of his own. Something unbreakable. So he created the following color code handbook:

Code Aquamarine: Civilian taking a threatening posture toward someone in uniform. (It could be anyone in uniform: a police officer, firefighter, nurse, mailman, or a Girl Scout—all in uniform must be respected according to Sheriff Somersby.)

Code Beige: Public nuisance after 3 p.m.

Code Electric Lime: Unlicensed throwing of missiles, grenades, or other WMD's

Code Carmine: Person with a gun

Code Ecru: Person with a knife

Code Fuchsia: Person with special powers (including, but not limited to, flying, X-ray vision, super speed, and Wonder Twin powers)

Code Clear: Person without clothes

Code Heliotrope: Rearranging the letters on the sign at the Greasy Spork to spell profane words

Code Maroon: Theft from the Greasy Spork

Code Mauve: Fire at the Lutheran Church

Code Periwinkle: Pop Jones is drunk again

Code Teal: Assault with a deadly weapon toward a civilian

Code Turquoise: Assault with a non-deadly weapon toward a non-civilian (usually applies to the local teenagers riling up cattle, ducks, cats, and gophers with weapons like BB, pellet, and/or paintball guns)

COWBOY JACK'S SONGBOOK

Cowboy Jack knew he had to sing something more than "Amazing Grace" and "Mr. Jones." He was the worship leader, and the church needed to sing songs that expressed the beauty and complexity of God. Of course, Cowboy Jack didn't understand the beauty and complexity of God. He didn't even know if God was beautiful and complex.

Still, singing the two same songs over and over seemed like it would grow old quickly. So Jack decided to write songs of his own. The problem was, he knew nothing about writing songs, so he took catchy songs with great lyrics and beats and chord progressions and rewrote them. He reclaimed them for the People's Church.

Cowboy Jack did this on many evenings sitting outside the horse stables at the ranch and staring at the sunset. He tried to think of the complexity and beauty of God when he wrote, but he usually couldn't fathom what that meant so he thought of Katherine instead.

Anyway, these are the titles of some of the songs he wrote. You can imagine how the lyrics went.

1. Britney Spears, "Save Me Jesus One More Time"
2. R.E.M., "Gaining My Religion"
3. Alanis Morissette, "God Oughta Know"
4. Hanson, "MmmGod"

5. Black Eyed Peas, "Let's Get Church Started"
6. Kelly Clarkson, "Since You've Been God"
7. Salt-N-Pepa with En Vogue, "Whatta God"
8. C+C Music Factory, "Gonna Make You Sweat (Everybody Praise Now)"
9. Tim McGraw, "I Like God, I Love God, I Want Some More of Him"
10. Foo Fighters, "There Goes My Holy Spirit"
11. Christina Aguilera, "Jesus in a Bottle"
12. Radiohead, "Fitter, Happier, More Christian"
13. The Fugees, "Saving Me Softly with His Song"
14. Sheryl Crow, "What Would Jesus Do (to Have Some Fun)"
15. Will Smith, "Gettin' Jesus Wit It"

CHAT WITH
AUTHOR ROB STENNETT

ROB STENNETT: Hey.

Z+: *Don't say a thing about* LOST. *I haven't seen it yet ...*

ROB STENNETT: Crap. I was just about to ask about ...

Z+: *NO.*

ROB STENNETT: I'd never do that. We'll debrief when you see it. That's all I will say about that.

Z+: *Okay. Here we go: Have you ever tried to start a church? Is that what inspired TATSORF?*

ROB STENNETT: My father was a minister. He planted a church when I was kid. That's when I really started to think, What makes people go to church?

Z+: *Did you ever find out?*

ROB STENNETT: Not sure. If I did, I'd write a church-planting book that'd sell like hotcakes. But I do think having a building helps. If it's the clothes that make the man, it's the church building that makes the church. We had to meet anywhere—schools, parks, and so on. It was tough for the church to develop an identity until it had a place of its own. I think Ryan realized this too. That's why he got so obsessed with where his church met.

Z+: *You have brothers and sisters?*

Rob Stennett: A brother and two sisters. I'm the oldest. But when I look in the birth order book about how the ages are supposed to act, I'm the middle child. So I don't know what went wrong.

Z+: Who acted as your older sibling then?

Rob Stennett: My sister. She's the second oldest. And she was always trying to rally to get us to do the right thing. Or at least she was the ringleader. I was too ADD for that. But not in an I-eat-lots-of-Pop-Rocks-and-drink-Coke-and-run-around-screaming sort of way.

Z+: So besides New Life Church, what else have you done with your life?

Rob Stennett: I've written several screenplays, studied screenwriting at UCLA, and about two years ago I was shopping around a TV show.

Z+: Sweet. What's it about?

Rob Stennett: It's sort of *Grey's Anatomy* meets *The Apprentice*, meets *Big Love*.

Z+: I don't even know what to say to that.

Rob Stennett: It was about a megachurch that was like the prime megachurch in the country, and these six apprentices had to compete to get a job as the church's newest pastor.

Z+: Cool. So, what kind of stuff do you like to read?

Rob Stennett: I love guys like Kurt Vonnegut and Christopher Moore and Douglas Coupland. I think I'm trying to write in the tradition they carved out. But I try to read all sorts of stuff. One guy whom I think about all the time is Tim O'Brien. His prose is unreal. *In The Lake of The Woods* blew my mind when I first read it. I thought to myself, I didn't even know you could do that with a book. I like to read novels that aren't as modern as well. I love George Orwell, Mark Twain, and Virgina Woolfe and Jane Austen. And I think my guilty pleasure is that I really dig Stephen King. Not that it should be a guilty pleasure. He's a heck of a writer. I think he writes great characters and puts them in awful situations, and that's one of the things that's great about reading fiction. It lets the reader ask, "What would I do?"

Z+: Do you have this story idea that someday you want to write, but you know you'll have to be really famous and successful before anyone will pay you to write it?

Rob Stennett: I know what you mean. I sort of thought Ryan Fisher was that story, to be honest.

Z+: *Why?*

Rob Stennett: Because when I was shopping around my TV show, everyone loved it. But they always said, "Who's this for? Is it for Christians? It seems too tough and gritty to be for Christians. But if it's *not* for Christians, then who's going to watch it?" And I said, "It's for people. You don't have to be a doctor to watch *Grey's Anatomy.* Or a lawyer to watch *Boston Legal.* And you don't have to be a Christian or a pastor to watch a show or read a book about Christians." Anyway, it was my same fear with Ryan Fisher. I was scared people would think it wasn't warm and bubbly enough for Christians and it wasn't dark and cynical enough for everyone else. Still, I had some hope because I think there are guys like Tom Perotta or Douglas Coupland who write really complex characters dealing with their faith. But I think Christians rarely do this, especially in fiction.

Z+: Why?

ROB STENNETT: Not sure. I think it's because we feel guilty. We're supposed to have all the answers. But that's what's great about Ryan. He doesn't have any answers. He just makes everything up. He's this great character who helped me explore all of these things that have always perplexed me, and he could look at them sort of innocently. Even though he's not very innocent at all.

Z+: So, what made you decide to write TATSORF?

ROB STENNETT: Well, like I said before, I was always drawn to these types of stories, these satires about faith, even when sometimes I didn't even want to write them.

Z+: You didn't want to?

ROB STENNETT: Sometimes I thought I'd rather write stories with lasers and robots. But they never turned out very well. I have a whole closet full of stories of the adventures of C3P0 and R2D2.

Z+: What's surprised you the most while writing TATSORF?

ROB STENNETT: Katherine. She's such a great character and I'd had this story rattling around in my head for a while, but I don't think it really started working until she came to life. Ryan, I knew pretty well, he was a combination of all sorts of people and things. But Katherine is the key that makes the story work. In ways it may even be more her story than Ryan's. But *The Almost True Story Of Katherine Fisher* just isn't as catchy. Actually, now that I think about it, it kind of is. Is it too late to change the title?

Z+: Yes.

ROB STENNETT: Never mind, then.

Z+: *Let's see, anything else you'd like to tell your readers about yourself?*

ROB STENNETT: I guess I'd like to say this is a work of fiction. My wife and I get along great. My mother-in-law is really worried everyone's going to think we're having marital problems.

Z+: *She'll be glad you cleared that up. Thanks for stopping by.*

Coming June 2009

Z+

EXCERPT FROM

The End Is Now

A Novel by Rob Stennett

Chapter 1

Above all, you must understand that in the last days scoffers will come, scoffing and following their own evil desires. They will say, "Where is this 'coming' he promised? Ever since our ancestors died, everything goes on as it has since the beginning of creation."

2 Peter 3:3–4

There are certain rules to surviving a horror movie ... Never, ever, ever under any circumstances say, "I'll be right back." Because you won't be back.

Jamie Kennedy, *Scream*

One month from tomorrow, at precisely 6:11 in the morning, the rapture or apocalypse or Armageddon or whatever else it is you'd prefer to call it, is going to occur.

But only in Goodland, Kansas.

The rapture will not take place anywhere else in the world. It will not crash the stock market, cause cars to wreck, and planes to be left without their pilots. Husbands will not leave for the kitchens to grab jars of pickles only to come back to the living rooms and discover that their wives are now nothing more than piles of clothes. Power plants will not shut down. Nuclear missiles will not be launched. Barcodes will not be tattooed onto wrists or foreheads. The number 666 will be nowhere in sight except for those rare instances when a customer of McDonald's buys nothing but a Filet-O-Fish and medium strawberry shake and the total comes out to be six dollars and sixty six cents. A world government will not be formed. Computers will not melt down because they are confused about what the year 2000 actually means. Running water will not be lost, forcing citizens to take baths in rivers and wash their clothes in lakes. Aliens will not blow up the White House.

None of this will happen.

That is, none of this will happen anywhere but Goodland.

This goes against conventional wisdom. Most think that when the end comes it will be widespread: Trumpets will sound and horsemen will appear and it will be a whirlwind of all kinds of tribulation—everything from pre-trib, to post-trib, to middle-trib. But that doesn't make sense. It's just not how such things work. It's not true to the pattern. There are always warning signs. God didn't simply destroy Nineveh—Jonah was sent warn Nineveh of its impending doom and then swallowed by a whale. Moses warned Pharaoh before the plagues hit—and even the plagues started out innocently enough, simple stuff like frogs and locusts before the heavy hitters like death angels. Peter warned Ananias and Sapphira—and in the end they were all destroyed to warn others about the dangers of wickedness.

This is what is happening in Goodland. Their rapture will be a signal flare to the world. They are a warning. A sacrificial lamb. Once everyone sees how powerful and completely overtaking the rapture is, they will be afraid, excited, they will hit their knees and repent of their sins. Everyone, everywhere, will know the truth. Not only that, but it will also provide God a chance to see how things go. He can look at the rapture and see what worked and what didn't. He can watch the good, the bad, and the ugly of the apocalypse so he can know how to do improve on it when it goes global.

Goodland is the test market for the rapture.
The warning sign for all to repent and change.

The sun set a Reese's Pieces orange as Jeff Henderson flipped down his dusty visor. His Ford Taurus was too old, clunky, and unfashionable for someone in his line of work to be driving. It was older than both his kids. If he had a promotion he could buy something much nicer and reliable and slick. But just as much, a promotion would validate everything: the hours away from his family, the stress, the phone calls, the hustling, the twisting and scheming, the smile he had to have plastered on his face forty hours every week, the nine to five, the long days without a sale; the blood-sweat-and-tears would all be worth it if he could just get promoted to senior sales rep. Even better, he wouldn't have to put "Junior Sales Rep" on his business card anymore. *Junior.* It was so embarrassing. He was a father of two, he was a husband, and he'd been in the business world for a little while now. And he still had a card that said *Junior.*

Still, worrying about things like business cards and titles was an entirely new thing for Jeff. A couple of months ago he didn't care what was on his business card. He was just happy to have a job. Well, maybe not just *a* job. He'd had lots of those — he'd been a farmhand, he'd framed houses, he'd been an assistant manager at Señor Clucks. For his whole life he'd been paid by the hour.

For Jeff's entire adult life he'd done whatever it took to survive. He'd been living in survival mode ever since his senior year of high school. It was second semester and he was ready to graduate. He was imagining a life in college. He didn't know what he wanted to study, didn't even care; he just wanted to live the college life. He'd take all the easy classes and party for a couple of years. He'd get serious about his major and figure out his life in his junior year. That was the plan.

But then, on one ordinary high school day, Amy came up to his locker and her face was pale. She was already pretty fair-skinned, but on that day she looked almost translucent.

"What's up babe?" Jeff said. He was wearing his letter jacket and chewing gum.

"I'm late," Amy said. And somehow her skin changed yet another color.

"So am I," Jeff answered.

"No, I'm *really* late," Amy said.

He gently grabbed her elbow and smiled. "Don't worry, I'll go to class with you."

"Is that your way of saying you'll marry me?"

"Wow. Um, okay, I don't know if I'm ready for that kind of commitment."

"Jeff, I don't think you're following—"

"Listen, you have history, right? Mr. Smith loves me. I'll give him some excuse of why you're late—"

"No, I'm late. *Late*, you know—"

Jeff stared at his girlfriend blankly.

"—Pregnant late."

And Jeff aged ten years. He'd never had a steady girlfriend and euphemisms like *late* just weren't in his lexicon.

But pregnant was. Everything came flooding in. He could hear the crying baby, smell the diapers, and he could see a tiny messy apartment overstuffed with cribs and rattles and toys that blipped, blinked, and beeped. He could also see his college life disappearing. He'd never get to drink beer while standing on his head, never get write a paper after thirty-six hours with no sleep, never get to tie sweaters around his neck and flirt with sorority sisters. His next eighteen years were etched in stone.

It didn't even matter that he never really saw himself as the family type. He knew what the right thing to do was. And if he had any doubt, Amy's parents knocked it away by insisting he make Amy an honorable woman. Jeff agreed that it was the reasonable thing to do. But as soon as they were married, he realized he was in over his head. All they could afford for a honeymoon was a weekend in Kansas City, and when they got home real life began.

Jeff didn't know how to act in real life. He'd never been anything but a student. He didn't know how to support a family or be a husband. There were a whole bunch of experiences like going to college that were supposed to get him ready for all of that. But there wasn't time anymore. It was as if Rocky had to go straight to fighting Apollo Creed without the jogging in sweats.

So, from the moment Emily was born, Jeff worked whatever job he could to support his family. To make sure Amy and the baby had food on the table, clothes to wear, and a roof to protect them at night.

Now, at Hansley, things were different. A friend had gotten him a job there about two years ago, and Jeff finally had a career. For the first time in his life he wasn't just paid by how many hours he spent at work. Now there was incentive. Selling pre-owned cars would mean he could double and triple his salary.

The problem was that every Friday, Dale Hansley Jr. (Mr. Hansley's son who'd never sold a car in his life) printed off reports of the top sales rankings of the week. The names of all the salesmen were listed, starting with the week's best salesman at the top. Jeff's name was always near the bottom. And that made him afraid. He worried that maybe Mr. Hansley would decide that Jeff didn't have what it took to be in sales. He lived in constant fear of a conversation that would start and/ or end with the words, "Maybe you'd be better off in another line of work."

Lately Jeff had decided to change. He could do this. He could be a top salesman. He'd just have to fight a little harder. He'd have to develop a killer instinct. He decided he needed to read business books—everything from motivational books, to books on time management, to books on improving his sales techniques and approach. So, long after Emily and Will had gone to bed, Jeff would sit in the dark with Amy sound asleep next to him, and with a reading light clipped to his book, he'd scour the pages for any insight they could offer to increase his sales.

Jeff stopped at his mailbox, opened it up, threw a pile of mail into his passenger seat, and continued down his long concrete driveway. Coming home always made everything worthwhile. He had a great house out in the country; the nearest neighbor was five hundred yards away. He had a large windmill that faced the Johnsons' cornfield. It was something he'd always wanted. The windmill didn't even do anything really, it was just there for decoration, but it was so great to own one. Sometimes he would just sit on his porch and drink lemonade and stare at it. It was mesmerizing.

And as odd as it sounds, it was always a relief to come home and see that his family was *alive*. That they were safe and un-harmed. There were lots of dull moments at Hansley automo-tive, lots of crossword puzzles and water cooler talk in between waiting for the next sale to walk through the door. Lots of time for Jeff's mind to wander. And that's when the fear came in. He couldn't help it, even though it was so irrational and bizarre—even though it did no good to think this way—that didn't stop the thoughts from coming. A tire blown and the car flipping over and over, or someone drifting into Amy's lane while Emily and Will were in the car, and *bam*, the end, Jeff would be left alone to plan the funeral for his entire family.

Sometimes the fears weren't even realistic.

Sometimes Jeff could see kidnappers or thieves in his house; his family tied to wooden chairs with coarse ropes and shotguns aimed at them. Other times he could see random ways his family could be harmed—Amy taking a bath and the hairdryer dropping in; Will landing on the trampoline wrong and snapping his leg; Emily parked with some drunk jock pawing at her after homecoming. It would be easy to say how morbid Jeff was for thinking about such things. And Jeff would agree, it was morbid, and he didn't want to dwell on things like this.

In fact, he didn't *dwell* on them at all. They just kind of popped up. Like flashes. Quick. He'd shut his eyes and the images would be gone. The fear would still be there, for a moment, and he would tell himself there was nothing to worry about. It's fine. He needed to stop. But then, just to make sure, he would call home.

"Hi," Amy would say. "What's going on?"

"Nothing. Just missing you."

"That's sweet."

He never told Amy it was the fear that made him call.

He hopped out of his car, walked into his house, and smiled as the smell of the roast Amy was cooking wafted toward him. It was Tuesday. That meant they were going to have a real meal. The type of meal that black-and-white television families had, the type where June and the Beav and Wally would laugh and share their day. The type where he could ask his kids, "How was your day at school?" where they could share the highs and lows of life, where they could be a family.

Jeff hated that this only happened on Tuesdays now. He hated that they were getting too old to be a family.

"Hey Dad," Emily said, glancing toward Jeff as he walked through the door.

"I'm home," Jeff said.

"Hey honey," Amy said, kissing her husband quickly and dutifully on the cheek. "How was your day?"

"I sold an H3," Jeff said.

"Wow, that's reason to celebrate."

"I sold it to Marsha Beckett."

"How can she afford a car like that?"

"She can't."

"Emily, Billy, come on, it's time for dinner," Amy said.

"What are we having?" Emily asked as she took a seat.

"Roast. Where's Billy?"

"I don't know. I'm not his babysitter."

"What time is it?" Amy asked.

Jeff checked his watch. "7:13."

Amy walked outside. Jeff followed.

"I'd say it's dark out, wouldn't you?" Amy asked.

"Pretty close."

"Billy asked if he could go to Nate's house. I told him yes, but he had to be home *before* dark. He said he would. I said, 'Do you promise?' and he said, 'Mom I *promise*.' Jeff, he's got to learn some responsibility."

And then a flash came: Will, listening to his iPod, singing along to whatever as he crossed the road at the exact wrong moment, as teenagers were speeding by in a Cadillac. They'd slam on the breaks, but they'd be going too fast, it'd be too late.

"Totally agree," Jeff said.

"You don't think he's hurt? Do you?"

"Course not. He got caught up playing at Nate's. Lost track of time."

"Well, he's got to learn his lesson."

Amy went back inside. Jeff walked in the kitchen to see her setting the table with the speed and determination of a pit crew.

"Mom, what are you doing?" Emily asked.

"We're going to sit here and wait for your brother. He's going to walk in and see us, with the table set, and the food on the table getting cold. He has to learn that there are other people in the world. He has to learn to concentrate. I know he has a hard time paying attention, but he's got to understand that sometimes it's hard work. That's why they call it *paying*."

"Sure, mom," Emily said.

She was reading *Cosmo*. Seventeen's got to be too young to be reading *Cosmo*. There's some pretty grown up stuff in there, Jeff thought. In high school he used to read *Cosmo* with his friends after school. They thought it would teach them the secret to understanding women. And understanding women was the key to getting women. They took its quizzes as if studying for the bar exam. And tonight Emily was reading *Cosmo*. Which meant there were boys out there, somewhere, reading *Cosmo* quizzes to get Emily.

"Put the magazine away, honey," Amy said.

Emily slid the magazine under her seat. Jeff grabbed a chair. Dinner looked great: baked potatoes in foil, green beans with bacon, fruit salad, and a roast in a crock-pot. Jeff hoped Will would get there soon. This was a lot of good-looking food just to waste on an object lesson.

As if reading her father's mind, Emily reached for the fruit salad.

"What are you doing?" Amy asked.

"I was going to get some fruit salad."

"Nobody eats until your brother gets here."

"But fruit salad's already cold. What does it matter if it gets *more* cold?"

"That's not the point and you know it."

"Well, what are we supposed to do until he gets here?"

"We wait," Amy said.

Share Your Thoughts

With the Author: Your comments will be forwarded to the author when you send them to *zauthor@zondervan.com*.

With Zondervan: Submit your review of this book by writing to *zreview@zondervan.com*.

Free Online Resources at
www.zondervan.com/hello

 Zondervan AuthorTracker: Be notified whenever your favorite authors publish new books, go on tour, or post an update about what's happening in their lives.

 Daily Bible Verses and Devotions: Enrich your life with daily Bible verses or devotions that help you start every morning focused on God.

 Free Email Publications: Sign up for newsletters on fiction, Christian living, church ministry, parenting, and more.

 Zondervan Bible Search: Find and compare Bible passages in a variety of translations at www.zondervanbiblesearch.com.

 Other Benefits: Register yourself to receive online benefits like coupons and special offers, or to participate in research.